Mapping Space, Sense, and Movement in Florence

Mapping Space, Sense, and Movement in Florence explores the potential of digital mapping or Historical GIS as a research and teaching tool to enable researchers and students to uncover the spatial, kinetic, and sensory dimensions of the early modern city.

The exploration focuses on new digital research and mapping projects that engage the rich social, cultural, and artistic life of Florence in particular. One is a new GIS tool known as DECIMA (Digitally Encoded Census Information and Mapping Archive), and the other is a smartphone app called *Hidden Florence*. The international collaborators who have helped build these and other projects address three questions: how such projects can be created when there are typically fewer sources than for modern cities; how they facilitate more collaborative models for historical research into social relations, senses, and emotions; and how they help us interrogate older historical interpretations and create new models of analysis and communication. Four authors examine technical issues around the software programs and manuscripts. Five other authors then describe how GIS can be used to advance and develop existing research projects. Finally, four authors look to the future and consider how digital mapping transforms the communication of research results and makes it possible to envision new directions in research.

This exciting new volume is illustrated throughout with maps, screenshots, and diagrams to show the projects at work. It will be essential reading for students and scholars of early modern Italy, the Renaissance, and digital humanities.

Nicholas Terpstra is Professor of History at the University of Toronto. His recent publications include *Cultures of Charity: Women, Politics, and the Reform of Poor Relief in Renaissance Italy* (2013) and *Religious Refugees in the Early Modern World: An Alternative History of the Reformation* (2015).

Colin Rose is a PhD candidate in the Department of History at the University of Toronto. He has published on petitioning the court in early modern Parma and on vendetta and judicial practice in Bologna.

Routledge Research in Digital Humanities

Mapping space, sense, and movement in Florence
Historical GIS and the early modern city
Edited by Nicholas Terpstra and Colin Rose

Mapping Space, Sense, and Movement in Florence

Historical GIS and the early modern city

Edited by Nicholas Terpstra and Colin Rose

LONDON AND NEW YORK

First published 2016 by Routledge

2 Park Square, Milton Park, Abingdon, Oxfordshire OX14 4RN
52 Vanderbilt Avenue, New York, NY 10017

Routledge is an imprint of the Taylor & Francis Group, an informa business

First issued in paperback 2019

Copyright © 2016 Nicholas Terpstra and Colin Rose for selection and editorial matter. © the contributors for individual contributions.

The right of the editor to be identified as the author of the editorial material, and of the authors for their individual chapters, has been asserted in accordance with sections 77 and 78 of the Copyright, Designs and Patents Act 1988.

All rights reserved. No part of this book may be reprinted or reproduced or utilised in any form or by any electronic, mechanical, or other means, now known or hereafter invented, including photocopying and recording, or in any information storage or retrieval system, without permission in writing from the publishers.

Notice:
Product or corporate names may be trademarks or registered trademarks, and are used only for identification and explanation without intent to infringe.

British Library Cataloguing-in-Publication Data
A catalogue record for this book is available from the British Library

Library of Congress Cataloging-in-Publication Data
Mapping space, sense, and movement in Florence : historical GIS and the early modern city / edited by Nicholas Terpstra and Colin Rose.
  pages cm. — (Routledge research in digital humanities)
  Includes bibliographical references and index.
  ISBN 978-1-138-18489-3 (hardback : alkaline paper) —
ISBN 978-1-315-63931-4 (ebook)
 1. Florence (Italy)—Historical geography—Data processing.
2. Geographic information systems. 3. Digital mapping. 4. Florence (Italy)—History—1421–1737—Research—Data processing. 5. City and town life—Italy—Florence—History—Research—Data processing.
6. Public spaces—Italy—Florence—History—Research—Data processing.
7. Spatial behavior—Social aspects—Italy—Florence—History—Research—Data processing. 8. Senses and sensation—Social aspects—Italy—Florence—History—Research—Data processing. 9. Walking—Social aspects—Italy—Florence—History—Research—Data processing.
I. Terpstra, Nicholas. II. Rose, Colin.
  DG737.4.M37 2016
  911'.455110285—dc23
  2015035186

ISBN: 978-1-138-18489-3 (hbk)
ISBN: 978-0-367-87582-4 (pbk)

Typeset in Time New Roman
by Apex CoVantage, LLC

Contents

List of figures vii
List of tables x
Acknowledgements xi
Abbreviations xiii
List of contributors xiv

Introduction 1
NICHOLAS TERPSTRA

PART 1
Creating a historical GIS project 13

1 **Thinking and using DECIMA: neighbourhoods and occupations in Renaissance Florence** 15
   COLIN ROSE

2 **The route of governmentality: surveying and collecting urban space in ducal Florence** 33
   LEAH FAIBISOFF

3 **From the *Decima* to DECIMA and back again: the data behind the data** 53
   EDUARDO FABBRO

4 **Shaping the streetscape: institutions as landlords in early modern Florence** 63
   DANIEL JAMISON

vi Contents

PART 2
Using digital mapping to unlock spatial and social relations 85

5 **Women behind walls: tracking nuns and socio-spatial networks in sixteenth-century Florence** 87
SHARON STROCCHIA AND JULIA ROMBOUGH

6 **Locating the sex trade in the early modern city: space, sense, and regulation in sixteenth-century Florence** 107
NICHOLAS TERPSTRA

7 **Plague and the city: methodological considerations in mapping disease in early modern Florence** 125
JOHN HENDERSON AND COLIN ROSE

PART 3
Mapping motion, emotion, and sense: using digital mapping to rethink categories and communication 147

8 **Seeing sound: mapping the Florentine soundscape** 149
NIALL ATKINSON

9 **Mapping fear: plague and perception in Florence and Tuscany** 169
NICHOLAS A. ECKSTEIN

10 **Locating experience in the Renaissance city using mobile app technologies: the *Hidden Florence* project** 187
FABRIZIO NEVOLA AND DAVID ROSENTHAL

Conclusion: towards early modern spatial humanities 210
NICHOLAS TERPSTRA AND COLIN ROSE

Index 217

Figures

0.1	The Buonsignori map of Florence, 1584 (1695 copy)	5
1.1	Florentine parish churches and *gonfaloni*, mapped over the city's *quartieri* at 80 per cent transparency	20
1.2	Florentine parishes as created from the *Decima* entries	21
1.3	Textile weavers in Santa Maria Novella and the assessed values of their household properties	23
1.4	Textile weavers in Santa Maria Novella and the rents they paid, in *lire*	24
1.5	Butchers, bakers, and barbers in Santa Maria Novella	25
1.6	The neighbourhood of Sant'Ambrogio	27
2.1	Via del Vecchio Parione	40
2.2	Five circuits walked in the quarter of Santa Croce	44
2.3	Detail of the first Santa Croce circuit	45
2.4	Third Santa Croce circuit, from Corso de' Tintori to Via degli Alberti ('F' to 'G')	46
2.5	Fourth Santa Croce circuit, from Via Torricelle to Via degli Alberti ('L')	47
3.1	18. Piero di Biagio, bottaio co*n* bottegha sotto	55
3.2	705. Religione di S*a*nto Jacopo, contigua a la s*u*det*t*a et a un' [*signum crucis*] tra di d*et*ta Religione 706. Casa del Capitulo di Santo Lorenzo, populo di S*a*nto Lore*n*zo, Via d'Argento, contigua a una altra sua et a uma di Piero d'Ant*on*io Signorini	55
4.1	Institutional properties in ducal Florence, 1561	76
4.2	Innocenti properties (x) on the corner of Via Guelfa and Via Tedesca	77
4.3	Congregazione Santa Maria del Fiore properties (x) around San Paolo	78
4.4	Camaldolesi properties (x) in Santo Spirito	79
4.5	Order of San Jacopo properties (x) near Piazza Santa Maria Novella	79
5.1	Two pages from the Florentine Convent Census (1548, 1552): report from Sant'Apollonia (left) and San Piero a Monticelli (right)	88
5.2	Location of four sample convents	92
5.3	Property holdings of selected nuns' families by surname, 1562	95

viii *Figures*

5.4	Property holdings of Canigiani family, 1562	99
5.5	Property holdings of Altoviti family, 1562	100
6.1	Prostitution zones (1547) with religious houses	112
6.2	Concentration of registered and unregistered prostitutes (1560)	115
6.3	Assessed value of properties owned by prostitutes, 1561	117
6.4	Registered prostitutes by parish, 1561	119
6.5	Mean property value by parish, 1561	119
6.6	Prostitutes and property values, 1561	120
7.1	Buonsignori map of Florence showing the quarter of San Giovanni/parish of San Lorenzo	130
7.2	Total plague morbidity in San Lorenzo parish, 1630–31	136
8.1	Map of the sixteen *gonfaloni* of Florence created after the political reforms of 1343	150
8.2	Leon Battista Alberti, *Descriptio Urbis Romae*, c.1450	152
8.3	Plotting Alberti's coordinates onto a circular projection results in an endlessly reproducible and highly accurate map of Rome	153
8.4	Map of the area around the Mercato Vecchio of Florence	155
8.5	Map showing the extent of the Rogation Day processions	156
8.6	The full map generated by DECIMA suggests that the larger outer parishes were extended from their churches, most of which lie close to the older circuit of walls	158
8.7	Author's first attempt to visualize the daily ringing cycle of the city's four principal bell towers as it was described in the city's statutes	159
8.8	Detail of the parish map created by Atkinson and Rose	161
9.1	Florence: intersection of Borgo Santi Apostoli with Piazza Santi Apostoli and environs	175
9.2	Notes on the household of Sandro di Vieri Altoviti	176
9.3	View of western Oltrarno, Florence, displaying selection of households reported in August 1630 'Visitation'	178
9.4	View of the area (*sestiere*) of San Giovanni, Florence, displaying selection of households reported in August 1630 'Visitation'	180
9.5	View of Florence displaying data from Figures 9.3 and 9.4	180
10.1	Via dei Pilastri, detail from Stefano Buonsignori, *Nova pulcherrimae civitatis Florentiae topographia accuratissime delineate*, 1594	188
10.2	*Hidden Florence* app user on Via dei Pilastri	189
10.3	Piazza della Signoria, detail from Stefano Buonsignori, *Nova pulcherrimae civitatis Florentiae topographia accuratissime delineate*, 1594	191
10.4	Canto di Monteloro: intersection of Via dei Pilastri and Borgo Pinti, detail from Stefano Buonsignori, *Nova pulcherrimae civitatis Florentiae topographia accuratissime delineate*, 1594, as viewed on screen in the *Hidden Florence* app	194
10.5	Canto di Monteloro: intersection of Via dei Pilastri and Borgo Pinti	195

10.6	Red City *potenza* stone on the corner of the church of Sant'Ambrogio	198
10.7	Red City *potenza* stone on the corner of the church of Sant' Ambrogio as viewed on the 'found it' screen in the *Hidden Florence* app	199
10.8	Vicolo del Giglio, detail from Stefano Buonsignori, *Nova pulcherrimae civitatis Florentiae topographia accuratissime delineate*, 1594, as viewed on screen in the *Hidden Florence* app	201

Tables

3.1	Details of the *Decima* manuscripts	53
4.1	Share of entries, assessed value, and population by quarter	67
4.2	Property value and population in the *Decima ricerche*	67
4.3	Instances of each primary holding type and their average value (in *scudi*)	69
4.4	Secondary holding types for properties under lease	70
4.5	Owner count and assessments in *scudi* by holding size	72
4.6	Number of institutions and total portfolio by holding size	73
4.7	Contract types used by the wealthiest institutional landlords	74
4.8	Rates of contiguity among institutional owners by holding size	75
7.1	Selection of John Henderson's original database	138
7.2	Reorganized data prepared for temporal mapping	138
7.3	Selection from attribute table of the DECIMA layer *San Lorenzo Streets*	139

Acknowledgements

A project built on conversations and collaborations among scholars, students, and technical experts generates debts, and it will become apparent very quickly to readers of this volume that we have many debts indeed.

We are grateful above all to those who have participated in those conversations from the beginning. Some are contributors to this volume, and we thank them above all both for their ongoing involvement and for their willingness to contribute articles to this volume under a very tight time line. Other interlocutors came to the various workshops and conference sessions that have been held as DECIMA developed. The Harvard Centre for Italian Renaissance Studies (Villa I Tatti) hosted the initial planning meeting in June 2011, and the University of Chicago hosted a small working group in 2012, while the Kunst-Historische Institut (KHI) in Florence hosted a conference, *Italia Illustrata*, out of which many of the chapters in this volume emerged. Our thanks to Lino Pertile, director of I Tatti; Alessandro Nova, KHI managing director; and Jan Simane, head of library, for their support. Sessions at annual conferences like that of the Renaissance Society of America have also periodically brought together interlocutors and triggered new collaborations.

We have benefited from exceptional technical support from different universities and granting agencies. We would like to thank Joseph Garver of the Harvard Map Library for his assistance in procuring the high-resolution scan of the Buonsignori map used in the DECIMA online tool, and Gianluca Belli and Amadeo Belluzzi of the University of Florence Faculty of Architecture for graciously sharing database materials with us. Ian Gregory of the University of Lancastershire joined us for the first consultation in Florence and provided excellent advice throughout the geocoding process. The University of Toronto has played a very large role in the success of the project. Philip Wright, Director of Information and Instructional Technology at the University of Toronto, mobilized vital technical support at a critical point in DECIMA's evolution, above all the programming assistance of Andreea Gheorghe, who developed the DECIMA Web presence. Marcel Fortin, GIS Map Librarian at the University of Toronto, and Byron Moldofsky, Manager of the University's GIS Cartography Office, provided important training and technical support throughout. The Social Sciences and Humanities Research Council of Canada has funded the bulk of the formal DECIMA project, while individual collaborators have received assistance from variety of national and institutional granting agencies.

The work of actually building up the database has been carried out by a team of exceptional research assistants at the University of Toronto. Within this group, Eduardo Fabbro, Leah Faibisoff, and Daniel Jamison have done the most to transcribe the *Decima* census documents and to populate the database upon which the map is built. Sara Patterson provided invaluable editing and formatting work as the volume came together. The evolving collaboration that animates the project began with the shared research interests of the coeditors; bringing different skills and backgrounds to the work of both the database and this volume, they are grateful for what they have learned from each other over the process, and still a bit surprised that it's all worked out as well as it has.

Abbreviations

ASF   Archivio di Stato di Firenze
CRSPL   Compagnie Religiose Soppresse da Pietro Leopoldo
fol./fols folio/folios
Sanità   Ufficiali di Sanità, Florence

Contributors

Niall Atkinson (University of Chicago) is an art historian whose monograph *The Noisy Renaissance: Sound, Architecture, and Florentine Urban Life* investigates the soundscapes of Renaissance Florence and the role of the acoustic environment in the meaning of built space and the construction of social communities. He is currently researching urban disorientation in the Renaissance city, looking at how Italians encountered and navigated the topographies and monuments of foreign territories.

Nicholas A. Eckstein (University of Sydney) is a historian whose principal area of research is the social and cultural history of Renaissance and early modern Italy, especially Florence. Among his articles and books is a recent major study, *Painted Glories: The Brancacci Chapel in Renaissance Florence* (2014). He is currently pursuing several thematically related projects on perceptions and uses of urban space in the early modern city.

Eduardo Fabbro (University of Toronto) is a historian of the Early Middle Ages who has published on early medieval historiography. He is currently finishing a project on society and warfare in Lombard Italy from the second half of the sixth century and through the course of the seventh and is also preparing an edition of the sixth-century *Copenhagen Continuation of Prosper*.

Leah Faibisoff (University of Toronto) is a specialist in medieval literary studies working on administrative and literary histories of thirteenth- and fourteenth-century Italy. Her current major project considers the role of notaries in the rise of the vernacular literary traditions of northern and central Italy and examines the manuscript tradition of the Latin *Apollonius of Tyre* and its vernacular translations in late medieval Italy.

John Henderson (University of London, Birkbeck College) is a historian of early modern medicine and hospitals and Professor of Italian Renaissance History at Birkbeck College. He is the author and editor of numerous works, including *Piety and Charity in Late Medieval Florence* (1994) and *The Renaissance Hospital: Healing the Body and Healing the Soul* (2006). He is currently completing a major study of the plague of 1630–31 in Florence.

Daniel Jamison (University of Toronto) is an economic historian conducting research on fiscal policy in the Italian commune of Lucca, using records of the city's gate tax (the *Gabella Maggiore*) to study trade dynamics and the development of tax policy. He has conducted research on bells as political symbols, the elaboration of governmental authority in the premodern state, and medieval urban provisioning.

Fabrizio Nevola (University of Exeter) is a cultural and architectural historian of early modern Italian cities with a special interest in public space and urban identity and in city streets as social spaces. He has written *Siena: Constructing the Renaissance City* (2007) and edited *Locating Communities in the Early Modern Italian City* (2010) and *Experiences of the Street in Early Modern Italy* (2013). He has also coproduced the geolocated walking app *Hidden Florence*.

Julia Rombough (University of Toronto) conducts research on the intersection of women's institutions, religion, urban life, and the senses in early modern Italy. Her current work considers the sensory regulations surrounding enclosed women's institutions in sixteenth-century Florence, analyzing how they shaped experience, caused conflict, and ordered space in the city.

Colin Rose (University of Toronto) is a social historian of early modern Italy. He has published on petitioning the court in early modern Parma and on vendetta and judicial practice in Bologna. His research explores why patterns of violence in North Italy cut across the grain of models used to explain the decline of violence elsewhere, looking at how the strength of social and institutional trust impacted social stability.

David Rosenthal (Edinburgh University) specializes in the social history of early modern Italy. His research on artisan urban culture and issues of class, gender, communication, and agency has appeared in numerous articles and in *Kings of the Street: Power, Community and Ritual in Renaissance Florence* (2015), which traces the rise and demise of Florence's carnivalesque artisan brigades c.1480–1630. He has also published on tavern culture and coproduced the geolocated walking app *Hidden Florence*.

Sharon Strocchia (Emory University) is a social historian who has written extensively on death, gender, sexuality, and the social history of medicine in Renaissance Florence. Her current work situates women as agents of health and healing within the rapidly shifting medical landscape of sixteenth-century Italy. She has published *Death and Ritual in Renaissance Florence* (1992) and *Nuns and Nunneries in Renaissance Florence* (2009) and edited *Women and Healthcare in Early Modern Europe* (2014).

Nicholas Terpstra (University of Toronto) is a social historian of early modern Europe who has worked on politics, gender, religion, and charity in early modern Italy, with an emphasis on institutional supports for marginalized groups. His recent publications include *Cultures of Charity: Women, Politics, and the Reform of Poor Relief in Renaissance Italy* (2013) and *Religious Refugees in the Early Modern World: An Alternative History of the Reformation* (2015).

Introduction

Nicholas Terpstra

This volume explores the potential of digital mapping or Historical GIS as a research and teaching tool with potential to describe the spatial, kinetic, and sensory dimensions of early modern urban societies. Other collections have compared different historical GIS projects in different cities. In this case we take the opposite approach and focus on one city – early modern Florence – where a number of new digital research and mapping projects, including a new GIS tool known as DECIMA (Digitally Encoded Census Information and Mapping Archive) and a cell-phone app known as *Hidden Florence*, have emerged. We explore three questions: how are such projects created; how do they facilitate more collaborative models for historical research into social relations, senses, and emotions; and how do they foster an interrogation of older historical interpretations and the creation of new models of analysis and communication, particularly around space, motion, and the senses?[1]

The authors gathered here to assess both the potential and the drawbacks of digital humanities include leading historians of Florence and younger scholars. Using both the DECIMA project and *Hidden Florence*, we describe how digitally inflected scholarship emerges and expands through technical challenges and ongoing revision. We show how emerging critical questions and expanding technical possibilities bring researchers back to the drawing board time after time. Approaches that seem feasible frequently have to be abandoned due to limits in the sources or technology. We demonstrate how digital projects can promote collaboration, allow scholars to extend their research within a field, and shift the questions and subject matter both within a particular area of research and in historical study generally. As the questions change and subject matter evolves, attention turns to how best to share findings and to whether there are new ways to bridge past and present and bring together academic creators and popular users.

This Introduction first sketches the historical and historiographical context for the DECIMA project and then explains how the project developed and briefly reviews the essays.

Sources and context: Duke Cosimo I, early modern big data, and mapping

Most projects in historical mapping and digital humanities deploy large bodies of data, and in practice this often means that they emphasize nineteenth- or twentieth-century phenomena or develop broad-ranging comparisons of earlier subjects. It is relatively rare to find a large body of statistical data for a single city before the eighteenth century. The exceptions are often the result of a particular ruler's or administrator's drive to inventory debts and resources, either to remake a society or simply to get a firmer grip on it. Renaissance Florentines developed one early example of this with the 1427 *Catasto* tax census, which emerged as the republican government was struggling to control its debts and manage its expenses. The comprehensive returns on household assets, investments, servants, and family generated by the *Catasto* became the basis for an ambitious statistical analysis by Christiane Klapisch-Zuber and David Herlihy, a methodological landmark that transformed our understanding of fifteenth-century urban society. Now available online, this enormous data set continues to be used by historians and social scientists studying Florentine social and economic life.[2]

A little more than a century later, Duke Cosimo I de' Medici (r. 1537–74) had similar needs and ambitions. Cosimo I came to the title after the assassination of a distant cousin, Duke Alessandro, in 1537. That murder marked a low point following four decades of frequent regime changes in Florence, which were themselves the culmination of this former mercantile republic's often violent progression over a century and a half from communal government through a steadily narrowing oligarchy towards rule by a single family. Few Florentines in 1537 would have thought that the eighteen-year-old Cosimo had much chance of surviving, much less of launching one of the most successful early modern absolutist regimes. Few tourists to Florence now have even heard of Duke Cosimo I, since guides and popular histories tend to focus on the artistic innovations of the fifteenth century and heroize the Medici of that period. Cosimo *Pater Patriae* and his grandson Lorenzo *il Magnifico* certainly did patronize many artists, thinkers, and writers. Yet, when modern visitors windowshop at the goldsmiths' shops on the Ponte Vecchio, or line up to enter the Uffizi, or marvel at the Ducal Palace and the Boboli Gardens behind it, or shuffle through the apartments of the Palazzo Vecchio, or crane their necks to see the rich frescos in the Cathedral dome and the largely bare walls around, they are in Cosimo I's city. Cosimo I remade the mercantile republican city state into a ducal capital. He directed a brain trust of now largely forgotten courtiers who acted through the city's governing bodies and a cluster of artists and engineers such as Giorgio Vasari, Bartolomeo Ammannati, and Baldassare Lanci, who saw large enterprises into being. This group reworked both the physical and the administrative fabric of the city in a burst of activity over the first fifteen or twenty years of Cosimo I's reign, and their efforts made both modern tourism and modern digital projects possible.

Cosimo I's early administrations used systematic surveys and data collection as a means of securing bureaucratic control over different parts of the Florentine state and its social life. In 1542 he launched an ambitious drive to create a more comprehensive welfare system that would regulate begging, expand services to needy children and the poor, and 'make poverty history'. Its framework of regulations and new institutions would rest on the financial foundation provided by the hundreds of small hospitals that dotted Florence and Tuscany. Cosimo I's assessors demanded systematic accounts of their holdings, revenues, and expenses so that excess funds could be channeled into support of the duke's new welfare system. Foot-dragging, avoidance, and creative accounting ensured that few surveys were returned and no funds were forwarded to Florence. Six years later, in 1548, he moved to reform the convents as part of a broader ecclesiastical reform strategy worthy of a contemporary Protestant German prince or English monarch. It began with the refusal to allow Archbishop Antonio Altoviti to take office and carried on to expelling Savonarolan friars from the Dominican house of S. Marco and curbing the activities of groups like confraternities and charitable institutions that had followed the firebrand friar. In 1560, Cosimo I created a new governing body, the Nine Conservators (*Nove conservatori del giurisdizione e del dominio fiorentine*), to oversee local administration throughout the Tuscan state. Learning from the frustrations of the poverty administrators of 1542, Cosimo I gave the Nine Conservators the mandate, staff, and disciplinary powers to conduct a comprehensive survey of local charitable and fiscal resources in 1561 and was rewarded with ten times the number of returns in one of the earliest surveys.

Censuses were part of this drive to count. In 1551 Cosimo I commissioned one man, Antonio di Filippo Gianetti, to prepare a count of 'households and souls' (*dischrezione delli fuochi et delle anime*) in the entire duchy. In 1561 he followed up with the even more ambitious *Decima ricerca*, which sent teams of notaries and scribes into the streets of Florence to collect detailed information on how many men, women, and children lived in each of its nine thousand households, how much those households were worth, and what they generated in rental income. Scribes then took the *Decima* results and produced, in 1562, a beautiful manuscript that conveyed a simplified version of the data in a form like that used for the 1551 census. On one level, we can think of the 1562 manuscript as simply a presentation copy of the 1561 *ricerca* for the duke's pleasure. But there was more to it than that. The 1561 *ricerca* was a survey of assets, while the 1562 census was a survey of liabilities. The 1551 and 1562 censuses tallied household population but gave only a general sense of urban geography and no record of property values or revenue. What they recorded were the open mouths – *bocche* – that Cosimo I had to feed. By contrast, the 1561 *ricerca* listed those revenue-generating properties that could be taxed to feed these mouths and the state itself.[3]

Cosimo I believed in big data. More to the point, he attracted a corps of administrators and bureaucrats prepared to argue for and to implement censuses and surveys as tools of governing. We can see one surveying initiative after another in the first fifteen years of his reign and trace them not only to the young and ambitious duke but also to this team of like-minded Tuscan administrators and aristocrats who were committed to ambitious social and institutional reform and who saw the duke as the man who could make it happen. It is this broader collective effort that allows us to frame governmentality in late Renaissance Florence as an elite's broad ethos rather than as a ruler's bold initiative. Florentines had long known that knowledge was power and that numbers were the key to knowledge. This conviction had driven merchants to adopt double-entry bookkeeping and governments to order new *Catasto* surveys in 1458 and 1480 to update the city's inventory of human, financial, and property resources.

Cosimo I also believed in mapping. In 1563, as he was renovating Florence's ancient Palazzo dei Priori into his own ducal palace, he planned a wonder-room that would demonstrate the cosmic significance implicit in his name – a connection he was quite conscious of and ready to exploit in his self-fashioning and public presentation. The room's walls would be lined with large painted maps of regions that were familiar, new to Europeans, or even only imagined: Europe, Africa, Asia, and the Americas, even the Polar Regions. The maps adorned the doors of the wonder-room's cabinets, and behind each door lay rare and exotic items from that particular part of the world. The crowning touches were two globes – one terrestrial and one celestial – that could be lowered from the ceiling. It was a fabulous, and fabulously expensive, testament to the duke's reach over land and sea and into the heavens.[4]

For a long time it seemed as though Cosimo I could indeed 'make it happen'. Thanks to his support for those who urged him to pay attention to the numbers, we have an extraordinary set of comprehensive surveys of mid-sixteenth-century Florence and its hinterlands. Thanks to his 'cosmic' ambitions, we have a map room that illustrates how mid-sixteenth-century Europeans imagined the world. Yet part of the duke's long-term success lay in his understanding that negotiations, brokering, patronage, and deals were ultimately more effective tools of governance than numbers and rules. He eventually abandoned many of the surveys and marginalized the bureaucrats and patricians who advocated them, reverting to the more direct horse trading and alliance building that made early modern governments function. There was no second convent census, no second *Decima ricerca*, no new comprehensive audit of charitable institutions. Cosimo I died before his cosmic wonder-room could be completed, and the two sons who succeeded him made only desultory efforts to finish it on the cheap before turning their attention to the more ambitious wonder-room that was the Uffizi. Little more than a year after his father's death, Francesco I dismissed the painter who had been preparing the wonder-room's maps and commissioned an Olivetan monk, Stefano Buonsignori, to complete that project and then also to prepare the 1584 aerial view that the DECIMA and *Hidden Florence* projects use as their visual interface.

The source base and aerial view employed in the DECIMA project demonstrate some of the frustrations that bedevil early modern mapping projects. Cosimo I's early efforts developed a bureaucratic apparatus often considered the paradigm of the early modern absolutist state. Judicial magistracies gained considerable powers to police and prosecute, and they sent violators to prisons or the galleys. New sets of regulations relocated economic activities according to sensory, aesthetic, and moral values. Prostitutes were redirected from a central brothel to a network of specific streets, orphans and the poor were segregated in a series of institutional enclosures, and Jews were confined to a ghetto. Large fortresses to north and south kept the city under close surveillance. 'Governmentality' was not an abstraction. The Medici dukes were regulating a new urbanistic order that, to an extent not seen previously, considered the city as a coherent whole. At the same time, thanks

Introduction 5

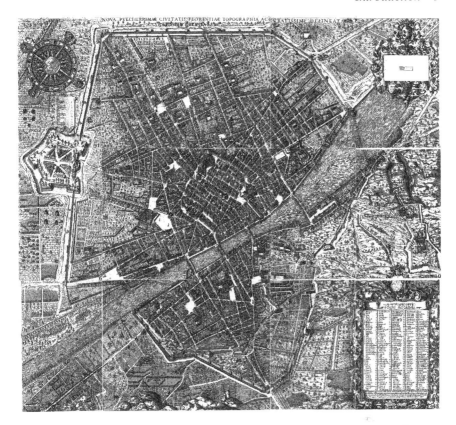

Figure 0.1 The Buonsignori map of Florence, 1584 (1695 copy), Harvard Map Library.

to the limits of early modern politics and bureaucracy, this was not – or at least not yet – the panoptic state of nineteenth- and twentieth-century dystopians. The Medicean Moment emerged thanks to the coming together of an ambitious young ruler and a corps of eager courtiers and bureaucrats. While it barely lasted to the end of Cosimo I's reign, it was a very real instantiation of modes of survey and surveillance that would become the keys to governing in the nineteenth and twentieth centuries and fodder for digital analysis in the twenty-first.

Mapping the *Decima*: pushing possibilities and exploring collaboration

The 1561 *Decima* offers an unparalleled comprehensive survey of an early modern city's population and resources, while the clarity and precision of the 1584 Buonsignori map make it among the best of those produced in the sixteenth century. It is not surprising that both have already been used in digital mapping projects. In 2008, Robert Burr Litchfield released *Florence Ducal Capital*, an ambitious survey of the state the Cosimo I was creating.[5] Litchfield's e-book included an online version of the Buonsignori map that superimposed a grid of eighty-seven equal squares and included a supplementary text noting the main public, ecclesiastical, and civic buildings in each, as well as the chief families and the most commonly represented artisanal activities. While a significant advance in joining this statistical and visual information for the first time, this was a static map that subordinated occupational data to an abstract grid. More dynamic approaches were already in the works. In this same year, Gianluca Belli and Amadeo Belluzzi of the Faculty of Architecture at the University of Florence were busy with a team of research assistants constructing an online atlas (*atlante digitale*) that would plot the locations of artisans' workshops as listed in the *Decima*. Because their longer-term interest lay in re-creating the built history of the city, they chose to use a nineteenth-century cadastral map of the city in place of the Buonsignori map. Shortly thereafter, Fabrizio Nevola and David Rosenthal began assembling their Taverns Project, working with the taverns recorded in the *Decima*. More recently, they have collaborated on the smartphone app *Hidden Florence*, described in this volume. *Hidden Florence* builds a modern city guide by using the Buonsignori map as a visual and kinetic frame for the extensive archival research of Nevola and Rosenthal into the physical texture and social life of the early modern city.[6] As described in their chapter in this book, users follow a fictional wool-worker of the 1490s through the city's streets and taverns and, through him, learn about politics, work life, arts, and entertainment in relation to the urban fabric.

With so many new projects emerging, DECIMA was designed from the outset to be a collaborative tool that would become available online at the earliest possible opportunity. In 2011 the Social Sciences and Humanities Research Council of Canada (SSHRC) provided a multiyear grant to fund the first stage of DECIMA as a project meant to allow the mapping of social historical, sensory, and spatial data. After an early consultation in Florence in 2011 with historical mapping consultants and possible collaborators, work began with data entry in the fall of 2011 and carried on to 2014. A formal consultation with Niall Atkinson and humanities computing experts at the University of Chicago in 2012 discussed how best to integrate sensory data, particularly around sound. A larger workshop in Florence in 2013 allowed DECIMA team members to give progress reports on results and to learn more about digital projects on other contemporary Italian cities, such as *Visualizing Venice*, *Orbis Urbis* (Rome), *Firenze Città Nobilissima*, and *Hidden Florence*, among others, This workshop also opened up collaboration with Gianluca Belli and Amadeo Belluzzi, who very generously shared their results in tabulating data on artisanal workshops (*botteghe*) and the built environment of early modern Florence.

Up to this point, Colin Rose had been taking primary responsibility for developing the technical dimension of DECIMA, designing and overseeing creation of the database and working out GIS georeferencing in consultation with Marcel Fortin, GIS Map Librarian at the University of Toronto, and Byron Moldofsky, manager of the University's GIS Cartography Office. Shortly after the 2013 Florence workshop, the University of Toronto also committed to offering technical assistance to major computing projects in the Humanities and so made available the services of a professional programmer, Andreea Gheorghe, who managed the critical movement to an online interface that was publicly launched in New York City and Toronto in 2014. The interface gives access to the data and map for the quarter of Santa Maria Novella, with the other three city quarters to follow shortly. In spring 2015, SSHRC approved funding to expand DECIMA by integrating 1551 and 1632 census data into the database and so allow longitudinal inquiries.

Spatial humanities: mapping space, sense, and movement in early modern Florence

The essays in this collection lay out in more detail some critical steps in the process already sketched. Four members of the research team explain technical issues around the software programs and the manuscripts used, illustrating how DECIMA employs *Decima* data for occupation and property ownership. Then three historians, working with DECIMA researchers and tools, demonstrate how a new GIS tool such as DECIMA can advance existing research projects in the social history of early modern Florence. Finally, three other historians look ahead to consider how digital mapping transforms both inquiry and the communication of research results and makes it possible to envision new directions and subject matter.

Part 1, *Creating a Historical GIS Project*, explores technical issues in the construction of a historical GIS for a particular city. In the opening essay, Colin Rose reviews some of the early decisions and revisions that gave DECIMA its current shape, while exploring geospatial patterns of work and residence in sixteenth-century Florence. Drawing data primarily from Santa Maria Novella, he shows that while the city was generally a mixture of rich and poor, distinct patterns emerge within this mixture. This quarter was dominated by textile workers, who themselves were stratified in both economic and residential ways. Networks of local services were regularly dispersed to provide for the daily needs of neighbourhoods. As a foil to the highly stratified modern city, the economically and professionally mixed neighborhoods of ducal Florence tell us much about the daily lives, networks, and relations of Florentines both male and female, old and young.

Leah Faibisoff sets the 1561 *Decima* against earlier tax surveys, such as the 1427 *Catasto*, that were based on neighbourhood and family. *Decima* surveyors walked through the streets of the city, assessing all real property *in situ* and recording detailed demographic information for every household. The physical movement of the surveyors themselves through 311 streets and 61 squares, measuring the demographic, occupational, and economic data for 8,726 households and their 59,216 inhabitants, sets out a 'route of governmentality'. This provides us with a conceptual model for understanding ducal governance as the projection of centralized power into urban space. It demonstrates how the totalizing bureaucratic eye of Duke Cosimo's emerging absolutist government viewed the city through an all-inclusive surveyance and axonometric collection of urban space. While the *Catasto* favoured family over geography, the *Decima* did the reverse, a telling instance of how a new way of seeing the state included a new way of seeing and mapping its spaces.

The DECIMA project is based on a rich collection of social data on sixteenth-century Florence, and Eduardo Fabbro discusses how the process of turning a detailed census into geocoded data points risks pasteurizing the diversity of the document, erasing the different approaches of individual surveyors and overlooking anomalous elements that, although statistically invisible, provide a rich, microscopic look into the social life of the city. Fabbro looks behind the DECIMA online database in order to explore the link between the manuscripts and the spreadsheets. The digital format provides a powerful tool to access the data from the manuscripts, but a paleographical analysis of the manuscripts can inform and detail the results provided by search engines and spreadsheets. Three different scribes worked on the 1561 census, and they proceeded according to somewhat different methods. Their distinct approaches produce slight variations in the kind of data generated for different quarters of the city, which could prove problematic for the macroscopic use of the database.

Daniel Jamison then explores the various forms of landholding and renting exercised in Florence, with a focus on the almost five hundred monasteries, convents, confraternities, and guilds that owned roughly one-third of all urban property. DECIMA invites a comparative study and allows us to visualize the distribution of landlords and tenants throughout the city. While private landlords possessed a mean of one and a quarter properties apiece, institutional entities leased out an average of five domiciles. Some owned nothing more than a home for their priest or gardener, while others managed scores of buildings. Some monasteries, guilds, and confraternities did more than manage scattered bequests – they shaped neighborhoods and controlled whole blocks. Jamison presents a statistical survey of institutional landholding to identify strategies of property management and the relationship between these strategies and the nature or size of the corporate landlords that employed them, and offers a visualization of a sample of them.

Part 2, *Using Digital Mapping to Unlock Spatial and Social Relations,* includes three essays by social historians that demonstrate how a new GIS tool such as DECIMA can advance ongoing research projects. All three historians employ historical mapping and manipulate large data sets; in their chapters, they show how their research has been expanded and reshaped through collaboration with the DECIMA research team.

Sharon Strocchia and Julia Rombough use the ducal census of Florentine convents taken between 1548 and 1552, together with DECIMA census data, to analyze networks linking Florentine convents and elite and middling families. What spatial and social strategies did families employ when enrolling a female member in a convent, and how did these change over the fifteenth and sixteenth centuries? The ties between convents and family residences built on and amplified broader networks of relationships – social, economic, political, and religious. Mapping placement strategies makes visible the ways in which these different interests intersected and coalesced. Strocchia and Rombough compare four convents, one from each quarter of Florence and representing cross sections of the city's districts, religious orders, and parishes, to explore how digital mapping can lead to new avenues of inquiry. They also explore how source limitations rooted in the complexities and richness of daily life and the intricacies of family dynamics around age and gender make relational mapping particularly difficult.

Nicholas Terpstra reviews the geography of the sex trade in early modern Florence and its conjunctions with the city's religious houses in order to explore how sensory and spatial history intersect. A civic brothel concentrated sexual services in the city centre from 1403, but Cosimo I emphasized a regime of registration and licensing that diffused the sex trade throughout the city, with regulations that demonstrate a concern that prostitution be both highly visible and highly restricted. The use of DECIMA to map where prostitutes lived and worked gives a better view of the competing worlds – geographically, visually, and aurally – of sex and the sacred and exposes the dynamics of compromise and accommodation in the experience of the city. The paradoxes and accommodations that define the boundaries between sex and the sacred become more clearly evident, and the tensions in their mutual exchange raise broader questions about the closed and open spaces of the early modern city.

John Henderson and Colin Rose review the plague of 1630–31, which killed nine thousand Florentines (12 per cent of the population) within a year. Previous studies have used government, church, and hospital records to gauge the official response in general terms. Using DECIMA to track weekly and monthly deaths street by street through the city's largest parish of San Lorenzo allows for geospatial analysis of rates of infection, the impact of infection in affected areas according to housing and population, and changes in plague virulence over the course of twelve months. Incorporating time as an organizing principle of analysis adds a new element to the DECIMA's scope and utility and shows how the plague decimated certain streets while leaving others relatively unharmed. The ability of historical GIS to draw demographic, geospatial, and temporal data into one unified analytical framework allows us to investigate why this was the case.

Part 3, *Mapping Motion, Emotion, and Sense: Using Digital Mapping to Rethink Categories and Communication*, steps back to consider how digital mapping transforms inquiry and makes it possible to envision new directions and subject matter. It raises broader questions of how space and mobility were experienced and how early moderns conceptualized their cities.

Niall Atkinson explores techniques of visualizing the soundscapes of early modern Florence by deploying the census data that the DECIMA group has plotted onto a digitally interactive platform representing the social topography of sixteenth-century Florence. This spatially coded environment allows him to show how mapping historical data sheds new light on how social relations are deeply embedded into urban space. It allows us to see that parishes in the premodern city were not fixed physical territories but imagined, fluid, and participatory psychogeographies through which social relations were continually realigned. From this emerges a more dynamic understanding of the ephemeral nature of sound and its role as a temporal and mobile but fundamental component of the city's physical and social geography. As such, visualizing soundscapes allows historians to apprehend the multiple, overlapping temporal and spatial zones within which early modern urban life was experienced.

Nicholas Eckstein asks, 'Can we map an emotion like fear?' Eckstein uses human movement, both actual and metaphorical, as a key to unlocking contemporary perceptions and understanding of Florence during the 1630 plague. Official correspondence of the city's health magistracy highlights fears about plagues in other towns and cities that threatened to engulf the Florentine population. Their advisories show how the anxiety produced by spreading disease and the measures that the government took to address this threat produced a spatialized vision of the Florentine state that we may understand as a mental map. Florence's neighbourhoods exhaled infection, while its walls could be breached in numerous places. Eckstein maps the highly spatialized language in which the health magistracy expressed its fears. By overlaying these maps with the social historical map of the DECIMA, we can produce a layered vision of the city informed by affect as well as geography, a map on which certain places and spaces assumed a different significance depending on the crisis through which they are described.

Fabrizio Nevola and David Rosenthal move into the area of knowledge mobilization with an explanation of how GPS technology delivered through smartphone apps can foster a new form of kinetic, experiential history. The *Hidden Florence* prototype investigates multiple sites through the city, constructed around the everyday itineraries of an artisan in the late fifteenth century. Using Buonsignori's map as the visual interface allows modern walkers to walk the streets of the past and directly confront the elisions and disjunctures between past and present. This chapter delves into the theoretical scaffolding and the social historical concerns underpinning *Hidden Florence* to reveal the ways it has been informed by recent thinking about the relationship among space, place, movement, and identity in the urban context. Nevola and Rosenthal explore the potential and drawbacks of this kind of application as a research methodology, as a pedagogical tool, and as a means of engaging a wide public in urban historical enquiry.

*

Florence has always held fascination as a site of artistic, intellectual, and cultural innovation. Ideas generated in the conflicted civic and political culture of the Renaissance period continue to resonate today. No other city of any size has data sets as complete or rich for a period before the eighteenth century. Having them for a major political, cultural, and economic centre with roughly nine thousand households offers an extraordinary research opportunity. The data generated by the 1427 *Catasto* give historians insight into the social structures of the fifteenth-century oligarchical republic. Data generated by the 1561 *Decima* speak not only to the expanding bureaucracy of a state that is a paradigm of early modern absolutism but also to that state's economic, social, sensory, and kinetic geographies.

Digital mapping projects offer statistically rich and socially complex comparative pictures of the key developments in Florence through the periods of its most transformative political, economic, and social change. It takes collaborative work both to bring together the underlying databases and to explore their potential with questions that may not have been on the minds of historians when they were first created. Describing the evolution of these projects through collaborative research and exploring the tensions, choices, frustrations, and questions that they generate can help anyone who aims to launch a similar project for other early modern cities. These digital tools are certainly powerful, but they also raise the question of what kind of city we are re-creating. Would sixteenth-century Florentines recognize it? Does the question even matter? Ideally, collaborative projects generate open-access tools that allow detailed comparative analysis on population and occupational distribution, economic development, social stratification, and mobility without losing a sense of the city as a lived and living environment rich in sensory dimensions. The rich mine of readily accessible comparative data that DECIMA opens up for mid-sixteenth-century Florence allows us to trace the dynamics of stability and mobility in an early modern city experiencing significant political, economic, and social change. As this online research and teaching tool evolves, it tests options for the advanced interdisciplinary spatio-temporal digital mapping of historical cities and even for understanding their sensory and emotional life. This is the city that digital historians have been aiming to recover, and the essays that follow here mark a further step in that process.

Editorial Note: In all the essays, we distinguish the 1561 tax record as the *Decima* and the modern digital tool as the DECIMA. More detailed versions of all maps and figures used in this book can be found on the DECIMA website: http://decima.chass.utoronto.ca

Notes

1 Access DECIMA at http://.decima.chass.utoronto.ca and *Hidden Florence* at www.hiddenflorence.org. See also N. Terpstra and C. Rose, 'DECIMA: The Digitally-Encoded Census Information and Mapping Archive, and the Project for a Geo-Spatial and Sensory Map of Renaissance Florence', *The Journal for Early Modern Cultural Studies* 13, 2013, 156–60.
2 D. Herlihy and C. Klapisch-Zuber, *Tuscans and Their Families: A Study of the Florentine Catasto of 1427,* New Haven, CT: Yale University Press, 1985. Access the online *Catasto* at cds.library.brown.edu/projects/catasto/. An example of a recent project working with this material is the 'Catasto Datamining Project': csis.pace.edu/~lombardi/sciences/computer/datamining/catasto (accessed 1 June 2015).
3 ASF, *Miscellanea Medicea*, 223 (1551) and 224 (1562). For the 1561 *ricerca*: ASF, *Decima Granducale*, 3780–84. S.M. Trkulja (ed.), *I Fiorentini nel 1562: Descritione delle Bocche della Città et stato di Fiorenza fatta l'anno 1562,* Firenze: Alberto Bruschi, 1991.
4 M. Rosen, *The Mapping of Power in Renaissance Italy,* Cambridge, UK: Cambridge University Press, 2015, 79–194.
5 R. Burr Litchfield, *Florence Ducal Capital, 1530–1630,* New York: ACLS Humanities E-Book, 2008. Online. Available <http://hdl.handle.net/2027/heb.90034.0001.001> (accessed 1 June 2015).
6 See http://tavernsproject.com and www.hiddenflorence.org (accessed 1 June 2015).

Bibliography

Manuscript sources

Archivio di Stato di Firenze (ASF), *Decima Granducale*, 3780–3784.
——— *Miscellanea Medicea*, 223 and 224.

Print sources

Herlihy, D., and Klapisch-Zuber, C., *Tuscans and Their Families: A Study of the Florentine Catasto of 1427,* New Haven, CT: Yale University Press, 1985.

Litchfield, R., *Florence Ducal Capital, 1530–1630,* New York, NY: ACLS Humanities E-Book, 2008. Online. Available <http://hdl.handle.net/2027/heb.90034.0001.001> (accessed 10 May 2015).

Rosen, M., *The Mapping of Power in Renaissance Italy,* Cambridge, UK: Cambridge University Press, 2015.

Terpstra, N., and Rose, C., 'DECIMA: The Digitally-Encoded Census Information and Mapping Archive, and the Project for a Geo-Spatial and Sensory Map of Renaissance Florence', *The Journal for Early Modern Cultural Studies* 13, 2013.

Trkulja, S.M. (ed.), *I Fiorentini nel 1562: Descritione delle Bocche della Città et stato di Fiorenza fatta l'anno 1562,* Florence, Italy: Alberto Bruschi, 1991.

Part 1
Creating a historical GIS project

1 Thinking and using DECIMA

Neighbourhoods and occupations in Renaissance Florence

Colin Rose

Can geospatial thinking about history improve our understanding of the past and the urban and rural worlds that early moderns moved in?[1] Historical Geographic Information Systems (HGIS) is a growing field that remains a specialists' game, yet some emerging platforms are flexible and multipurpose, employing a range of data provided by and serving historians in many subfields.[2] This is the concept and intent behind DECIMA. More than simply a tool, it aims to encourage historians working from various methodologies and in various subfields to begin thinking and practicing spatial history.[3] This chapter reviews how the DECIMA evolved and uses some test cases to demonstrate how the spatial dimension it facilitates allows historians to see both their documents and Renaissance Florence in a different light.

The DECIMA GIS allows us to focus progressively closer on individual Florentines as they described themselves to a scribe inquiring after their property. At its outermost resolution, DECIMA provides a new way of conceiving of Florence's parishes, for example, by mapping them as polygons according to parishioner's self-identification. This exercise revealed that Florentine parishes, as conceived and described by their members, were vastly more complex than the city's political divisions into *quartiere*, *sestiere*, and *gonfalone*, spatial divisions that were instituted by civic authorities for administrative purposes. Parishes, as lived and conceived by their members, were bound less by geography or church location than by local identity and relationships, as demonstrated by the wildly intricate parish map generated by DECIMA and discussed further later.

Tightening the lens, DECIMA shows that within each quarter and parish, life was similarly complex: a bustling mix of labourers, launderers, and artisans rubbed shoulders with the high and mighty, with sumptuous courtesans, and with some of Europe's most notable dignitaries. In the westerly cloth-weaving quarter of Santa Maria Novella, concentrations of industrial labourers crowded out almost everybody else except the bakers and butchers. DECIMA's occupational and economic data reveal how Florentine neighbourhoods could be highly mixed yet dominated by single groups. In the same quarter, occupational groups appear in fascinating patterns, revealing that Florentine neighbourhoods avoided an overconcentration of services such as baking or barbering. By design or self-interest, these were evenly distributed geographically. Yet not all artisans lived adjacent to their places of work, and DECIMA allows us to move yet further into the data and compare workplace and residence among these skilled workers and professionals. Geographic, economic, and social stratification reveals that these groups were themselves heterogeneous. Difficult-to-penetrate neighbourhoods become more visible in the DECIMA HGIS, and its ability to analyze multiple variables such as property ownership, occupation, and property value in a single frame allows far more sophisticated comparative queries into place and space.

Moving closer to street level, we see individual Florentines, from Michele the plumber to Mona Alessandra de' Medici, in the physical landscape of ducal Florence. We can map their residence, their occupations, their places of employment and investment, and their familial and working networks. We learn who their neighbours were, what industries operated along their streets, and what sights, sounds, and smells they experienced in their daily lives. DECIMA allows for a micro-analysis of the inhabitants of streets, bringing individual and otherwise unremarkable Florentines such as the mason Chimenti into relief and taking him through his neighbourhood of Sant'Ambrogio, where we learn about the highly mixed group of characters inhabiting this working-class district. DECIMA's fiscal data reveals retired courtesans living in quarters rented from local nuns, next to the *palazzi* of well-to-do townsmen and in comparative decrepitude. We can follow Chimenti as he moves through the neighbourhood, using tax estimates to establish a socioeconomic profile of the houses and taverns he passes on his way to church or tavern. As we zoom in even closer with DECIMA we are able to re-create different levels of socioeconomic and geographic context and appreciate the value of spatialized socioeconomic data to even the most micro- of microhistories.

Early modern data and modern data analysis

The translation of a rich though inconsistent body of materials from a manuscript and a map produced in the sixteenth century to a digitized platform combining a robust database and a georeferenced map of early modern Florence has been a difficult process. The challenges encountered are instructive both for its use and for early modern historians interested in pursuing similar projects. Broadly, the DECIMA team encountered two major problems. First, how could we effectively organize a database, which relies on discrete categories of information reduced to their most comparable variables, out of a data set that is, by the nature of its project, inconsistent?[4] Some *Decima* entries describe a building and the people inhabiting it in detail, while others give a more minimalist sketch of a street's properties. Second, how could we reconcile our conception of geographic space, based on the Cartesian plane and defined by degrees, minutes, and seconds, with the very different notions of urban space that we can see in the period's manuscripts and visual renderings? While Stefano Buonsignori's surveying and cartographic methods were technically advanced and equal to the best of the sixteenth century, he was not building a modern highway map.[5] Would his cartography be compatible with modern software?

Initially, we had the choice of a modern road map of Florence, to which census data could be relatively easily attached, or a contemporary map that would represent more fully the urban makeup of sixteenth-century Florence. We opted for the latter: the highly detailed *Nova pulcherrimae civitatis Florentiae topographia accuratissime delineata* produced by the Olivetan monk and Medici court cartographer Stefano Buonsignori in 1584. We faced the challenge of placing this map into Cartesian geographic space and then placing the completed database onto that map as a 'layer' of point-based vector data. Each point represents one of the approximately nine thousand properties surveyed by the ducal notaries in 1561. There were three challenges in georeferencing the map and the census: could we make a meaningful connection between Buonsignori's cartography and modern GPS coordination? Would our two data sets, the written data from 1561 and the visual presentation of the city from 1584, be compatible? Finally, in the absence of numbered addresses that modern historians can work with, how would we map the locations of some nine thousand properties in any meaningful or accurate manner?

Given that we were using an updated 1695 printing of the 1584 map, provided by the Harvard Map Library, there was also a real fear that changes in the city's urban fabric would have rendered the map inaccurate.[6] On this question, our fears were rapidly assuaged: colleagues at the University of Florence Faculty of Architecture assured us that the period 1561–84 was bereft of major changes to the urban fabric. Those elements of the city updated in the 1695 reprinting of the Buonsignori map, such as the labelling of the Ponte Vecchio as the goldsmiths' district, do not change the layout of streets and gardens that dominate the map. In fact, Florence's urban fabric remained largely unchanged from the late sixteenth century until the major changes of the nineteenth century when demographic growth and its brief status as the capital of the new Italian state (1865–71) triggered a boom in demolition and construction.[7] It is thus neither a stretch of the imagination nor a manipulation of historical reality to place the 1561 census entries on the 1695 printing of the 1584 map, aligning the streets described in the manuscript with those drawn by Buonsignori. We still needed to decide how to do it and whether our map would suffer in the process of georeferencing (the placing of a topographic image onto its corresponding Cartesian coordinates, represented in two-dimensional space).

Fortunately, Buonsignori was a good surveyor. He relied on newly developed techniques to ensure that streets met at the correct angles, that distances were proportional across the map, and that the mathematical apportionment of space represented the 'bird's-eye view' with fair accuracy. We find minor inaccuracies in the map when we compare it to our modern depictions of space: the working-class neighbourhood stretching along the southern bank of the Arno on the eastern side of the city suffers from some distortion, as does its corresponding neighbourhood across the river in Santa Croce. This is attributable partly to physical changes in the riverbed between the 1500s and today and partly to the limitations of Buonsignori's surveying techniques. Here again, ArcGIS was able to accommodate these limitations through a transformation process that reshaped the map image to fit more accurately the physical layout of the physical city. Those who access the map online will see that it appears on the diagonal. This helped to create the visual interface and to orient the map image on a north-south axis, the demands of which were not present in early modern cartography.[8]

We were still left with the challenge of overlaying thousands of property holdings onto the visual platform. HGIS platforms constructed with later data have two major advantages in this respect: fire plans and numbered address systems.[9] Both are highly accurate, and GIS platforms are capable of 'reading' both of these historical sources and matching tabular data on residency and address to the visual platform with considerable automation. Early modern Florence had neither fire plans nor numbered addresses on streets; the location of residences is always relational – next to a monastery, around the corner from the church, by the gardens of the Signore.[10] Mapping residences point by point was impractical with some nine thousand properties to locate. After consultation and discussion with Niall Atkinson and humanities computing experts at the University of Chicago, we decided against attempting to locate precisely each and every building in the census, as this would result in an unintelligible warren of properties stretching back into gardens and crowding major street corners. Instead, we would seek a 'route-based' accuracy that reflected the relative position of properties to one another as they appeared in the census; the gardener's shed is thus placed not in the garden but in line with the houses on the street. To achieve this, we developed a method for extracting Cartesian locational data (X,Y coordinates) from the descriptions of the routes taken by the team of *Decima* surveyors.

These surveyors were assiduous at marking the corners of streets and the directions they travelled along them throughout the census. This proved critical. Rather than locating by eye the approximately nine thousand census entries, we placed all corner properties on the map and extracted their XY coordinates to the census database. Using MS Excel©, I automated the creation of XY coordinates for all entries between the corners. The result is the unrealistically neat but extremely legible map of Florentine social geography that places properties in their correct location in the census, on the correct street, though not necessarily at the exact location on that street where the physical edifice stood. To accommodate the difficulties of geolocating early modern properties lacking coded address information, we used the census notes as a locational guide to ensure that neighbours are next to neighbours, that corner properties are appropriately located, and that the tangible experience of walking through the streets was reproduced as faithfully as possible in two-dimensional representation. The results were pleasantly surprising: many of the houses described as 'next to a garden' indeed ended up next to a garden.

Working with early modern sources in Historical GIS presents particular challenges that modernists are unlikely to face but that will be immediately recognizable to anyone familiar with the urban history of the sixteenth and seventeenth centuries. Early modern peoples conceived of their cities in different ways than we do; they were not just areas of transit, or employment, or residence. They were working, living, and ritual spaces described and depicted according to the work, life, and ritual needs of their societies. The *Decima* was an exercise in a ritual of power undertaken at a time when information and the ability to track that information were becoming ever more important for governments. This project of power proved highly compatible with our own aims as digital historians, despite or, indeed, because of the unique challenges presented by our early modern sources.

The city from above: official and local demarcations of space

Building the DECIMA system required translating the two early modern sources just mentioned, the *Decima* manuscripts of 1561 and the 1584 Buonsignori map, from their paper forms to a database of spatialized entries. Each of these sources contains spatial information, either in text or presented visually, that provides an *official* view of the city's major physical features, administrative borders, and spiritual and political centres. Neither is a neutral document. In Buonsignori's map, the cathedral of Santa Maria del Fiore, or Duomo, appears even more outsized and monolithic than in real life. Buonsignori gives it a scale that dominates the nearby churches of Santa Maria Novella, San Lorenzo, and Santa Croce. The Palazzo Vecchio and the Palazzo Pitti, governmental spaces close to the Medici dynasty, are similarly prominent in Buonsignori's view of the city. The map highlights both the religious and the political spaces of the city, depicting them with considerable realism and faithfulness to their appearance, whereas residences, most *palazzi*, and *botteghe* are drawn pro forma, with a standardized 'model' of what a Florentine home looked like. These depictions give the city a uniform look, with significant public spaces associated with sacred and secular order being made important by their size and detail. When using the map, then, we recall that *it has a purpose*; we should not lose sight of that purpose, which was the presentation of an early modern city to its ruler as a drawn representation of his domain and power.[11]

The census notes should be viewed much the same way.[12] Beyond the political motivations of the census, we see that demarcations of space in the census notes reflect official conceptions of the city, its administrative divisions, and its physical landscape. Thus it is organized by quarter and by street; spatial references are given by familiar landscape markers that are often religious: a house was 'next to one owned by the monks of the *Chiarito*' or 'between the walls of the monastery and the walls of the Hospital'.[13] The structure of parishes is an exception to this rule. The notation of neighbourhoods, or parishes, sometimes placed at the top of a page, is often embedded within the entries, hinting that the residents themselves supplied the information. Within this document, shaped by Cosimo I's fiscal purposes and the *Decima*'s administrative needs, there are flashes of local colour that complicate our understanding of the spatial organization of the early modern city.[14] The structure or, to be more accurate, the lack of structure of Florentine parishes is one such element of the census; only by combining the textual and the visual sources do we notice and begin to query this messy clash of official borders and social geography.

A review of parish boundaries highlights this clash of cartography and identity.[15] Figure 1.1 shows the location of the forty-nine parish churches across

20 *Colin Rose*

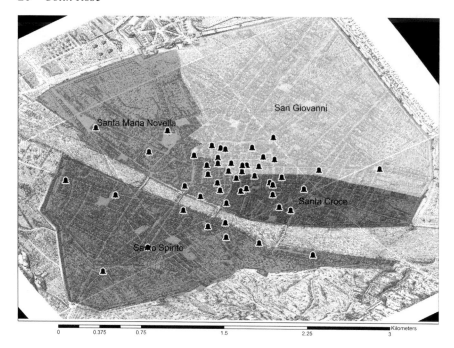

Figure 1.1 Florentine parish churches and *gonfaloni*, mapped over the city's *quartieri* at 80 per cent transparency.

Florence, mapped against the city's four quarters and sixteen *gonfalone* administrative districts. Most of the parish churches (32) lie within the old centre of the city, either within or just outside the ancient Roman grid that includes the area stretching from the Duomo west to San Lorenzo and from there down towards the river on either side. The grid is clearly visible on Buonsignori's map, just another means for the map to show the city's change over time and its historical phases. As we see from the concentration of parish churches within the historic city core, these structures emerged at an early stage in Florence's urban development. They were built in and for a smaller city, with a smaller population, and were poor markers of local communities, overshadowed by preexisting family territories and turfs.[16] By the late sixteenth century, when the city had expanded well beyond the core and houses, convents and suburban *ville* had consumed many intramural suburban gardens, and new parish churches had been added in pockets radiating from the city centre, though none were built in the northern quarter of San Giovanni. The newest churches tend to be located on the south bank, in the quarter of Santo Spirito, and are found on major transit routes through the neighbourhood and clustered along the riverbank. Prior to building the parish boundary polygon layer, DECIMA hypothesized that these churches would generally lay in the centre of parishes, with residences of parish dwellers located radially around them.

Figure 1.2 shows the parish churches mapped against the geography of Florentine parishes as defined by the census takers and the subjects of their inquiry. It

Thinking and using DECIMA 21

Figure 1.2 Florentine parishes as created from the *Decima* entries.

is immediately clear that there is a significant difference between the geography of civic administrative district known as the *gonfalone* and that of the ecclesiastical neighbourhood districts known as parishes. To create a parish map based on the borders of parishes as defined by the *Decima* scribes, I worked backwards from the point-based visualization of the census entries. By setting the residential layer's symbology to represent the parish ascribed to each entry, I achieved a rough visualization of census borders. I then drew polygons over these borders to create a shape-based map of Florentine parishes. The result is a map of Florentine parishes that abides by the borders of parishes identified by the *Decima* scribes and the subjects of their fiscal survey.

The complexity of Florence's social geography is immediately apparent in Figure 1.2. The city centre, where the oldest and most established parishes were located, is a warren of interlocking, overlapping social geographies that existed primarily in the minds of the scribes and of the people living there. Extracting parish data from the census entries revealed that residence was not the primary criterion of parish membership; other factors were at work, more important than proximity to one's parish church. What is perhaps most striking about parish geography is that many parish churches in the old centre, such as San Remigio, lie outside the parish boundaries as these were identified by parish members themselves. This complexity would not be apparent if we were not able to juxtapose the census entries and the Buonsignori map. The analytical and cartographic capacities of Historical GIS bring out the disjunction of administrative and social boundaries. Social histories of the past four decades have led us to realize that the social geography of Florence is vastly more difficult to understand than its administrative or political geographies would indicate. DECIMA's cartographic and analytic capabilities allow us now to document and visualize this.

This stage of DECIMA analysis relies on *vector data*, the points, lines, and shapes that overlie the map's *raster data*, the image of the map itself that has been georeferenced to Cartesian GPS coordinates. It is primarily a visual analysis. The labels of churches and parishes have been excluded from Figures 1.1 and 1.2 to avoid cluttered images, to demonstrate visually how the social geography of Florentine parishes differs from its administrative divisions, and to show that the latter do not track in any meaningful way to the former. We see that instead of, for instance, occupying the central territory of a parish, the older parish churches are clustered around major streets of the old Roman city, while the newer churches south of the Arno and west and east of the old Roman core act as gateways lying on the borders of parishes, their own parishes stretching behind them, their neighbours ahead of them, and the church demarcating the boundaries. The physical church is more liminal than central to the parish, and it is the visual capabilities of DECIMA that allow us to see this and to ask new questions about how early modern cities organized their populations and how their populations organized themselves.

Professional and economic stratification within Santa Maria Novella

Who lived and worked in Renaissance Florence? How much did they pay in rent, and who owned the houses they lived in? Where did artisans, labourers, and courtiers call home throughout the city? How much did cobblers interact with weavers in the course of their work week? Geospatial patterns of work and residence can tell us much about the quotidian sociability of early modern Florentines. The tightly knit family networks that constituted the city's upper class were embedded in the very real brick-and-mortar geography of the cityscape, no less than were the lives of the masons, weavers, prostitutes, and gardeners whose work supported the elite. Yet, for all we know about ducal Florence's highly ritualized civic life, its messy bureaucracy operating under an unspoken tolerance of graft, and the importance of charity and other social welfare for the peaceful existence of its elite citizens, we lack a firm picture of precisely who participated in that civic life, who stood to lose significantly from the habitual theft of grain reserves, or who watched from their windows as babies were passed through the turn-wheel at the foundling home of the Innocenti.[17] Ducal Florence was a city in which public life loomed large, and having a better idea of who constituted the Florentine 'public' helps us understand the myriad ways in which Florentines of vastly different social stripes cohabited in a densely packed city of fifty to sixty thousand people.

The quarter of Santa Maria Novella, at the city's western end on the north side of the Arno, is instructive here. We know already from Robert Burr Litchfield's earlier work employing these sources that Via Palazzuolo was home to a high concentration of textile weavers.[18] The layering of census data onto the Buonsignori map makes clear that large numbers of weaver households also lived on Borgo Ognissanti and on Via Gora, pressed between Ognissanti and the Arno River. There was also a large grouping of weaver households near the end of Via della Scala and a small cluster on Via Nuova di San Giuliano. The number of weavers on any given street is less important than their geospatial and economic distribution along that street, which Litchfield's method was unable to account for. While he divided the Buonsignori map into eighty-seven equal squares laid out in a grid in order to plot in rough terms where workers' households were located, DECIMA's street-level analysis allows for a more detailed accounting of these patterns. Using assessed taxes as a rough estimate of household wealth, we understand that economic stratification within the textile industry was played out in geospatial residential patterns.

There are a total of 172 textile weaver households identified as such in Santa Maria Novella, 10.3 per cent of all the quarter's households.[19] Only fourteen of these weavers owned their own homes. At the same time, only twelve weaver households were at the opposite end of the economic scale, occupying sublet housing (DECIMA has termed these 'Third Renters'). These poorer weavers were identified only as *tessitori*, while weavers who owned their homes were more often identified by specialized skills, such as *tessitori di drappi* (wool weavers), who made up half of the owners, or *tessitori di broccati* (silk weavers – two of the fourteen owners) The majority of weavers (95/172, or 55 per cent) held their properties under a *livello*, a lease whose term could be anywhere from a few

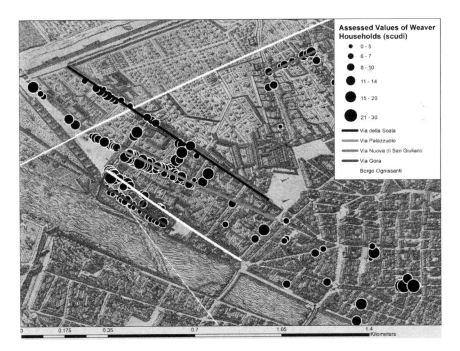

Figure 1.3 Textile weavers in Santa Maria Novella and the assessed values of their household properties.

months to a lifetime.[20] These patterns demonstrate the range of wealth within the textile industry: seventy-seven weaver households have an assessed value ranging from 8 to12 *scudi*, while fifty-seven fall below this assessment and thirty-eight are above it. While there were more poor weavers than rich, there were more middling weaver households than any other kind.

This could all be deciphered working with the *Decima* manuscripts and a spreadsheet. DECIMA enhances the analysis by locating the individual weaver households and allowing for geospatial analysis of these patterns (see Figure 1.4). The poorest weavers lived in rented quarters on Via Gora, which they either leased or sublet from widows, artisans, or religious institutions such as the Umiliati monastery of Ognissanti; the friars of Ognissanti had introduced textile work to the area centuries earlier and continued to take an active interest in it. So, for example, they apparently accepted responsibility for the widows of weavers, four of whom were clustered in cheap housing next to the convent itself on Borgo Ognissanti. Along Via Palazzuolo to the north, where Litchfield noted the highest concentration of weavers, two patterns stand out. The first is that the weaver households are most densely packed at the western end of the street, on both the north and the south sides. Here and at the western end of the Borgo Ognissanti lived weavers of the middling sort, who tended to rent their homes from artisan leaseholders. They paid higher rents than their colleagues two streets to the south, between 70 and 105 lire *per annum*. At the western end of Via della Scala and along Via Nuova di San Giuliano lived more weavers of this middling sort who paid medium rents on properties assessed at medium values. There were extremes of wealth within the

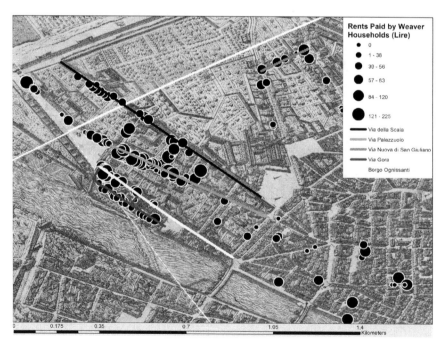

Figure 1.4 Textile weavers in Santa Maria Novella and the rents they paid, in *lire*.

weaver class: in the southeastern corner of Figure 1.3 are larger condominiums, represented by two large diamonds. One was owned by a group of four weavers (three siblings and one other, who occupied the house) with an apartment let to another weaver, while the second was owned by the confraternity of Orsanmichele and occupied by a weaver named Batista who apparently lived free of charge. Both of these properties had assessed values of 30 *scudi*, which was on the very high end of declared property values in Florence. If we take advantage of DECIMA's geospatial analytical prowess, we see that the fairly intense economic stratification among weavers becomes a spatial issue as well as an economic one: the poorest weavers lived by the river, on the outflow side of the city. This is one major difference between the early modern and the modern cities: an apartment on Via Montebello, formerly Via Gora, can currently be rented for €1010 a night, while in 1561 the outbound riverside was filthy, odorous, and manifestly unhealthy. This undesirable property was where the poorest of textile weavers clustered.[21]

DECIMA can also reveal the spatial distribution of particular professions and their dispersal across the city. Using it to track the locations of three types of professional workshops across Santa Maria Novella reveals a regularity of geospatial distribution that cannot be coincidental. Renata Ago argued that networks of Roman artisans operated primarily on personal experience and personal credit; that is, you patronized whom you knew and whom you trusted.[22] I would suggest that something similar was at work among the guild bakers, barbers, and butchers of Santa Maria Novella. The locations of ovens, barbershops, and butchers' homes are shown in Figure 1.5.

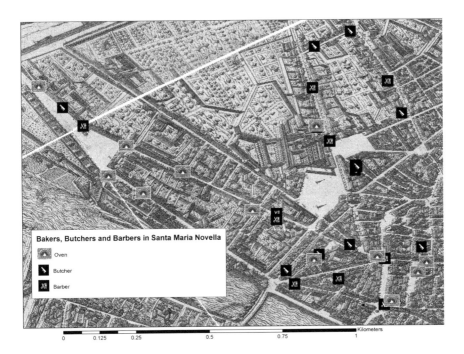

Figure 1.5 Butchers, bakers, and barbers in Santa Maria Novella.

The oven icons in Figure 1.5 represent *forni* where locals could buy their daily bread. The butcher's cleavers represent the homes of butchers, who mostly would have operated stalls in the Mercato Vecchio. The saw-and-scissor icons represent barber-surgeons, who worked primarily from home or travelled to their clients and patients. Litchfield assigns each of these professions, for the year 1551, a 'distance from centre' co-efficient of zero, meaning that the homes of these professionals were dispersed regularly throughout the city.[23] Here, again, DECIMA takes the analysis a major step further by placing these professions and their workshops individually into the geospatial landscape of Florence, using the 1561 data extracted from the *Decima* of that year. Figure 1.5 shows exactly how regular the distribution of ovens was across the quarter of Santa Maria Novella. These locations are more precisely plotted than the average household in the DECIMA, because so many of them, as is plainly visible, were located on street corners and thus formed part of the census takers' locational data that guided the geocoding of the *Decima* properties. Along Via Palazzuolo, the ovens are dispersed at intervals of no more than 300m and no less than 150m. That is to say: one never had to walk more than 150m, and usually substantially less, to buy one's daily bread.

Butchers and barbers are equally well dispersed through the less-industrial areas of Santa Maria Novella. The streets Gualfonda and Faenza, leading north from the churches of Santa Maria Novella and San Leonardo, respectively, have butchers at both their north and south intersections and barbers about halfway along the street. The radial distance here is important: once again, no inhabitant of these streets, and indeed of most of the quarter, was ever more than 150m from someone who could set a broken bone, suture a wound, or stuff a sausage. DECIMA's geolocation, representative rather than realistic, emphasizes the highly regular dispersal of these basic professions, shown in their workshops, the ovens, and, curiously, the homes of butchers.

Florentines lived in highly stratified, economically diverse communities that nonetheless placed the poorest members on particular streets and allowed the wealthier members to collect rents from their less well-off colleagues in undesirable areas of the city. The stratification is horizontal, not vertical: no weaver would be considered 'wealthy' in comparison to the economic elite of Florence or to wealthier artisans such as a successful goldsmith. But the weavers of Via Palazzuolo would have taken comfort that they were not as poor as those of the Borgo Ognissanti, who themselves would have turned their noses up at the maliferous odours of the Arno wafting into the homes of their colleagues on Via Gora. Fortunately, when it came to feeding one's family there were no 'food deserts' in poor areas – everyone had an oven nearby. For the poorest weavers, finding a barber in an emergency might have been difficult, and it may have been a trek to buy meat but even then, the maximum distance to walk was some 375m. Florentine neighbourhoods, hosting dense communities of like workers, were well served by the basic industries of food and emergency medical care/barbering.

Quarter-wide occupational analysis is relatively straight forward, but it shows how simple analyses in HGIS can provoke unexpected interpretations. The questions guiding this section are not complex or difficult – where did barbers or weavers live? – but from these simple questions emerge fascinating patterns that have hitherto been described only anecdotally or very locally in nonvisualized spatial analyses of the occupational structure of Florentine neighbourhoods. Though the questions are simple, answering them required selecting attributes across five fields for simultaneous analysis, something that cannot be done in conventional spreadsheet programs or by the historian poring over manuscripts. DECIMA's GIS analytical power, backed by its robust database of historical information, makes feasible these sorts of analyses.

DECIMA as a micro-historical lens

On a given morning in 1561, Chimenti di Luca Piccardi, a mason, might have stepped out of the house he owned on the north side of Via dei Pilastri northeast of the Florentine city centre, turned to the left, and walked southeast towards the parish church of Sant'Ambrogio at the triangular convergence of Pilastri, Via dei Sbanditi, and Via Pietrapiana.[24] He may have been accompanied by some of the six women, presumably his wife and children, who lived with him. Hoping to avoid the harsh Tuscan sun or perhaps to stay out of a winter's chill, he would have huddled close to the tall walls of the house next door, owned by the Camaldolese

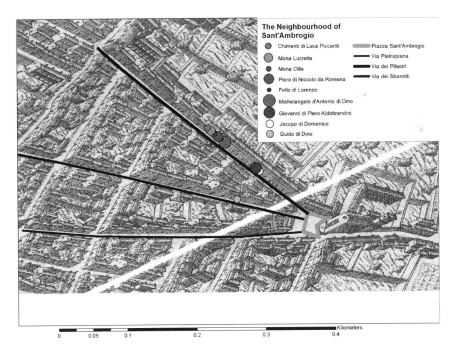

Figure 1.6 The neighbourhood of Sant'Ambrogio, including the parishes of Sant'Ambrogio and San Piero. Proportional dots indicate the relative locations of the owners and tenants discussed in this section, scaled to the assessed tax value of their residence.[25]

Monaci degli Angeli. Chimenti's neighbor, Michele the tailor, had passed away, and his widow, Lucretia, now rented the house from the monks, supporting herself and two other women by working as a *meretrice*, a courtesan; neighbours would assume that her two female companions shared the occupation as well as the house.[26] Chimenti hurries his daughters past this house and the next, a building crowded with twelve people from two households: one of Andrea di Francesco Larucci and the other of his landlord, Cilia, the widow of Andrea the cloth dyer.[27] Cilia herself has leased the building from the Monastery of S. Pietro, which charges her less than half the 7 *scudi* per annum that her neighbour Lucretia pays to the friars of the Angeli.

Chimenti and his daughters may have slowed down for the next house, the palazzo of Piero di Niccolo da Romena, who lives here alone and whose extensive garden is tended by Fello di Lorenzo, who lives in the cottage behind.[28] Next door is the even larger Dino residence, where Michelagnolo d'Antonio lives with a small family.[29] The Dino home is part of a long stretch of narrow row houses leading towards the Piazza Sant'Ambrogio; many of these are home to families large and small, many are owned by local religious confraternities, and many are rented cheaply to local widows. Perhaps Chimenti doffed his cap to the wealthy Giovanni di Piero Aldobrandini as he passed his home about ten doors away from the church.[30] It is more likely that he stopped to bad-mouth the *pezzi grossi* (big shots) with Jacopo di Domenico, a *legnaiolo* (carpenter) who rented an apartment from Aldobrandini's neighbour Raffaello di Guccio Pallaio, before carrying on past the wool carders, cobblers, cloth dyers, widows, and patricians who filled in his short walk to the church down the road.[31] At S. Ambrogio, he may have shared a joke and some wine with Guido di Dino, a wool carder who lived around the corner on Via dei Sbanditi.[32] On his way home he would have run a similar gauntlet on the south side of Via dei Pilastri, where another cadre of assorted neighbours made their homes. Chimenti's short walk of some 375m took him through a world of lords and labourers, children and widows, all tightly packed into the narrow row housing that dominated Florence's eastern district.

HGIS allows us to follow Chimenti's short walk and to explore urban neighbourhoods with him. It allows us to reconstruct the spatial and social experiences of living in late Renaissance Florence in a unified analytical framework. This is not just for imaginative fun: behind the narrative of Chimenti's walk lie the socioeconomic data that track the composition of his neighbourhood. The DECIMA platform allows for a spatial interrogation of data that are inherently spatialized. It represents the very real experience of Duke Cosimo I's census takers as they travelled the city collecting information throughout 1561. The brief narrative of Chimenti's walk to Sant'Ambrogio, like the locating of bakers, barbers, and butchers in S. Maria Novella, relies on the analysis of vector data, the points representing census entries layered onto the Buonsignori map. It shows how the platform can analyze multiple data sets at a time, in this case the names of property tenants (owners, letters, and renters), the assessed values of their homes, and their location in Florence. It also reveals the strength and weakness of our visual source.

The Buonsignori map has been scanned at an extremely high resolution, allowing us to achieve a clear image at close zoom, down to individual houses occupying our frame of view. Yet the process of reconstructing the map from nine individual sheets is imperfect. As the edges of the physical paper have crinkled and warped over the centuries, a seamless digital stitch of the images proved impossible without sacrificing the geospatial integrity of Buonsignori's cartography.

This section also shows the benefits of working in tandem with the database of census information and the visual source and guiding the visualization by one's own interests. Tracing individual Florentines from the vast body of social history dealing with the sixteenth-century city and placing them in their homes, hitherto a painstaking process of archival shuffling though familial, governmental, and ecclesiastical records, can now be done more readily through queries to the DECIMA database. There can be confusions, particularly if the person one is searching for has some utterly common Florentine name like 'Giovanni di Giovanni'. Generally speaking, the more details known about the individual, the quicker and more reliable the results of one's search will be. But broadly, with the correct data and an understanding of how to work the database, historians can deeply enrich their understanding of the socioeconomic profiles of their research subjects, expanding on the information available in traditional social historical sources to include a spatial analysis that reveals unexpected patterns hitherto understood only in outline. DECIMA gives us great analytical prowess as well as insight into the geosocial composition of the early modern city and its inhabitants across the entire socioeconomic spectrum.

Conclusions and future work

The DECIMA platform is a powerful research tool because of how it helps the researcher to visualize social conditions and relations. In this way, it can prompt new queries while also providing a means of answering them.[33] It allows the broadest and the deepest inquiries into contemporary social visions of sixteenth-century Florence, though, as this volume demonstrates, some of these visions are suspect or even sinister. Apart from the projects described in this volume, DECIMA has already been used in research dealing with madness and families, with merchant families spread across Tuscany, and with the role of alcohol and taverns in early modern Florence.[34] The range of research that can be stimulated and improved by use of HGIS is more than can be listed here.

This chapter has shown how simple analyses of the DECIMA vector data (the dot-points representing census entries, the lines that form the street map used in Figures 1.3–1.6, and the polygon data that inform Figures 1.1 and 1.2) can reveal unexpected patterns. As the parish map demonstrates, DECIMA provokes questions about how exactly parishes were defined, if at all, and shows that Florentine laity and clergy may have had different ways of approaching those definitions. As the mapping of weavers' households in Santa Maria Novella shows, DECIMA can improve our understanding of how the households of textile workers were concentrated on three streets. Those three streets showed significant social and economic stratification, with the poorest weavers huddling in the stench of the riverbank where million-dollar apartments now stand. And as Chimenti's walk to Sant'Ambrogio shows, occupational clustering was not uniform throughout the city. This mason's neighbours were a highly mixed group of wealthy patricians, carpenters, prostitutes, and monks all living in what must have been less than perfect harmony. Each of these three analyses has employed a different set of DECIMA's analytical capabilities, and the platform is really just getting started. As data sets are added, coding improves, and the body of work that informs DECIMA continues to grow, the powerful research capabilities of this innovative HGIS will continue to improve together with these changes, demonstrating patterns and juxtapositions that can take the study of the early modern city in new directions.

Notes

1 J. Martí-Henneberg, 'Geographical Information Systems and the Study of History', *The Journal of Interdisciplinary History* 42, 2011, 1–13; D.A. DeBats and I.N. Gregory, 'Introduction to Historical GIS and the Study of Urban History', *Social Science History* 35, 2011, 455–63.
2 The list of quality HGIS platforms is growing. An excellent first resource for historians interested in developing basic HGIS knowledge is *Geospatial Historian*, an offshoot of *The Programming Historian* written and maintained by J. Clifford and J. McFayden. J. Clifford and J. McFayden (eds), *Geospatial Historian*. Online. Available <https://geospatialhistorian.wordpress.com/> (accessed 13 May 2015).
3 A.K. Knowles, 'Introduction', *Social Science History* 24, 2000, 451–70; A.K. Knowles and A. Hillier (eds), *Placing History: How Maps, Spatial Data, and GIS Are Changing Historical Scholarship*, Redlands: ESRI Press, 2008; I. Gregory and A. Geddes (eds), *Toward Spatial Humanities: Historical GIS and Spatial History*, Bloomington: Indiana University Press, 2014; I. Gregory, *A Place in History: A Guide to Using GIS in Historical Research*, Oxford, UK: Oxbow, 2003; M. Fortin and J. Bonnell (eds), *Historical GIS Research in Canada*, Calgary: University of Calgary Press, 2013; A. von Lunen and T. Charles (eds), *History and GIS: Epistemologies, Considerations and Reflections*, Dordrecht: Springer, 2013, 1.
4 For the process of constructing and modifying the database, see E. Fabbro's contribution to this volume.
5 On Renaissance cartographic techniques and motivations, see U. Lindgren, 'Land Surveys, Instruments and Practitioners in the Renaissance', in J.B. Harley and D. Woodward (eds), *The History of Cartography*, Chicago, IL: University of Chicago Press, 1987, 477–508, as well as L. Rombai's chapter in the same volume, 'Cartography in the Central Italian States from 1480 to 1680', ibid., 931–39.
6 Harvard's Map Librarian, J. Garver, was of indispensable help in providing the extremely high-resolution map employed in the DECIMA platform.
7 G. Fanelli, *Firenze, architettura e città*, Florence: Mandragora, 2002.
8 Cf. the beautiful collection of urban maps produced in the sixteenth-century by G. Braun and F. Hogenburg, in which North-South polarity is not important to the cartography. Bologna, for example, is consistently shown oriented with the southern end of the city at the top of sixteenth-century maps. G. Braun et al., *Cities of the World*, Cologne: Taschen, 2008.
9 Cf. *Addressing History*, which relies on Scottish Post Office data from the nineteenth and twentieth centuries to track people and professions across Scotland.
10 The value of these modern tools is demonstrated well in M.J. Novak and J.A. Gilliland, 'Trading Places: A Historical Geography of Retailing in London, Canada', *Social*

Science History 35, 2011, 543–70. In their article, reliable and consistent addressing systems allow for multi-annual analysis of the changing geography of retailing as it changed over the nineteenth and twentieth centuries in London, Ontario.
11 M. Foucault, *Discipline and Punish: The Birth of the Prison*, New York, NY: Vintage Books, 1995.
12 See L. Faibisoff's contribution to this volume.
13 Archivio di Stato di Firenze, *Decima Granducale*, 3783, ff. 2v, 4r.
14 Cf. C. Friedrichs, *The Early Modern City 1450–1750*, Toronto, Ontario, Canada: Longman, 1995, for a broad survey of the characteristics of early modern cities and the relationship between religious, political and public spaces.
15 N. Atkinson explores this further in his contribution to this volume.
16 R.C. Trexler, *Public Life in Renaissance Florence*, New York, NY: Academic Press, 1980, 13.
17 Trexler, *Public Life in Renaissance Florence*; J.-C. Waquet, *Corruption: Ethics and Power in Florence, 1600–1770*, University Park, Pennsylvania: Pennsylvania State University Press, 1992; N. Terpstra, *Abandoned Children of the Italian Renaissance: Orphan Care in Florence and Bologna*, Baltimore, MD: Johns Hopkins University Press, 2005; N. Terpstra, *Lost Girls: Sex and Death in Renaissance Florence*, Baltimore, MD: Johns Hopkins University Press, 2010, P. Gavitt, *Gender, Honor, and Charity in Late Renaissance Florence*, New York, NY: Cambridge University Press, 2011.
18 R.B. Litchfield, *Florence Ducal Capital, 1530–1630*, ACLS Humanities E-Book, 2008, Renaissance Society of America Digital Books, para. 284. Online. Available <http://quod.lib.umich.edu/cgi/t/text/text-idx?c=acls;cc=acls;view=text;idno=heb90034.0001.001;rgn=div3;node=heb90034.0001.001%3A12.3.2.> (accessed 13 June 2015).
19 Here again we see some of the limits of early modern data. Across the entire city, about 50 per cent of households reported occupational data; there are surely more weavers in Santa Maria Novella than the *Decima* indicates.
20 See D. Jamison's chapter for more on these divisions.
21 <www.florenceapartmentitaly.com/florence-apartments-via-montebello-frecobaldi-32.html> (accessed 13 June 2015).
22 R. Ago, *Economia barocca: Mercato e istituzioni nella Roma del seicento*, Rome, Italy: Donzelli, 1998, 181–90.
23 Litchfield, *Florence Ducal Capital, 1530–1630*, para. 32, Table 1.1.
24 Archivio di Stato, *Decima Granducale*, 3783, f. 152r. See Figure 1.1 for the neighbourhood of Sant'Ambrogio.
25 Archivio di Stato, *Decima Granducale*, 3783, f. 152–159; S. Buonsignori, *Nova pulcherrimae civitatis Florentiae topographia acuratissime delineata*.
26 Ibid.
27 Ibid., f. 152v.
28 Ibid.
29 Ibid.
30 Ibid., 153r.
31 Ibid., 153r-v.
32 Ibid., 159v.
33 I. Gregory and A. Geddes, 'Introduction', in *Toward Spatial Humanities*, xii–xv.
34 For which see Fabrizio Nevola and David Rosenthal's contribution to this volume, and download their fantastically enjoyable *Hidden Florence* app.

Bibliography

Manuscript sources

Archivio di Stato di Firenze, *Decima Granducale*, 3780–3783.

Print sources

Ago, R., *Economia barocca: Mercato e istituzioni nella Roma del seicento*, Rome, Italy: Donzelli, 1998.

Braun, G., Hogenberg, F., Füssel, S., and Taschen, B., *Cities of the World*, Cologne: Taschen, 2008.

DeBats, D.A., and Gregory, I.N., 'Introduction to Historical GIS and the Study of Urban History', *Social Science History* 35, 2011.

Fanelli, G., *Firenze, architettura e città*, Florence: Mandragora, 2002.

Fortin, M., and Bonnell, J. (eds), *Historical GIS Research in Canada*, Calgary, Canada: University of Calgary Press, 2013.

Foucault, M., *Discipline and Punish: The Birth of the Prison*, New York, NY: Vintage Books, 1995.

Gavitt, P., *Gender, Honor, and Charity in Late Renaissance Florence*, New York, NY: Cambridge University Press, 2011.

Gregory, I., *A Place in History: A Guide to Using GIS in Historical Research*, Oxford, UK: Oxbow, 2003.

—— and Geddes, A. (eds), *Toward Spatial Humanities: Historical GIS and Spatial History*, Bloomington, IN: Indiana University Press, 2014.

Harley, J.B., and Woodward, J. (eds), *The History of Cartography*, Chicago, IL: University of Chicago Press, 1987.

Knowles, A.K., 'Introduction', *Social Science History* 24, 2000.

—— and Hillier, A. (eds), *Placing History: How Maps, Spatial Data, and GIS Are Changing Historical Scholarship*, Redlands, CA: ESRI Press, 2008.

Lindgren, U., 'Land Surveys, Instruments and Practitioners in the Renaissance', in J.B. Harley and D. Woodward (eds), *The History of Cartography*, Chicago, IL: University of Chicago Press, 1987, 477–508.

Litchfield, R.B., *Florence Ducal Capital, 1530–1630*, ACLS Humanities E-Book, New York, NY: Renaissance Society of America Digital Books, 2008. Online. Available <http://quod.lib.umich.edu/cgi/t/text/text-idx?c=acls;cc=acls;view=text;idno=heb90034.0001.001;rgn=div3;node=heb90034.0001.001%3A12.3.2> (accessed 13 June 2015).

Martí-Henneberg, J., 'Geographical Information Systems and the Study of History', *The Journal of Interdisciplinary History* 42, 2011.

Novak, M.J., and Gilliland, J.A., 'Trading Places: A Historical Geography of Retailing in London, Canada', *Social Science History* 35, 2011.

Rombai, L., 'Cartography in the Central Italian States from 1480 to 1680', in J.B. Harley and D. Woodward (eds), *The History of Cartography*, Chicago, IL: University of Chicago Press, 1987, 909–39.

Terpstra, N., *Abandoned Children of the Italian Renaissance: Orphan Care in Florence and Bologna*, Baltimore, MD: Johns Hopkins University Press, 2005.

—— *Lost Girls: Sex and Death in Renaissance Florence*, Baltimore, MD: Johns Hopkins University Press, 2010.

Trexler, R.C., *Public Life in Renaissance Florence*, New York, NY: Academic Press, 1980.

von Lunen, A., and Charles, T. (eds), *History and GIS: Epistemologies, Considerations and Reflections*, Dordrecht, The Netherlands: Springer, 2013.

Waquet, J-C., *Corruption: Ethics and Power in Florence, 1600–1770*, University Park, PA: Pennsylvania State University Press, 1992.

2 The route of governmentality
Surveying and collecting urban space in ducal Florence

Leah Faibisoff

Let us suppose that a Shade [. . .] is standing on the famous hill of San Miniato, which overlooks Florence from the south [. . .] and as he looks at the scene before him, the sense of familiarity is so much stronger than the perception of change that he thinks it might be possible to descend once more to the streets and take up that busy life where he left it.

George Eliot, *Romola* (1863)[1]

One of George Eliot's main priorities in her historical novel about the city of Florence, which opens in April 1492, is the perception of historical change. In the introduction, a Florentine 'Shade' that lived in the sixteenth century appears on the hill of San Miniato behind the south bank of the river Arno in the present day – 1863. As the Shade gazes down at Florence, the urban changes he sees there, though certainly evident, do not inhibit the sense of familiarity he feels towards his city. He longs to return to the city streets, to hear their familiar sounds, to see their familiar sights, and to know their political and social developments. From up above, it seems to the Shade possible to walk once again in the streets of Florence. But the changes at street level, the narrator warns, are considerable. 'Go not down, good Spirit! for the changes are great and the speech of Florentines would sound as a riddle in your ears.'[2]

Questioning the perception of urban change, Eliot introduces the novel by revealing an opposition between two different perspectives on the city: a bird's-eye view of Florence on the one hand and the view of a walker in the city streets on the other. Throughout the book, Eliot deliberately draws attention to a series of correspondences between the time in which the novel is set and the time in which it was written, questioning the idea of history, how we understand it, and why we are so interested in it.

This question concerning the difference between the seemingly static, built environment of the city of Florence as it is perceived from above and the everyday processes that continuously work to form and reform the social geographies of the city streets is of particular relevance to the DECIMA project. Much of Florence still looks from above as it did to Stefano Buonsignori in 1584. Yet for those who walk its modern-day streets, the sense of the past is one of nostalgia and empty verisimilitude, despite attempts to revive the feel of the period.[3] The disconnect between the way that the city appears from above – as, for example, to a shade standing on the hill of San Miniato or to the period eye of the historian – and the way the city feels down below is clear. Yet, for the historian of Florence searching the Buonsignori map to find the home or workplace of his subject of study, there is a certain familiarity with the city and an accompanying desire to know the imperfections and improvisations of life on the street as his subject knew it. Similarly, for the shade in *Romola*, familiarity with the still-identifiable, physical city as seen from above is what provokes a desire to walk its streets once more and to know its changing social geographies.

The relationship between the city as a physical phenomenon and the city as a social dynamic is a distinction that DECIMA meets head on as it seeks to assess the spatial and sensory dimensions of early modern Florence. Yet, the DECIMA project uncovers many different layers of historical dynamics and processes of change. This essay offers evidence for another such layer, arguing that an aspect of the sixteenth-century city that plays an inextricable part in the physical and social worlds of the city is its bureaucratic world. This is evident in the sixteenth-century project to survey Florence, an attempt to fiscally and demographically organize its social characteristics by way of the city's physical geography.

Legislation passed in the summer of 1561 mandated that four head surveyors and four scribes chosen by Cosimo I de' Medici and his counsellors complete a survey of all the houses and families in the city of Florence – the second such survey completed under Cosimo I.[4] According to this legislation, each head surveyor and his scribe were assigned to one of the four quarters of the city.[5] Knocking on each door they came across, they examined the residential particulars of every household and recorded its fiscal information. The surveyors were charged with determining the amount of taxable income that owners were making on their immovable property by asking those residing on the property how much they paid in rent. This is not to suggest that the Florentines interviewed did not attempt to conceal their property holdings. The figures listed in these records must be taken with a grain of salt and measured against other sources. Yet, administrators would have acknowledged that residents paying rent were in the best position to either corroborate or contradict the tax declarations of property owners. Thus, the 1561 survey demonstrates an official attempt to gauge the value of all immovable property throughout the city in order to determine the amount of tax that Florence's fiscal offices – the *Magistrato della Decima* – ought to be collecting from income on immovable property. This marked a distinct change from Florence's better-known fiscal innovation of 130 years earlier – the *Catasto*, which was based on declarations of assets and liabilities that individual taxpayers submitted and that neighbourhood committees then confirmed or challenged.

On the basis of detailed notes about the circuits that the *Decima* surveyors and scribes walked through the city, what may have been a separate set of officials working in the fiscal offices compiled a series of geographically encoded registers that record comprehensive demographic and fiscal information for every residence and place of business in the city. Assembled according to how properties were situated along the streets of the city, these registers, labelled '*ricerche*', or surveys, are unlike the bound registers of taxpayers' *Catasto* declarations submitted to the earlier, republican (that is, pre-ducal) fiscal offices. Administrators of the Florentine Republic conceived of the world they managed sequentially and hierarchically. Maps were rarely, if ever, used to delineate any taxable land or immovable property. More important, fiscal information regarding the property holdings of taxpayers was ordered according to an alphabetical sequence of names residing throughout the administrative units of the city and countryside, for example, according to city quarters or to the *gonfaloni,* officially named neighbourhoods within the city quarters.

Similarly, in the versions of the 1561–62 ducal survey there is no recourse to sketch, diagram, or partial map in order to delineate property boundaries. Yet, there is something fundamentally different about the development and organization of the registers of the 1561–62 survey from earlier censuses. Though these registers are sequential, they are not hierarchical. Here, order is based on the geographic locations of properties relative to other properties in the city streets. The document is so precise in descriptions of location that it allows historians today to superimpose with some accuracy its data onto the urban geography of Florence.

This survey ultimately served to facilitate the ducal state's assertion of the fiscal obligations of its citizens. The administrative mindset that envisioned and created the 1561–62 survey thus fashioned a textualized topography of the fiscal and residential data of Florence. While unofficial visions of urban space and social geographies do not easily accommodate official attempts to delineate and control urban space, bureaucratically conceived urban geographies – like the 1561–62 textualized topography – are mechanisms that facilitate the organization of vast amounts of information.

The ability to organize and portray a large multitude, as in a map, plays an important role in what Michel Foucault termed 'governmentality',[6] the dramatically expansive way that modern European states administer their populations relative to earlier models of administration. In his analysis of power structures Foucault specifically noted the ability to delineate different perspectives of power and to organize and reinforce boundaries and territories of that power. He suggested that contenders for power manipulated certain mechanisms and technical procedures that worked to organize and manage the 'details' of a human multiplicity.[7] Michel de Certeau expanded on this idea with the claim that his term 'panoptic administration', or the way that space is organized from above by some 'all-seeing power', is reciprocal to Foucault's management mechanisms.[8] De Certeau elaborated further, stating that, despite efforts by administrators and governments to organize, generate, and define the city, the walker at street level moves in ways that serve to spontaneously create the social geography of his city. The walker's movements are incompatible with the plans of organizing bodies, even as he continuously creates and re-creates the social geographies of his city through the complexities of his understanding of life at street level in any given moment.

Nicholas Eckstein demonstrates the veracity of de Certeau's assumption in his study on the urban district of *Drago Verde*, or the 'Green Dragon', within the early modern city of Florence. He shows how a single district such as *Drago Verde* was, in the eyes of walkers in the street, a complex area of overlapping, fluid, and semipermeable micro-communities.[9] His source is the 1427 *Catasto*, which, he argues, captures a single moment during *Drago Verde*'s long-term process of class stratification within its individual neighbourhoods. The social geography of Florence, he argues, is vastly more difficult to understand than its administrative or political geographies would suggest, largely because of this constant flux in urban geographies. Thus, although the viewer from above may be able to see the city as if in a fixed geography, the truth of the city's social geography lies in the movement of the streets themselves and in the constant change of social realities at street level. The spectacle of the panoptically conceived city has its own purposes, though. It is useful in the administration of a state, and, as we will see, one of the concerns of the ducal government of Florence was the 'panoptic administration' of its parts.

In chapter 1 in this volume Colin Rose compellingly demonstrates how official borders clash with social geography, namely through the inclusion in the 1561–62 census of certain unofficial micro-units within the city quarters.[10] He argues, much as Eckstein has done, that Florentine life at street level – that is, the way that everyday people moved through the streets and understood their surroundings – is far more complex than the parameters that administrative documents would have us accept. The present chapter, however, is particularly concerned with those official parameters. It establishes the official boundaries envisioned by Cosimo I's census officials as they walked the city in an ordered manner by revealing the 'official' route they followed. It also aims to acknowledge administrators as legitimate city walkers with their own motivations and observations concerning the varieties of the Florentine urban fabric through which they walked. The documented surveys are textualized urban topographies that relay fiscal and demographic information and ultimately give form to a panoptic and bureaucratic perspective of the city; they are aspects of ducal organization and management of the urban multiplicity of Florence. As 'mechanisms' of ducal governmentality, the documented surveys, or '*ricerche*', are themselves generated through the movement of officials along an officially demarcated route through the city of Florence in 1561.

The survey is extant in two versions: a working copy, which was likely the *Decima* office's own version (Archivio di Stato di Firenze, *Decima Granducale*, 3780–3784), and a clean display copy, abridged from the former and presented to Duke Cosimo I in 1562 (Archivio di Stato di Firenze, *Miscellanea Medicea*, 224).[11] The surveyors' original lists and descriptions of their itineraries are now lost. Nevertheless, the set of registers created for and by the *Decima* offices and the presentation copy created for the duke bear testimony to the original route of the survey. Together, these documents reveal the idea of ducal administration – a governmentality that uses an officially travelled route and its resulting textualized topography as a means of organizing bureaucratic documentation.

The *Decima* survey

The *Decima* was a mode of taxation introduced in 1495 with the restoration of republican governmental forms following the death of Lorenzo de' Medici and the expulsion of his heirs.[12] It was based on the principle that only the income on immovable property should be subject to levy. The tax was calculated on the estimation of income generated by real property and confirmed by the republican government according to normative market prices. Rather than being based on total capital wherever it was found, as the earlier *Catasto* had been, the *Decima* was a direct tax based on income raised from real assets. When Cosimo I de' Medici, from a cadet branch of the family, became duke in 1537, he retained the *Decima* because it was still considered the most equitable and stable mode of taxation, largely preferable to the earlier *Estimi* and *Catasti* taxes.

Cosimo I did, however, introduce significant procedural reform, as he did in many other areas of Florentine administration where the general centralization of power was apparent.[13] In 1551, for example, the magistracy of the *Decima* absorbed the older magistracy of the *Prestanze*, and in 1560 Cosimo I combined the *Otto di Practica* and the *Cinque Conservatori* into the new magistracy of the *Nove conservatori*, nine citizens who were to examine and supplement the economic and administrative supervision of local chancellors and *camerlenghi* (chamberlains) throughout ducal territory.[14] In 1561 Cosimo I did away with the *Arbitrio*, a tax introduced in 1508 in order to finance the recapture of Pisa. This tax was based not on immovable property but rather on liquid assets and on conjecture about the total income a citizen might raise during the year. It was widely considered to be neither equitable nor particularly useful (Pisa had surrendered to Florentine hands in 1509) and hence was abandoned, although Cosimo I did periodically introduce wartime levies, such as during the protracted war with Siena through the 1550s.[15]

Fiscal reform, however, also involved the reform of record keeping within the fiscal offices. We see, for example, an attempt to simplify the Florentine filing system in 1534. As *Decima* officials seem to have discovered early on, it was becoming increasingly difficult to organize and keep track of the mass of papers related to property holdings and their fluctuations for every head of house in the city of Florence. Basing the *Decima* on immovable property for every citizen required officials to wade through innumerable registers virtually blind because citizens were not necessarily required to file under the *gonfalone*, or official city neighbourhood, in which they resided. As it became ever more difficult to navigate the multitude of tax records, in 1534 *Decima* officials compiled a series of registers specifically to facilitate the process of keeping track of the amount of all citizens' tithes and their acquisitions and alienations of property.[16] These new registers recorded limited but essential fiscal information for every citizen in alphabetical order according to quarter; next to each name was the *Decima* each citizen paid on his income. These entries were eventually cross-referenced with the registers containing information about the property itself and with registers recording various interim acquisitions and alienations.

Under Cosimo I, the purpose of more centralized mechanisms for collecting and organizing fiscal information was to generate more complete, accurate, and easily accessible knowledge about property-based taxable income in Florence. These mechanisms are indicative of the way that the ducal state administered its citizens – its govern-mentality – and they demonstrate the totalizing impulse of governance that lay behind the 1561–62 ducal census.

Surveys of Florence's urban and rural households and their fiscal obligations to the state reached back to the early years of the Republic in the thirteenth century. Yet, the 1561–62 survey suggests a different mentality of governance. The surveyors' practice of collecting urban information on site and the fiscal officials' methods of organizing that information within the offices themselves were the most critical differences. Prior to this survey, demographic and fiscal information for the *Catasto* and *Estimo* was collected indirectly through tax declarations written by heads of house and individually deposited at the fiscal offices. This information was then bound in large, alphabetically ordered registers systematized by year and by the general location of the property (according to *gonfalone* for city properties and parish for country properties).

Though these earlier registers are rightly considered 'surveys', the 1561–62 survey aimed for greater regulation and supervision than the alphabetized, holographic tax declarations and the registers of fiscal data compiled for the *Catasto* and *Estimo*. The comprehensive survey taken *in situ* by civic officials is a 'description'[17] of the trajectory of residential and fiscal information as it actually sat, parallel to the streets of every quarter. As a description of spatially delineated data, it portrays both the movement along an official route through the city and the officially examined and confirmed data along that route. As a narrative of residential and fiscal information, it provided its users within the *Decima* offices with a textualized map that functioned to keep track of, organize, and confirm fiscal data.

The 1561–62 document and its 1551 model

There were three stages involved in the completion of the 1561–62 survey: (1) the examination of the city completed by assigned officials and scribes, (2) the collection of their labours into bound office registers, compiled according to the trajectory of streets in each of the city's quarters and used exclusively by the offices of the *Decima*, and (3) the registration of the residential information of the city into an official, ducal presentation copy. The *Decima* offices likely created the final presentation copy, although there is no definitive evidence as to who created that codex. As already noted, the preliminary lists and notes compiled by officials during their labours during the first step are missing, but the codices of the second and third steps are extant.[18]

In the office copy of the survey (the second step described), every individual residence is given an entry number, which is followed immediately by the name of the owner of the property. This is the person who received any income generated on the property and who was expected to declare it to the offices of the *Decima*. The entry numbers correspond to specific properties on the street, though the streets themselves lacked property numbers. Each entry number or data point is linked to the next via information explaining the walked trajectories. Every residence is described as coterminous on its first side to the property or land that lay before it and on its second side to the property that lay after it. Properties are relational, but the document is directional, and each property was localized in relation to those immediately adjoining. Indeed, very few entries in the document are lacking this essential localization information, which is what within the registers establishes the directional lines, or trajectories between data points on a conceivable 'plane' of urban space, mapping the residential geography of the city.

The surveyors textually rendered their movements in the city streets. Later, *Decima* compilers registered the surveyors' progression through the city into an all-encompassing, textualized topography of the residential and financial patterns of the city. This process, however, was not always straightforward. The physical geography of the city was often rather complicated, and the process of translating the surveyors' trajectories resulted in some confusion within the *Decima* office registers. For example, heavily built-up and compacted spaces of the city were often areas where the compilers of the office registers would make mistakes trying to follow the surveyors' descriptions of the properties.

In the register recording the survey of Santa Maria Novella at entries 1348–1354,[19] a batch of properties is inserted out of order. At entry 1348, we read:

> [. . .] having passed the arch of the Minerbetti, this house, along with those following up to the sign should be included in the circuit which begins at 1317 because they were left out by mistake, and they should to be followed by number 1325 [. . .] ([. . .] passato la volta de' Minerbetti questa casa con le seguenti sin' al segno deve esser compresa nel circuito che comincia 1317 per essersi queste per error' lasciate, et devea seguitar' dopo 'l numero 1325 [. . .])[20]

Explained as a mistake, this insert gives us a good deal of insight into how the compilers of the *Decima* office copies worked with the notes of the surveyors. Eight properties that lay in the cramped area along Via Parione Vecchio (today Via del Purgatorio) from the Arch of the Minerbetti to Via del Limbo and that should have been written on the pages immediately preceding were instead inserted into the text out of order, thus breaking the 'circuit'. Turning back a page, we find a marginal note at entry 1325 explaining that 'the rest of this circuit is at number 1348 until number 1353' ('Il resto di questo circuito è a' numero 1348 sin' numero 1353'). Apparently, the office compilers would receive surveyors' notes explaining 'circuits' they walked on any given day. The compilers would then organize the movements of the surveyors such that an official, unbroken route was recorded in the final fiscal registers.

On the day when surveyors were meant to record the fiscal and demographic information for these eight properties, however, something must have happened to confuse the usual documentation of the trajectory of the route. Either the surveyors forgot or missed this back street or the scribes in the *Decima* offices mislaid the original notes containing the information pertaining to this circuit. The possible reasons for this break in the circuit are made clearer when we look to the Buonsignori map, where the portrayal of the layout of these homes is indeed rather peculiar. The map clarifies that Via del Vecchio Parione was not – and a walk through the streets today confirms that it indeed is still not – a thoroughfare.

Judging from the appearance of the map, it was an area that had to be recorded separately because the surveyors coming down Via dei Tornabuoni did not have access to Via del Vecchio Parione. Surveyors were unable to easily access those eight properties during the circuit that ought to have recorded their information – that is, immediately following the final property at the corner of Via dei Tornabuoni and Via del Vecchio Parione. So they went back to survey these properties later, perhaps misplacing the information for the end of the circuit amongst the notes taken for the next circuit.

There is no seeming rhyme or reason as to why these eight properties had to be included in the circuit following from Via dei Tornabuoni. It is certain, however, that this small and awkward area in urban space presented the surveyors at street level with some difficulty in completing this particular circuit of their official route and thus presented the compilers of the office copies with similar difficulties. Still, this mistake suggests how the office copies may have been compiled: the surveyors

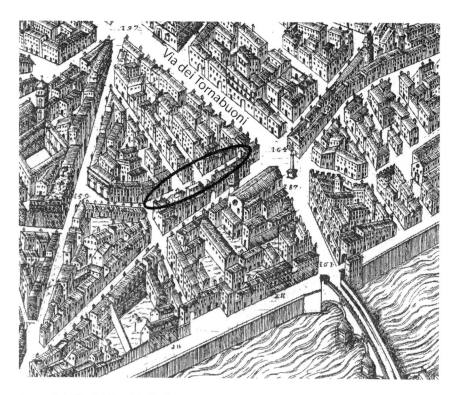

Figure 2.1 Via del Vecchio Parione.

The route of governmentality 41

daily submitted their notes to the *Decima* offices, where either they or, more likely, another set of officials would immediately copy into the registers of the *Decima* the information gathered during the surveyors' circuits of the city. It is, of course, also possible that the surveyors and their scribes walked all the circuits of streets in their assigned quarter before handing their complete notes over to the *Decima* offices, in which case their circuits were finally copied into large bound registers all at once. It seems more likely, however, given the proximity of the misplaced circuit, appearing only one page after the place where it should have been inserted, that the surveyors' notes were daily registered in the fiscal office registers. Whatever the case, it is clear that in compiling the office copies, the office officials' concern was primarily with the circuits that the surveyors walked through the streets, because it was through descriptions of these circuits that *Decima* officials were able to create a textualized urban geography of coterminous residences.

The description of residential and fiscal information is composed entirely of individual data points collected during the examination of properties along each street. Each data point includes localization information that places the surveyor in urban space as he moved through the streets. Listed thus, individual data points trace an official trajectory through the residential cityscape. This description is what encourages the registers' readers to comprehend the cityscape geographically, that is, as a successive series of data points running parallel to the streets and marking out the walkable trajectories of those streets. The individual data points within the working copy of the survey, set in uniform and successive progression as they are, work together to cast the urban plane in geographic relief before the reader's eye. This representation of collected and complete data in textually encoded, parallel perspective is the real novelty of the survey.

There was a third step involved the preparation of the same material – the creation of a presentation copy for the duke of the information collected in the streets. In this third copy, the scribes did away with the bulk of the information recorded in the fiscal office's copies. Without that fiscal and localization information, the copy presented to the duke functioned primarily as a directory of the names of Florentine heads of household and a tally of the number of Florentine men and women living in individual residences. Only limited amounts of that information are actually recorded there in three columns: the number of hearths (designated by 'h'), followed by the number of men in the first column and of women in the second. Entries in the official, presentation copy appear as follows:[21]

	h.	m.	f.
Bartolomeo of Berto Berti, gardener, parish of Santa Lucia sul Prato	1	3	5
Alesso of Hannibale from Pistoia	1	1	1
Luca of Batista, Genovese Madonna Lucretia of Stagio and Madonna Agniola of Mariotto	1	3	4

For the purposes of comparison, here is a transcription of the same data as it is portrayed in the fiscal office copy:

		m.	f.
1	Madonna Francesca, the wife of Marco of Giovanni Benedetti. Parish of Santa Lucia sul Prato. Before this property lies the Prato, after this property, the Nuns of Santa Maria sul Prato. Living there and paying rent, Bartolomeo of Berto Berti, a gardener. Eight mouths. He says that he pays eight *scudi*. The property is estimated at 8 *scudi* ——— *scudi* 8.	3	5
2	A house of the nuns of Santa Maria sul Prato in said parish. Before this property, the Prato, after this property, a house belonging to said nuns. Living there and paying rent for the restaurant is Alesso of Annibale from Pistoia [paying] 16 ½ *scudi*. The property is estimated at 16 *scudi*; with two mouths. ——— *scudi* 16.	1	1
3	A house of said nuns, said parish. Before this property, the Prato, after this property, a house belonging to said nuns. Living there and paying rent, Luca di Battista Genovese, Mona Lucretia di Stagio, and Mona Agniola di Mariotto – for 7 *scudi* and 7 mouths ——— *scudi* 7.	3	4

The fiscal office copy of the survey provides information about property owners, renters, and inhabitants. The presentation copy, in contrast, relates only the names of renters and the total number of men and women living on the property. Unlike the purpose of the *Decima* office's working copy of residential and fiscal data, the purpose of the presentation copy was apparently not to ensure the validity of the amount of income that property owners were declaring on their holdings. Rather, it was meant to reveal population numbers and the names of all the heads of house. Significantly, this copy does have a clear model in a series of surveys completed ten years prior.

In 1541 Cosimo I commissioned Ser Antonio di Filippo Giannetti, to complete various *descrizioni* of the populations and strongholds found throughout the Duchy.[22] The result of his labours was a codex completed in 1551 and now held in the Biblioteca Nazionale, the 'Description of the people and hearths of the Dominion of His most Illustrious Excellence' ('*Descriptione delle persone e fuochi del Domini di Sua Eccellenza Illustrissima*').[23] Shortly after the completion of this first '*Descriptione*' Ser Antonio completed two other codices, which provided the model for the presentation copy of the 1561–62 survey: 'The Hearths and People of the Florentine State' ('*Fuochi e anime dello Stato fiorentino*') and the 'Index of all the houses and people living in Florence according to quarter and street' ('*Indice di tutte le case e persone abitanti in Firenze secondo i quartieri e le vie*').[24] The similarities between the codices completed by Ser Antonio and the display copy of the 1561–62 survey are striking, right down to the very layout and type of data represented. The earlier 1551 census was also focused only on demographics, and if a fiscal version ever existed there is no evidence of it. It too registers demographic information on a street-by-street basis. The administrative mindset behind the survey completed by Ser Antonio was to geographically record information about the city's inhabitants. Extant letters exchanged between Ser Antonio and Cosimo I's *maggiordomo*, Pier Francesco Riccio, reveal strategies for surveying populations in such a way.[25]

While this first census of 1551 shows Cosimo I as concerned primarily with demographics, the extensive financial information contained in the second of 1561–62 shows a far wider ambition. In legislation at least, if not in practice, he quadrupled the number of surveyors, perhaps to speed up the process, and outsourced the compilation of the final copies to scribes in the offices of the *Decima Granducale* to facilitate the restructuring of the fiscal administration of the city. One point remained the same: both for Ser Antonio and for the 1561 surveyors and *Decima* officials, urban geography had a specific utility for the surveillance and organization of mass data sets.

The 1561–62 route of governmentality

'Governmentality' allows for the study of a specific dimension of history constituted of practices, habits of mind, strategies, and technologies inherent in managing a multitude of people. It is particularly useful for teasing out the motivating factors behind the creation of single administrative documents such as the 1561–62 *Decima* survey of the city of Florence. Mentalities of governance can be inferred on the basis of certain management practices within the bureaucratic offices of the state – in this case, a cartographic practice of management. In this final section, elaborating on these methods and practices of organization within the Florentine fiscal office, I trace parts of the 1561–62 surveyors' route on the Buonsignori map of 1584. The purpose is to highlight the underlying cartographic impulse in the design and creation of the survey as a mode of ducal administration and, further, to suggest that those same impulses are synonymous with actual cartography, or chorography, as it was then called.

Recreating the 1561–62 route may seem artificial because we do not have the notes and lists written out by the surveyors themselves as they walked the city streets. We must rely solely on the *Decima* office's working copy of the survey to determine their route. This historical document is full of relevant economic data about the city of Florence in a specific year but does not narrate the sensory experiences that administrators experienced on their journey through the streets of Florence. Nonetheless, fiscal administrators envisioned and practiced fiscal governance of the city of Florence in a cartographic way.

On the Buonsignori map, it is possible for the urban geography to be seen as a totalized urban space. However, in the fiscal survey, a textualized urban geography unfolds only gradually and capillary-like by means of the description of the official route through urban space. In the *Decima* registers, surveyors describe what they call 'circuits' through the city. They would set out on their circuits from city gates: in the quarter of Santa Maria Novella, they began at the Porta al Prato; in Santa Croce, at 'the fortress at the Gate of Justice' ('*alla fortezza della porta a giustitia*'); in San Giovanni, at the 'old Gate at San Gallo' ('*della porta vecchia à San Gallo*'); in Santa Spirito, at the gate at Borgo San Niccolo.

44 *Leah Faibisoff*

In Figure 2.2 I outline the first five circuits walked by the surveyors in the quarter of Santa Croce, using the Buonsignori map and alphabetical coordinates. The surveyors for this quarter began, as already mentioned, at the Porta a Giustitia; they proceeded west along the south side of what the census describes only as the 'street of the Fortress of the Gate of Justice' (Via della Fortezze della Porta a Giustitia), the modern Via Torricelle.

They started with a small house described as being 'behind the Fortress of the Gate of Justice',[26] exactly as it appears in the Buonsignori map, labelled 'A'.

Figure 2.2 Five circuits walked in the quarter of Santa Croce. Alphabetical coordinates indicate their routing beginning at the Porta a Giustitia.

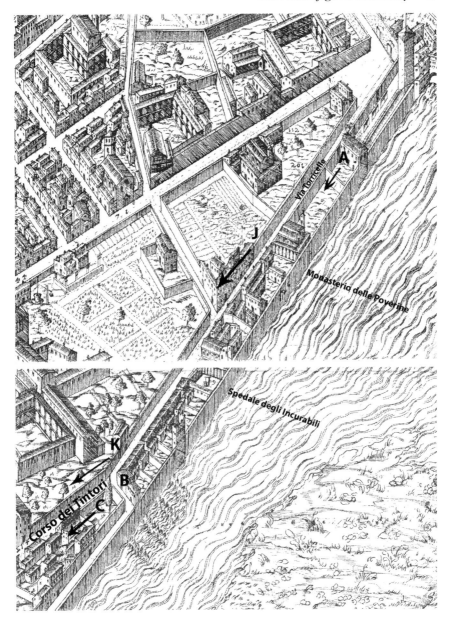

Figure 2.3 Detail of the first Santa Croce circuit. First house ('A') marks the house at which the surveyors began.

The text of the survey describes this house as 'contiguous to the monastery' ('*a primo detto monasterio*'), as Buonsignori also shows. From here, the surveyors continued walking west along the south side of the street, skipping the monastery (a practice common throughout with ecclesiastical properties) to collect and register fiscal and demographic information from the properties lying just west of it.

46 *Leah Faibisoff*

One at a time, and in the order as they appear to the surveyors walking down the street, the register individually describes all properties to the west down the plane of the street. For example, the house just west of the monastery is described as sitting next to said monastery ('*è acanto al detto monasterio*'). It is immediately followed by another house belonging to the monastery ('*a secondo, una casa del detto monasterio*'). Next follows a house of the *Abbandonate*, a shelter for abandoned girls, then the twenty-five properties after it lying along the south side of the street. All properties are registered in the order in which the surveyors encountered them as they walked down the street. Each property is described as contiguous to the ones before and after it, allowing for a reader who is tracing the trajectory of the surveyors' circuit in the registers to follow them down the street. Their first circuit ends with a description of the '25th property' (labelled 'B' on the map provided).

The twenty-sixth property, the beginning of the surveyors' second 'circuit'[27] (labelled 'C'), is the next house in the same street, which here is named Corso dei

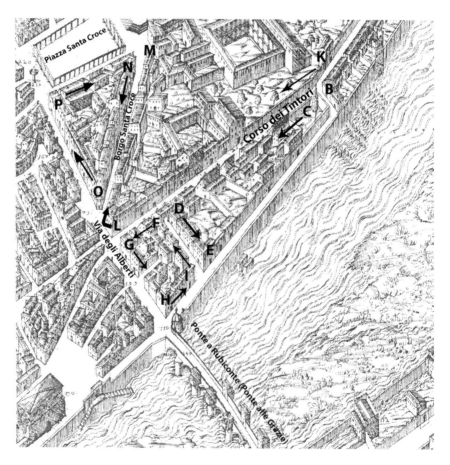

Figure 2.4 Third Santa Croce circuit, from Corso de' Tintori to Via degli Alberti ('F' to 'G').

The route of governmentality 47

Tintori. It is 'a house with a garden on the corner of the Corso dei Tintori where the street exits back towards the Arno'.[28] The surveyors continued west along the Corso dei Tintori until they reached 'a small arch which leads to the Arno' (*'volticina che va al Arno'*; on the map at 'D'). Turning left under this arch, they continued down the east side of this small street (in the text referred to as the 'small archway which passes to [Via] Lung'arno') until they reached the river ('E'). Here they turned left again to collect the few properties along the back of Via Lung'arno, so concluding another circuit.

They returned to the Corso de' Tintori to begin the third circuit, collecting the properties remaining along the south side of the street, from the small arch to Via degli Alberti ('F' to 'G').

Turning left on Via degli Alberti, they walked south to the Rubaconte bridge, the modern Ponte alla Grazia, marked by the Church of Madonna delle Gratie ('[. . .] *sulla coscia del Ponte a Rubaconte al incontro della Madonna delle Gratie* [. . .]'; 'G' to 'H'). Along the way, they passed what they call 'a small piazza' (the small open space visible on the Buonsignori map halfway between

Figure 2.5 Fourth Santa Croce circuit, from Via Torricelle to Via degli Alberti ('L').

'G' and 'H'). They collected information about the properties lying within this little piazza before continuing south again along Via degli Alberti ('H'). From here, they turned left and head east along Via del Lung'arno, turning left again to walk north along the west side of the small street under the small arch mentioned in the previous circuit.

The fourth circuit (beginning at 'J') lies back along Via Torricelle, this time referred to in the text as Via della Fortezza Vecchia. Returning west and having already gathered information on the properties on the south side of the street during their first circuit, the surveyors registered the properties along on the north side of the side until they reached Via degli Alberti ('L').

At the end of the Corso de' Tintori, they completed this circuit, by turning right onto the Borgo Santa Croce, registering the properties along its east side up to the Friary of Santa Croce ('L' to 'M'). Checking back west along the north side of the Borgo Santa Croce, they began their fifth circuit around the triangular block south of the Piazza ('N'/'O'/'P').

Following these first five circuits through the quarter of Santa Croce underlines how deliberate the surveyors and their scribes were in setting out through the city streets to register the city's inhabitants one by one. It was their task to gather and record fiscal and demographic information for every property in the city wherever they were, keeping track of each separate property according to where it actually was located within the urban fabric.

Reading map and document in tandem highlights the underlying cartographic quality of both. In republican Florence, administrators did not prioritize urban space – public or private – in the same geographic or dimensional way. Rather, the ownership of urban space in hierarchically ordered texts like the *Catasto* was individual and relational. In their *Catasto* tax returns, individual taxpayers described their residence and then listed the neighbours or properties surrounding theirs. These tax returns provide a far more fragmented picture of urban geography. Though the 1561–62 *Decima* survey contains primarily verbal accounts, with no recourse to map or diagram, the trajectory of the official route is geographically linear and descriptive. This ultimately enabled administrators, who would have had an intimate knowledge of the city streets, to imagine the city's fiscally governable urban geography. Fiscal information was collected in 'parallel' perspective. In architectural rendering, 'parallel projections' are two-dimensional renderings of affine planes. These projections are defined by the relationship of points and lines to a collateral, parallel plane.

On the Buonsignori map, the buildings sit parallel to the plane of the street; that is, the trajectory of buildings runs continuously atop the street plane through to a dead end, city wall, or contiguous street. In the document, we experience a similar phenomenon where the entry numbers of coterminously listed properties function to guide the reader alongside the surveyors, parallel to the street plane, stopping at every house along the way. The main difference between document and map lies in the portrayal of urban space, that is, in the actual signs by which the city is visualized (on the map) or conceived (in the document). Where the map can show the entire geography of the city at once, in the text the residential and fiscal geography emerges gradually out of descriptions of circuits around city blocks.

The Buonsignori map of the city and the textualized *Decima* 'map' of the city betray a cartographic frame of mind. The objective of the mapmaker is not to create the impression of perspective through the portrayal of a vanishing horizon. Rather, all perspectival interest is shifted onto the ground and into the streets themselves, where individual points and buildings become the viewer's points of perspectival reference. The 1561–62 street-level survey and Buonsignori's 1584 'parallel' vision of the streets both do exactly that. Thus, the cartographic conceptualization in parallel perspective of the city's properties becomes a way of registering and administering information obtained about the private and public space of ducal Florence, which is particularly effective for what we might call the panoptic purposes of governmentality.

The five registers drawn up by *Decima* officials in 1561–62 had two practical purposes, both related to the business of keeping track of and ensuring citizens' fiscal obligations. In the first instance, they organized data within the fiscal offices for greater ease of access. This is suggested by the periodic but consistent cross-referencing to other *campioni* (registers) within the fiscal office throughout the document. Second, the document allowed officials to double-check what property owners declared as the income on their houses and shops. The 1561–62 investigation into citywide yields on property was, in essence, a ducal reform of the fisc. It was a snapshot of the taxable assets available within the city during that year.

Though the surveyor's circuits can be recreated only through the locational relationships between properties given within the document, what the fiscal offices preserved in the working copy of the survey is a vision of the city based on an essential, on-site experience of its streets. The route upholds an official view of fiscal and demographic information throughout the city, thereby creating a textualized map. There is little evidence that use of this particular document was particularly long lived. More traditional methods of organization continued to be used in the form of alphabetically organized registers of holographic tax declarations for every administrative unit of the city and countryside. So, while the *Decima* survey may not mark the emergence of a sixteenth-century mode of governmentality that permanently replaced earlier approaches, it reflects an early instance of the cartographic conceptualization of the ducal state as a governable urban whole.

When George Eliot's imagined Shade looked down over the city from San Miniato in 1863, it beheld a city on the verge of major urban change. Florence was soon to become the capital of the new nation of Italy, and from 1865 to 1871 it underwent significant urban reshaping. In the spirit of revivalism, the transformations of the city were attempts to recreate the city's Renaissance past, and so it came to resemble a nineteenth-century vision of what the Florentine Renaissance was. Historical consciousness and the desire to recreate and reassemble visions of the Renaissance city have equally shaped DECIMA's own attempts at recapturing social and bureaucratic visions of Florence through Historical GIS and the digitization of historical data. The danger in digital mapping projects is to do as Buonsignori did – or the 1865 national government as it tried to re-create historical perspective in certain places of the city – and turn the city into a fixed, monumental space. From the beginning, the challenge of the DECIMA project has been to build a motion-based system of urban mapping, made possible by the georeferential parameters and kinetic nature of the 1561–62 *Decima* survey in order to restore the motions and senses of the Renaissance city as a living, human place.

Notes

1. G. Eliot, *Romola*, in D. Barrett (ed.), New York, NY: Penguin Books, 1996, 2.
2. Ibid., 7.
3. N. Terpstra, 'Creations and Recreations: Contexts for the Experience of the Renaissance Street', *I Tatti Studies in the Italian Renaissance* 16, 2013, 221–29.
4. L. Cantini, *Legislazione Toscana, raccolta e illustrata*, 4 vols, Florence, Italy: Fantosini 1802, 171–72. 'Imperò Sua Eccellenza Illustrissima insieme con gli suoi Magnifici Consiglieri han provvisto, deliberato, et ordinato che in vertù del presente Decreto, e s'intendino essere, e sieno eletti quattro Capi Maestri con quattro Scrivani da nominarsi li uni, e gli altri per quelli Cittadini che Sua Eccellenza deputerà, li quali Capi Maestri ciascuno in un Quartiere con il suo Scrivano sarà tenuto, e debba visitare, e descrivere diligentemente tutte le case, e abitazioni che si trovano dentro la Città con lor famiglie, et abitatori in quel tempo [. . .]' ('His most Illustrious Excellence ruled, and together with his Magnificent Counselors, saw to it, decided, and ordered that, by virtue of the present Decree, four chief masters and four scribes should be instated and elected, each of them to be nominated by the citizens that His Excellence will designate. Each chief master, together with his scribe, will be assigned to a Quarter, and he must visit and diligently describe all of the residences and habitations found within the city, including the families and all the current residents.') All translations are my own.
5. For an examination of how this survey may have been carried out in practice however, see E. Fabbro's chapter in this volume.
6. G. Burchell, C. Gordon, and P. Miller, *The Foucault Effect: Studies in Governmentality, with Two Lectures by and an Interview with Michel Foucault*, London, UK: Harvester Wheatsheaf, 1991. Foucault later extended the meaning of the term beyond the level of political administration to the conduct of individuals and groups at every level – self-governance, the management of the family, the organization of corporations, and so on. The basic units of study in the analytics of governmentality are the practices and habits inherent and specific to various governing forces.
7. M. Foucault, *Surveiller et punir: Naissance de la prison*, Paris, France: Gallimard, 1975.
8. M. de Certeau, *L'invention du quotidian*, Paris, France: Gallimard, 1990, vol. 1, esp. ch. 7.
9. N.A. Eckstein, *The District of the Green Dragon: Neighbourhood Life and Social Change in Renaissance Florence*, Florence, Italy: Leo S. Olschki, 1995.
10. On the phenomenon of social geographies as incompatible with administrative geographies, see Colin Rose's chapter in this volume; also Eckstein, 'Addressing Wealth', and *The District of the Green Dragon*.
11. A facsimile of the presentation copy is found in S. Meloni Trkulja, *I fiorentini nel 1562: Descrizioni delle Bocche della Città e Stato di Firenze fatta l'anno 1562*, Florence, Italy: Bruschi 1991.
12. On the *Decima* tithe, I primarily consulted G.F. Pagnini del Ventura, *Della Decima e di varie altre gravezze*, vol. 1, Lisbon and Lucca, 1765.
13. R. Burr Litchfield, *Emergence of a Bureaucracy: The Florentine Patricians, 1530–1790*, Princeton, NJ: Princeton University Press, 1986, passim.

14 Pagnini della Ventura, *Della Decima*, 107. Also Litchfield, *Emergence of a Bureaucracy*, 104–5 on the *Decima*, 72 on the formation of the *Nove Conservatori*, and 110 on its provincial concerns.
15 Pagnini della Ventura, *Della Decima*, 62.
16 These registers are described in ibid., 48.
17 The operating word in the running headings on the first pages of the registers is 'Description': '*Descrizione del quartiere di Santa Maria Novella*', '*Descrizione del quartiere di Santo Spirito*', '*Descrizione del quartiere di San Giovanni*', '*Descrizione del quartiere di Santa Croce*'.
18 The fiscal office codices are: Archivio di Stato di Firenze, Decima Granducale 3780 (Santo Spirito), 3781 (Santa Croce), 3782 (Santa Maria Novella), and 3783 (San Giovanni). The final presentation copy is Archivio di Stato di Firenze, Miscellanea Medicea, 224.
19 ASF, *Decima Granducale*, 3782, 77v-80r.
20 ASF, *Decima Granducale*, 3782, at 80r.
21 For a facsimile, see Meloni Trkulja, *I fiorentini nel 1562*, 57.
22 For an analysis of the *descrizioni* of Antonio del Mucione, see D. Lamberini, 'Strategie difensive e politica territoriale di Cosimo I dei Medici nell'operato di un suo provveditore', in A. Calzona, F.P. Fiore, A. Tenenti, and C. Vasoli, (eds), *Il Principe Architetto: Atti del Convegno internazionale, Mantova, 21–23 ottobre 1999*, Florence, Italy: Leo S. Olschki, 2002.
23 Biblioteca Nazionale Centrale di Firenze, *Fondo Nazionale*, II.I. 120.
24 ASF, *Miscellanea Medicea*, F. 264; ASF, *Miscellanea Medicea*, F. 223. Also see ASF, *Miscellanea Medicea*, F. 224, and ASF, *Manoscritti*, 181.
25 Lamberini, 'Strategie difensive', 125–27.
26 [. . .] una casina del monasterio delle poverine dietro alla fortezza della porta a giustitia [. . .]
27 In the *Decima* volumes, horizontal lines periodically appear between descriptions of properties. On close examination, these lines tend to occur at city intersections or at the ends of roads. With the aid of the Buonsignori map, it becomes clear that they actually mark out the beginnings and ends of circuits around city blocks. Scribes copying the surveyors' notes into the registers of the *Decima* must have struck horizontal lines in the text at points in the text where the surveyors ended circuits and began new ones.
28 [. . .] una casa con orto nel Corso dei Tintori [. . .] trafossi [*sic*] che riesce su arno [. . .].

Bibliography

Manuscript sources

Archivio di Stato di Firenze (ASF), *Decima Granducale*, 3780–3783.
―――― *Miscellanea Medicea*, 224, 264, 223.
―――― *Manoscritti*, 181.
Biblioteca Nazionale Centrale di Firenze (BNCF), *Fondo Nazionale*, II.I. 120.

Print sources

Burchell, G., Gordon, C., and Miller, P. (eds), *The Foucault Effect: Studies in Governmentality, with Two Lectures by and an Interview with Michel Foucault*, London, UK: Harvester Wheatsheaf, 1991.
Canestrini, G., *La scienza e l'arte di Stato, desunta dagli atti ufficiali della Repubblica fiorentina e dei Medici – Ordinamenti economici. – Della finanza, Parte I. – L'imposta sulla ricchezza mobile e immobile*, Florence, Italy: Felice Le Monnier, 1862.

Cantini, L., *Legislazione Toscana, raccolta e illustrate*, 4 vols, Florence, Italy: Fantosini, 1802.
de Certeau, M., *L'invention du quotidian*, vol. 1, Paris, France: Gallimard, 1990.
Eckstein, N.A. *The District of the Green Dragon: Neighbourhood Life and Social Change in Renaissance Florence,* Florence, Italy: Leo S. Olschki, 1995.
—––––– 'Addressing Wealth in Renaissance Florence: Some New Soundings from the *Catasto* of 1427', *Journal of Urban History* 32, 2006, 711–28.
Eliot, G., *Romola (1862–63)*, D. Barrett (ed.), New York, NY: Penguin Books, 1996.
Foucault, M., *Surveiller et punir: Naissance de la prison,* Paris, France: Gallimard, 1975.
Lamberini, D., 'Strategie difensive e politica territoriale di Cosimo I dei Medici nell'operato di un suo provveditore', in A. Calzona, F.P. Fiore, A. Tenenti, and C. Vasoli (eds), *Il Principe Architetto: Atti del Convegno internazionale. Mantova, 21–23 ottobre 1999,* Florence, Italy: Leo S. Olschki, 2002.
Litchfield, R., *Emergence of a Bureaucracy: The Florentine Patricians, 1530–1790,* Princeton, NJ: Princeton University Press, 1986.
Meloni Trkulja, S., *I fiorentini nel 1562: Descrizioni delle Bocche della Città e Stato di Firenze fatta l'anno 1562,* Florence, Italy: Bruschi, 1991.
Pagnini della Ventura, G.F., *Della Decima e di varie altre gravezze imposte dal comune di Firenze,* vol. 1, Lisbon and Lucca, 1765.
Terpstra, N., 'Creations and Recreations: Contexts for the Experience of the Renaissance Street', *I Tatti Studies in the Italian Renaissance* 16, 2013, 212–30.

3 From the *Decima* to DECIMA and back again

The data behind the data

Eduardo Fabbro

The 1561–62 *Decima*, elaborated by order of Duke Cosimo I (1519–74), produced a fine-tuned account of the population of Florence that gave ample information about demographic and fiscal conditions. It is only because the sixteenth-century compilers of the *Decima* organized their data so well that in the twenty-first century we were able to assemble the geocoded data that produced the digital rendering of Cosimo I's Florence. Plotting those records on a GIS map – which provided a visual expression for all the names and numbers – did not, in principle, transform the *Decima* data into something new. It simply opened a window into the geographic knowledge that sixteenth-century Florentines already possessed, providing a glimpse into their daily lives and producing a link to their spatial experience otherwise lost to us. It did, nonetheless, transfer the data from one cultural milieu to the other – from a notarial and manuscript tradition to a digital one. This translation – like any good translation – was not a straightforward shifting from one language to another; it required a process of negotiation and accommodation as we grafted the information from one media onto the other. This article highlights the practical dimensions of this transition, showing how the DECIMA team produced a digital database from the manuscripts of the *Decima*. First, it provides a description of the four manuscripts in which the *Decima* was preserved; second, it shows what the *Decima* records looked liked; and finally it turns to how the information was transferred into the DECIMA database and what how this transfer changed the shape of the data.

Descriptio codicum

The *Decima* was organized in four manuscripts, each containing the census for one of the four quarters of Florence, namely Santo Spirito, Santa Croce, Santa Maria Novella, and San Giovanni. Table 3.1 shows the details of each manuscript in the Florentine State Archive deposit for the *Decima Granducale*, with the number of folios and of entries:

Table 3.1 Details of the *Decima* manuscripts

Quarter	Hand	Folios	Entries	People (Male + Female)	People/entry
Santo Spirito ASF, *DG*, 3780	A	155	2,315	(6,143 [44.08%] + 6,792 [55.91%]) = 12,935	5.587

(*Continued*)

54   Eduardo Fabbro

Table 3.1 (Continued)

Quarter	Hand	Folios	Entries	People (Male + Female)	People/entry
Santa Croce ASF, DG, 3781	A	108	1,336	(4,807 [54.20%] + 4,062 [45.79%]) = 8,869	6.638
Santa Maria Novella ASF, DG, 3782	B	101	1,654	(6,073 [55.39%] + 4,891 44.60%]) = 10,964	6.628
San Giovanni ASF, DG, 3783	B + C	223	3,437	(11,218 [44.41%] + 14,037 [55.58%]) = 25,255	7.347
Total	–	–	8,742	(28,241 [48.67%] + 29,782 [51.32%]) = 58,023	6.637

Each entry preserved the owner's and tenants' names, the estimated value of and rent on the property, and the number of mouths in the household (i.e. total number of residents), amongst other information. The quarter of San Giovanni contains the largest number of entries, followed by Santo Spirito, Santa Maria Novella, and Santa Croce. San Giovanni, with 7.34 people/entry, is also the quarter with the largest demographic density per entry, compared to the overall concentration of 6.63. The census produced a total of 8,742 entries, each reporting to a property, and a total of 58,023 people, with the female population slightly surpassing the male one (51.32/48.67 per cent). It is impossible, however, to establish how comprehensive this list was and whether all social categories were, indeed, accounted for.

The production of the *Decima*: the palaeographic evidence

The *Decima* was produced by order of Duke Cosimo I in the summer of 1561. The decree, published on 17 June, established that four *capi maestri* and four *scrivani* were to be selected to survey all the landed properties in Florence.[1] Each *maestro*, together with his *scrivano*, would be responsible for one of the four quarters of the city. The result of the survey was registered first on a working copy for the *Decima* office and subsequently on an official, abridged presentation copy offered to the duke.[2] The evidence in the manuscripts, however, suggests that Cosimo I's command was not followed to the letter, and the survey was carried out not by four but instead by two teams, each comprising three different scribes. The first group worked in Santo Spirito and Santa Croce, the second in Santa Maria Novella and San Giovanni. Furthermore, the specific details of the entries in the different volumes point to a gradual development of the methodology, suggesting that the parameters of the collection of data were adjusted as the data were collected.

The first indication for the production of the *Decima* comes from the palaeographical evidence of the codices. The four manuscripts were produced in a chancellery hand, most likely from original notes taken house by house by the census team. Three different scribes worked on our manuscripts: a first hand ('A') worked on Santo Spirito and Santa Croce; a second ('B') worked on Santa Maria Novella

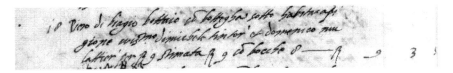

Figure 3.1 18. Piero di Biagio, bottaio co*n* bottegha sotto. Habita a pigione Cristo*f*ano di Michele, tintor*e* et Domenico, mulattier*e*, p*er* s*o*ldi 9, stimata s*o*ldi 9 co*n* bocche 9 – s 9:3:5.

[Santo Spirito, 2v. 18. Piero di Biagio, cooper, with a store below. Cristofano di Michele, dyer and Domenico, mule driver rents for 9 soldi. Estimated value 9 with 9 mouths. – s9:3:5].

and on the first 705 entries on San Giovanni; and a third hand ('C') worked on the remaining entries on San Giovanni. Apart from slight differences in the *ductus*, each scribe presents a few individual characteristics. Hand A is a very cursive hand with a great number of Tuscanisms (e.g. the Tuscan 'ch/gh' before a, o, u: *Marcho, tenghono*) as well as a more conservative spelling for some names (e.g. *Baptista, Catherina*).

The very angled style of A makes it significantly different from B and C, which are more vertical and clear. B and C, although clearly distinct hands, share several traces, in form, use of abbreviations, and spelling (see Figure 3.2). The Tuscanisms present in C are absent from both hands (e.g. *Marco, tengono*), and both favour a spelling of names closer to modern Italian (e.g. *Battista, Catterina*).

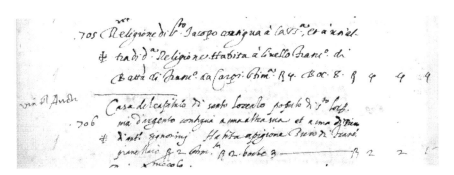

Figure 3.2 705. Religione di S*a*nto Jacopo, contigua a la s*u*det*t*a et a un' [*signum crucis*] tra di de*t*ta Religione. Habita a livello Franc*es*co di Batti*s*ta di Franc*es*co da Carpi. Stimata s*o*ldi 4 Bocche 8. – s.4:4:4.

706. Casa del Capitulo di Santo Lorenzo, populo di S*a*nto Lorenzo, Via d'Argento, contigua a una altra sua et a uma di Piero d'Ant*o*nio Signorini. Habita a pigione Piero di Franc*es*co pianellaio, s*o*ldi 2, Stim*a*ta s*o*ldi 2. Bocche 3 – s.2:2:1.

[San Giovanni, 45v. 705. Order of Saint James, next to the one mentioned above and another of the same order. Francesco di Battista di Francesco da Capri lives by *livello*. Estimated value 4 soldi; mouths 8. – s.4:4:4.

706. House of the Chapter of Saint Lawrence, populo of St. Lawrence, in Via d'Argento, next to another house of the same owner and to one belonging to Piero d'Antonio Signorini. Piero di Francesco, seller of chopines, lives there by rent, 2 soldi. Estimated value 2 soldi; mouths 3 – s.2:2:1].

Apart from the subtle different in *ductus*, B and C differ mostly by the use of distinct terminologies for widows: unlike A (and also C), B consistently favours 'moglie' over 'donna'. Figure 3.2 shows B's last entry and C's first one.

The fact that three scribes were involved in copying the surviving manuscripts does not, however, immediately guarantee that the scribes represent different teams involved in the collection of the data. It could be argued that the role of the three hands identified earlier did not go beyond merely copying the finished carried by the *capi maestri* and the (original) *scrivani*, which would definitely separate their intervention from the actual *ricerche*. The differences among the hands, however, appear to go beyond the style and orthography and suggest, as we will argue later, that hand A was working under different supervision from hands B and C. Although the details of the interaction between the collection of the data and the registering in our manuscripts remain obscure, a close reading of the entries points to a gradual evolution of the style and methodology, which suggests that changes in the collection of data were reflected in the entries preserved in the *Decima*.

Comparing the entries of different hands, we can observe that the entry style recorded by hand A changed progressively in Santo Spirito, only to stabilize halfway through. The entries in the beginning of Santo Spirito report simply the owner, estimated value, and number of mouths. For example, the second entry reads (2r):

> 2. Francesco di Bartolomeo del Macha, sarto, habita Giuliano di Guglielmo da Verrazzano, a pigione per s. 8; Stimata s. 8 co' bocche 5 – 8   4   1.

Hand A slowly started introducing more information about the location of the houses. A major shift occurs after entry 338 (ASF DG 3780, 19r). After this point, entries include full names of owners of houses on both sides, as well as more details on the building. Similarly, occupations are now often noted (usually to differentiate homonyms). From time to time, the scribe added workplaces; hence we know that Filippo, who rented a house in Via Ghibellina from the Monastery of S. Ambrose traded chickens in the Mercato Vecchio or that the taciturn Andrea, just down on Borgo Allegri, was a spicer at the Ponte Vecchio (Andrea was know as 'il Burbero', the Surly, adds our scribe). The geographic location is also spelled out in details: each household is described in relation to its neighbours. Thus, il Burbero has '*a primo Matteo Guiducci, a secondo Giorgio di ser Giovanni Battista Vivaldi*', that is to say, Matteo lived on one side, Giorgio on the other. This new style is carried on to Santa Croce.[3] The entries often provide rich details of the buildings, such as accesses and even the internal division of a few houses.[4]

Hands B and C are quite similar in their entry style, and the transition from one hand to the other is not followed by a change in methodology.[5] The entry style is stable throughout the two quarters and includes the basic information (owner, tenant, estimated value, rent, and number of residents), with the occasional mention of occupation of owners or tenants and details of the houses, amongst others. The entry includes a geographic location similar to those entered by hand A, stating that the house was '*contigua a la sudetta*', that is, next to the previous house. The fact that the scribe working on Santa Maria Novella (hand B) carried the work into San Giovanni suggests that the two quarters were done in succession.

The evolution of the entries allows us to advance some conclusions about the assembling of the *Decima* manuscripts. In the first place, the changes in entry style most likely reflect a change in the process of collection and sorting of data, suggesting a direct connection between the different scribes in the manuscripts and the survey on the streets. It seems clear that hand A worked on Santo Spirito and Santa Croce, and it is safe to assume that the two quarters were produced in succession by the same team. The data used by hands B and C in Santa Maria Novella and San Giovanni, however, are slightly different from those for Santo Spirito and Santa Croce, suggesting that the collection of information for these two quarters was carried by a different team. In addition to that, the similarities between the entries from hands B and C point to a single system of data collection behind the two different hands – in other words, Santa Maria Novella and San Giovanni were likely produced by the same team but registered by two different scribes. In the second place, we can argue for a tentative chronology of composition for the four volumes. The evolution in style observed in Santo Spirito suggests, as we mentioned, that that team first composed Santo Spirito and later Santa Croce, while the fact that hand B starts in Santa Maria Novella and continues half the way through San Giovanni indicates that Santa Maria Novella was finished before San Giovanni. Furthermore, unlike Santo Spirito and Santa Croce, Santa Maria Novella and San Giovanni seem to be operating under a stable and well-established system of entries, which suggests that by the time data were being collected for those quarters the system had already been satisfactorily tuned up, presumably by the experience in Santo Spirito and Santa Croce.

In sum, we can argue, on the basis of the manuscript evidence, that the *ricerche* was carried out by two different teams, supposedly composed of a *capo maestro* and a *scriptor*. The first team started in Santo Spirito, moving then to Santa Croce. As the collection of data proceeded, experience prompted changes in the methodology, as the surveyors realized the need for more extensive and explicit information for each entry (including a more evident spatial markers), leading to a turning point after entry 338 in Santo Spirito (ASF DG 3780, 19r), after which a relatively standardized style was established. This style was carried over to Santa Croce. The second team started in Santa Maria Novella, using a modified version of this standardized style, which this team also used in San Giovanni, even after hand C replaced hand B.

From the *Decima* to DECIMA

To produce the geocoded picture of Florence from the *Decima*, the DECIMA team worked in two distinct phases. As Colin Rose describes in his chapter in

58   *Eduardo Fabbro*

this collection, the first step was to transfer the data from the *Decima* into a digital format, creating a database. The DECIMA team established the basic categories from the entries to build our own entry system, which initially was not unlike the one used by the original census. We established fields for the standard information provided in the entries, namely 'owner', 'holder', and 'holding type', including rent (if the owner was not resident), 'estimated value', the number of people ('bocche'), 'street name', and 'populo'. To these basic categories, we added two fields with metadata, 'location information' and 'other', in which we registered data that, although not evident in the final database, could inform the geolocation. To these fields we soon added others that were not part of the information directly relevant to the *Decima* but that were often present incidentally in the original entries. At this point we added three fields for 'other residents' and one for descriptions of the building and of shops that might be connected to the property. These fields of data were entered into a FileMaker entry file. This example shows the steps from the manuscript to the FileMaker database:

1) The manuscript entry:

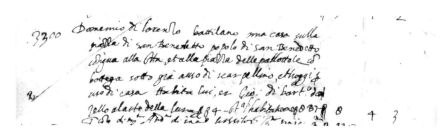

Figure 3.3
(By permission of the Ministero dei Beni e delle Attivita Culturale e del Turismo).

2) Transcription:

3300. Domenico di Lorenzo, battilano, una casa sulla Piazza di san Benedetto popolo di san Benedetto, contigua alla s*ude*tta et a la Piazza delle Pallottole, co*n* bottega sotto gia a uso di scarpellino, et hoggi per uso di casa. Habita lui, et Gio*va*nni di Bart*olome*o, donzello al Arte della Lana, p*er soldi* 4; S*ti*ma*ta* l'habitatione s*oldi* 8; b*ocche* 7. – .8:4:3.

[San Giovanni, 212v. 3300. Domenico di Lorenzo, wool beater, a house in the Piazza di San Benedetto, popolo of San Benedetto, next to the previous one and to the Pizza delle Pallottole, with a shop below, formerly a shoe shop, now used as a residence. Domenico lives there together with Giovanni di Bartolomeo, squire at the Wool Guild, who rents for 4 soldi. Estimated, only the house, 8 soldi; mouths 7. – s.8:4:3.]

From the Decima *to DECIMA* 59

3) Breaking down the information:

3300. Domenico di Lorenzo, battilano, una casa sulla
entry #   owner   occupation   building description

Piazza di san Benedetto popolo di san Benedetto,
  street   popolo

contigua alla sudetta et a la Piazza delle Pallottole, con
             location info

bottega sotto gia a uso di scarpellino, et hoggi per
          shop info

uso di casa. Habita lui, et Giovanni di Bartolomeo, donzello al Arte della Lana,
 holding type   resident   occupation

per soldi 4; Stimata l'habitatione soldi 8; bocche 7. -----s.8:4:3
 rent   estimated value   mouths   male/female

Figure 3.4

4) FileMaker entry:

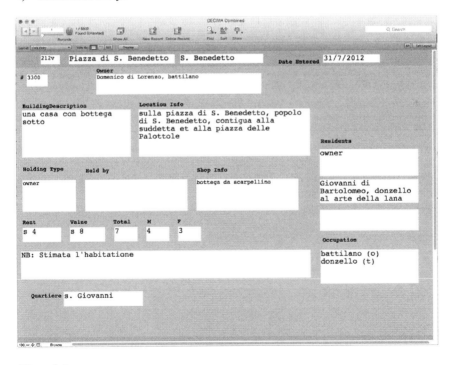

Figure 3.5
(© FileMaker).

Once we established the fields and the entry system, we produced an edition of the *Decima*, formatting it through FileMaker. The transcription of the manuscripts was certainly the most time-consuming part of the process and resulted in a diplomatic edition of the text, laid out in FileMaker entry format. The next step was to standardize the text, both to adjust the language to modern Italian and to ensure that similar items in the database were spelled in the same way in every instance, regardless of the number of variants under which they appeared in the manuscript. We removed all the 'Tuscanisms' from hand A, as well as older spelling of street names, locations, and occupations (such as '*ofizio*' for '*uffizio*' and '*cancellario*' for '*cancelliere*'). At this point, for example, all mentions of the 'Spedale delli Innocenti' or simply 'Innocenti' were replaced by the modern 'Ospedale degli Innocenti', and so on. During this process we also attempted to add any extra information we had available for people who were mentioned in multiple entries to every single entry in which they appear so that details such as patronymic or occupation, often present in only one of the entries, could be seen in all the entries in which they were mentioned.

As the database took shape, we noticed that those broad fields, often dependent on the entry style found in the manuscripts, fell short of the computational capacities to which we had access. For instance, while the 'occupation' field allowed us to map the distribution of specific trades in the city, we realized that if we connected someone's occupation with his situation in the house (that is, whether he owned, rented, or leased it), we would be able to plot occupations not only in a spatial but also in a social grid. For that, we split the occupation field into 'owners', 'holder', and 'residents', making it possible to search for 'butchers' who were also 'owners', for example.[6] In addition to that, we also established that occupations of deceased persons (such as dead fathers or husbands) would be marked with an asterisk, making occupations the first element that can actually be projected into a different generation, an avenue of inquiry that we will further explore in the next phase of the DECIMA project. Likewise, we partitioned all the five nominal fields ('owner', 'tenant', and the three 'residents' field) into 'title', 'cognomen', 'patronym', 'avonym', and 'surname', using a script run through Microsoft Excel. As a result, the database now unveiled kinship networks and their use of the urban space.[7] At this point, the database was ready to be geocoded and plotted into Buonsignori's map.[8]

Back from DECIMA to the *Decima*: what was lost, what was gained

Looking back from the digital database to the sixteenth-century manuscripts, we can ask what was lost and what was gained to enable digital access to all the information contained in the census. Obviously, DECIMA, as an online database, makes the data collected in the *Decima* easily available in a fully searchable edition of the text. From five rather obscure codices in the Archivio di Stato in Florence that were accessible only to specialists who could travel to consult them directly, the DECIMA project produced a resource that offers not only the data together with several research tools for specialists but also easy access for secondary and postsecondary teachers and curious amateurs. What was lost and what was gained in our perception of the data preserved in the manuscripts is, however, a more complicated question. As we have seen, translating the notarial notes of our codices in a geocoded digital database demanded adjustments, adaptations, and, above all, standardization of the data, as well as the inclusion of information that went beyond what was initially available through the manuscripts. The result was *not* a digitization of the *Decima* but the creation of a different kind of database.

The most significant loss in the process of creating DECIMA is the erasure of the individuality of the teams and scribes working on the original document. This individuality includes both linguistic particularities and the evolution of style in the collection of the data. DECIMA removed every trace of the distinction between the 'Tuscanisms' of hand A and the more standardized Italian of hands B and C, as well as every other difference in redaction and in the presentation of the three hands. Furthermore, the necessary standardization removed the initial inconsistencies of the entries, erasing the temporal dimension in the production of the manuscripts. The collection of data as a learning experience disappeared, giving way to the pure data. Finally, the database format shifted the fluidity of the practice of the collection of data to the background. While reading through the *Decima* – admittedly a somewhat unnatural task, given that it is after all a repetitive series of entries – one is often taken into the daily process of walking the city. When reading, one is transported to the practical experience of the scribes. For example, in Via del Sole, the team collecting data in Santa Maria Novella pointed out a depiction of the Virgin.[9] By choosing to focus on the data, the DECIMA database deemphasized the human experience behind the elaboration of the *Decima*, and, on that account, a return to the manuscripts can still be extremely rewarding.

The contributions of DECIMA, however, go beyond expanding the availability and navigability of the tax census. Once combined in a full database and displayed on a map, the data in the census assume a different form from their original presentation. The *Decima* was a fiscal presentation, not a map or a blueprint of the city. It certainly indicated the streets that were covered, as well as the location of each house, but the information answered mostly to the practical demand of ensuring that the collection of data had been thorough – the pragmatic character of such information is made clear by the fact that it was removed from the final presentation copy. By skimming through the various entries in the *Decima*, the modern reader has no immediate perception of the geographic dimension of the work, either in its physical (that is, the layout of streets and houses) or in its social character (the distribution of neighbours and the social boundaries of space). The lack of a clear spatial orientation, however, highlights the fact that spatial and social orientation in the city was part of a practical knowledge that our scribes shared with the rest of the population. As such, it remained unstated in the background. In other words, the *Decima* team (and the intended audience) did not need a clearly articulated definition of space because contemporary Florentines already knew the city, not as a graphic representation, but as an experienced reality. This 'feeling of the city', which the sixteenth-century inhabitants had for Florence, is a sensation or understanding that the modern reader certainly lacks.

It is in accounting for this lack that DECIMA provides one of its most interesting contributions. Unlike the *Decima*, the DECIMA database is *not* a fiscal representation of the city but a geographically precise depiction of social data. Once plotted onto the map, the combined data from the census create a visual understanding of the city that goes beyond the intentions in the *Decima*. This collection of space-oriented data provides the modern reader a theoretical understanding of the city that can help emulate to a certain extent the practical spatial experience of sixteenth-century Florentines. The GIS representation of the census allows the social historian to artificially reproduce the 'feeling of the city' particular to the contemporaneous experience. In other words, the amount of spatial data made available through DECIMA provides some access to the practical mastery that Florentines had of their city but that eludes many modern scholars. Every entry from the *Decima* received a spatial context (both physical and social) in DECIMA, making our understanding of the *Decima,* through the enhanced lenses of DECIMA, closer to what Florentines would have experienced from their daily life in the city. Spatializing the data, by connecting the *Decima* to DECIMA, allows us to read these documents as they were conceived by their creators in their survey of Florence's social geography.

Notes

1 The decree is recorded in L. Cantini, *Legislazione Toscana, raccolta e illustrata*, vol. 4, Florence, Italy: Stampa Albbiziniana, 1802, 171–72.
2 Archivio di Stato di Firenze (ASF), *Decima Granducale* (DG), 3774–3780, and ASF, *Micellanea Medicea*, 224, respectively. On the elaboration of the *Decima,* see L. Faibisoff, 'Route of Governmentality', in this volume. A facsimile of the presentation copy is available in S. Meloni Trkulja, *I fiorentini nel 1562: Descrizioni delle Bocche della Città e Stato di Firenze fatta l'anno 1562*, Florence, Italy: Bruschi, 1991.
3 ASF, *DG*, 3781 (Santa Croce), 41r 493 (Fillipo), Santa Croce 41v.504 (Andrea).
4 For example, ASF, *DG*, 3780, 151r 2273.
5 For example, ASF, *DG*, 3783, 45v 705–6.
6 See C. Rose, 'Thinking and Using DECIMA', in this volume.
7 S. Strocchia and J. Rombough, 'Women behind Walls', in this volume.
8 Rose, 'Thinking and Using DECIMA', 3–5.
9 ASF, *DG*, 3782, 66v 1144.

Bibliography

Manuscript sources

Archivio di Stato di Firenze (ASF), *Decima Granducale,* 2273 and 3774–3780.
——— *Micellanea Medicea,* 224.

Print sources

Cantini, L., *Legislazione Toscana, raccolta e illustrate*, vol. 4, Florence, Italy: Stampa Albbiziniana, 1802.
Meloni Trkulja, S., *I fiorentini nel 1562: Descrizioni delle Bocche della Città e Stato di Firenze fatta l'anno 1562*, Florence, Italy: Bruschi, 1991.

4 Shaping the streetscape
Institutions as landlords in early modern Florence

Daniel Jamison

If we look at Florence from the high perspective provided by Stefano Buonsignori's 1584 etching, its people are invisible. From above, we cannot divide the city into the parishes and neighbourhoods that were sensible to its inhabitants. On the other hand, when we increase magnification too much, the engraving's rich detail becomes overwhelming and distorted: separate buildings flow into one another, rooflines are jagged and meet at odd angles, and our view is cluttered with shrubs, chimneys, and hatched shading. The manuscripts of the 1561 *Decima* present similar flaws to the modern investigator. The summary statistics derived from them fall short of depicting the actual shape of the city's residential property market, but the document's level of detail becomes both baffling and irregular if one draws closer and reads from entry to entry. Using the DECIMA interface effectively as a research tool means navigating the shortcomings of these two sources, and one solution to oversaturation is to narrow the range of visible data, in this case to examine only certain sections of the city, types of properties, or kinds of residents and owners.

The goal of this essay is to provide a survey of the property market in 1561 Florence, which requires addressing all four quarters and the range of buildings present in the city. In order to achieve this breadth while avoiding both the general and the infinitesimal, I focussed on property in the *Decima* owned by institutional landlords: convents, churches, and other corporate entities. This approach confers several advantages. First, Florentine institutions controlled a respectable portion of the urban residential property – almost one third. Institutional landlords are also representative of the propertied class as a whole insofar as they employed the same tenancy arrangements and owned the same kinds of properties as other landlords. Finally, there are far fewer institutions than private owners in the *Decima*, and institutions on average managed much larger estates; focusing on institutions thus limits the number of subjects in view and provides more significant results than would a survey of all landlords in 1561 Florence. Because of these limited numbers, we can group institutions into close-fitting categories with some confidence; as we will see, different types of organizations had different profiles in the property market. For example, parish churches managed fewer parcels of land than convents and monasteries, and their respective approaches to exploiting these properties naturally differed. But the physical location of property also impacted how these landlords disposed of them, as two institutions with estates of similar size might not employ the same tenancy contracts if their estates were not similarly consolidated (e.g. along the same block, within the same quarter). Given the sizeable proportion of the property market, and especially the rental market, that was under institutional management, the impact of these considerations on Florentine urbanism cannot be disregarded.

This chapter works through concentric rings of data that describe the residences of 1561 Florence, beginning with the city as a whole, moving to institutions as a group, and ending with specific institutions as economic actors. On each level, we can draw tentative conclusions about the shape of the urban property market, the strategies of the landlords active in it, and ultimately the effect that these strategies might have had on the life of the average Florentine. At this last stage especially, the DECIMA map enhances the census's statistics and allows us to see that a few institutions were large enough to dominate entire neighbourhoods. The interests of institutional landlords imposed patterns of consolidation, standardization, and development upon the urban fabric of sixteenth-century Florence. These strategies had an impact on street life because they affected the appearance and occupants of the structures that served as its backdrop.

*

Elsewhere in this volume, Leah Faibisoff and Eduardo Fabbro describe the practices employed by the head surveyors and scribes to arrange their census of taxable properties into a novel geographic scheme. To work with these entries in the aggregate, we must address the strengths and limitations of the product, the *Decima ricerche* themselves. The men sent by the *Magistrato della Decima* intended to provide a usable description for all residential property within the city of Florence in order to complement the payer-submitted tax returns collected and organized by the fisc (in the *campioni*).[1] But, while we can be reasonably sure that these investigators dutifully went door to door and gathered the basic details on every property, their exact methods can only be guessed at, and each team appears to have had a slightly different *modus operandi*.[2] Generally, it seems that they conducted brief interviews with residents, but they may have consulted the *campioni* for more technical information such as property values.[3] The result of their work is a document that clearly demonstrates the geographical relationship between buildings in the city but reflects an unsystematic method of inquiry into each residence.

This lack of standardization makes the *Decima* no different from other early modern Italian sources, but its effects need to be recognized.[4] One of the advantages of looking at institutional landlords is that the owners identified as 'Congregazione di Santa Maria del Fiore', 'Capitolo di Santa Maria del Fiore', and 'Congregazione dei Preti di Santa Maria del Fiore' can be reduced to a single entity, namely the cathedral chapter.[5] This isn't the case with many 'private' owners, such as a certain merchant named Francesco who is listed as the owner of a house in Via della Morte; he may or may not be the same 'Francesco di . . . merciaio' who appears as owner in two other entries, or indeed he might be the same man as any Francesco either described as a merchant or listed without an explicit profession.[6] While one large church could house multiple institutions, such as chapel endowments, confraternities, and the fabric itself, each possessed a distinct name insofar as it appeared to its tenants as an independent landlord. This means that the properties of each can be found under the same name in Santo Spirito as in San Giovanni. But, just as tenants supplied 'Francesco the merchant' because the name sufficed to identify a single man on a local level, there are yet a few entries bearing incomplete names for their institutional landlords.

The contractual arrangements between owners and tenants are often ambiguous as well. The scribes did their best to be thorough, but they also tried to be concise and lacked a standard vocabulary; as a result, they distinguished between types of holdings with distinct phrases but rarely supplied enough detail for comparisons across the city. Next to Michelangelo Buonarroti's shop on Via Mozza, the children of Biagio di Lorenzo Benvenuti, a deceased glassmaker, held a house from the Carmelites 'under lease by the masculine line' ('*a livello a linea masculina*'), which is to say that the lease devolved upon them from their father.[7] Across the river at the Canto al Lione in Santo Spirito, the heirs of Giuliano di Benedetto Bati were living in another house owned by the Carmelites 'by the [masculine] line' ('*a linea*').[8] But were these heirs paying periodically to renew their hereditary lease, as were the glassmaker's sons? The fact that the terminology in use depends on the entry's situation in the manuscript make a clear answer to this question impossible, since each scribe may have been trying to represent legal distinctions or, as seems more likely, simply employing an idiosyncratic vocabulary. This unevenness problematizes any attempt to compare and contrast across the city, but some lines can be drawn; *Decima* scribes and surveyors knew the difference between a *livello* contract and a *pigione* contract, for example, as this had implications for how a subject property's assessment would be factored into the owner's total tax.[9] This is the primary reason why I use such broad categories for contract type later in this chapter.

Another issue raised by the *Decima* is the question of property value. As part of their survey, the fiscal scribes noted the *stima*, or estimated tax burden, of each property on their route. This was equivalent not to the total value of the structure but to its potential yearly return, and this estimate concerned only the residential aspect of multi-use buildings.[10] Moreover, the *stima* was not established with every new survey but referred to a property's value as it was established in the *Magistrato della Decima* in one of its previous surveys, possibly as early as 1532–34.[11] But officials also attempted to learn, presumably from the occupants themselves, the rent that was actually being paid for the property in each entry; reported rent, the actual income derived from a property over a year, and *stima*, the official record of that income, should ideally line up – but they often do not.[12] Of course, these two amounts were not always directly related, such as in the case of homes attached to businesses or shops.[13] For example, an innkeeper named Jacopo di Bastiano, called Corsetto, rented a building at the Canto alle Rondine to serve as both a home and his *osteria* from Piero d'Antonio Carnesecchi; he paid 45 *scudi* in rent, but the residential section of the structure was only worth 20 *scudi*.[14] In this case, and in the case of many other properties with shops below or beside, the reported rent was being paid for the building as a whole, while the *stima* was assessed for the residence alone.

If we exclude such mixed-use structures, in which rent is almost always higher than the *stima*, we can find many other properties for which the tenants claimed to have paid rent well below the assessed value of the property. Limiting our search to property in which only rent-paying tenants were resident, we still see that about 25 per cent garnered rents worth less than 90 per cent of their *stima*.[15] Allowance may have to be made for the different currencies in use, as the 'silver' *scudo d'argento* used for the *stima* was a centrally determined money of account, whereas the various monies reported by tenants in rental fields (mostly *lire*, *soldi*, nonspecific *scudi*, and *scudi d'oro*) were likely pegged to other rates fixed by contract.[16] It is also possible that some rental (*pigione*) properties entailed another form of remuneration that was not recorded by the scribes or that they carried an entry cost that was amortized over several years of rent payments, although long-term contracts of the latter sort should have been recorded as leases (*livelli*). Because of these uncertainties, in this chapter I always use the *stima*, rather than reported rents, to describe the value of urban property.

Related to value is the issue of overall wealth and urban land ownership. While the *Decima campioni* can provide statistics on the total wealth of individuals and institutions, at least insofar as they reported their holdings, the *ricerche* concern urban property only. Many individual landlords and most institutional landlords owned land outside the city walls, and for some this formed the larger part of their estate. As a result, my study addresses only the management of urban portfolios, and my comparisons between groups are limited to the context of the city.

For the sake of greater clarity, I have also devised six categories of contracts on the myriad forms present in the *Decima*: *Free/Office*, indicating buildings for which no rent was due (e.g. *senza pagamento*); *Linea/Lifelease*, including all holdings held *a vita* or *a linea* and their variants; *Livello*, denoting a long-term lease; *Owner/Res*, meaning all holdings in which the owner was the *sole* occupant; *Pigione*, a periodic rental arrangement with weak tenancy rights, by and large the sole category of homes for which rent was recorded; and finally *Uninhabited/ Other*, which includes all empty homes and several dozen entries that cannot be slotted into the aforementioned categories. These six categories reflect but cannot pretend to encompass the variety of contracts actually used in mid-sixteenth-century Florence. They are useful insofar as they provide a matte finish for the source material's fine grain.[17] I have similarly divided 'private' owners into three groups (Heirs, Women, and Men) and institutional owners into a number of types to be explored later. With the six categories noted earlier, we can pull back and see the contours and contexts of the property market in 1561 Florence.

*

We can begin with broad comparison of contrasting markets in the city's four quarters. Santa Croce, San Giovanni, Santa Maria Novella, and Santo Spirito differed significantly in density and in the average value of housing stock, as summarized on Table 4.1.

Table 4.1 Share of entries, assessed value, and population by quarter

Quarter	% Entries	% Value	Wealth Index	% Population	Crowding Index
SC	15.16%	16.15%	106.5	15.11%	99.7
SG	39.22%	40.50%	103.3	40.03%	102.0
SMN	19.06%	20.59%	108.0	19.63%	103.0
SS	26.55%	22.76%	85.7	25.23%	95.0

San Giovanni contained the most households by far, followed by Santo Spirito, Santa Maria Novella, and finally Santa Croce, and consequently it contained the most taxable wealth and the highest population.[18] By comparing each quarter's share of assessed value and population to its number of registered households, we can derive two more indices. The wealth index is the ratio between each quarter's total assessed taxable value and number of entries, and thus it indicates how much the property in each quarter was worth on average. Property in Santa Maria Novella was most valuable, while property in Santo Spirito was worth 15 per cent less than its number of homes would suggest. The second index, the crowding index, shows the ratio between population and households, and so we can see that San Giovanni and Santa Maria Novella had properties that housed, on average, slightly more people than those in Santa Croce, which was nearly balanced, and that Santo Spirito was underpopulated in comparison.

The differences among the four quarters in the *Decima* certainly merit further investigation, particularly given that different personnel handled each quarter's survey and that reporting methods differed somewhat depending on the scribe. Indeed, much more can be done with these indices in the DECIMA interface, which allows a user to chart quality-of-life criteria such as crowding and wealth along particular streets and between neighbourhoods. In the interest of looking at landlords across the city, and especially large institutional landlords whose urban portfolios contained properties in multiple quarters, I will present statistics for Florence as a whole for the remainder of the chapter.

Turning then to a closer comparison of institutional and individual property-owning patterns, we start by noting that *Decima* officials recorded slightly fewer than 52,000 people, about 25,000 men and 27,000 women, living in the city in slightly more than 8,700 residential properties.

Table 4.2 Property value and population in the *Decima ricerche*

	Entries	Assessment	Ass./Entry	Population	Pop./entry
Institutional	2,340	24,114	10.42	13,870	5.93
Private	6,379	109,945.5	17.34	37,774	5.92
Women	869	11,664	13.44	4,755	5.45
Heirs	664	14,066	21.25	4,261	6.42
Men	4,846	84,215.5	17.51	28,758	5.93
Grand Total	8,719	134,059.5	15.49	51,644	5.92

Some 14,000 people lived in the 2,300 homes owned by institutions, while the remaining 38,000 were resident in 6,400 privately owned structures. Houses managed by institutions were estimated to have a total tax burden of around 24,000 *scudi*, or an average of just over 10 *scudi* per dwelling, versus the average 17 *scudi* tax levied on 'private' property, collectively worth about 134,000 *scudi*. This disparity is the most striking difference between institutional and private owners, as the average population per dwelling is more or less the same in both categories. At the outset, then, we find a significant distinction between institutions, which owned cheap properties for rent or lease to lower-class Florentines, and private owners, who held the city's more valuable properties.

Most noninstitutional property owners in 1561 Florence were individual men (~76 per cent), but around 14 per cent were women and 10 per cent were collective groups of heirs, identified as the *redi* (from *heredi*, or heirs) of a deceased owner. Hereditary properties were assessed a higher average tax burden than buildings owned by individual men or women. This is no surprise given that the least divisible portions of estates were often the most valuable and therefore fodder for lengthy legal disputes. For example, the *redi* of Girolamo di Francesco da Sommaia jointly managed a mansion assessed at 150 *scudi* on the Borgo Allegri, in which his one unmarried daughter, Hippolita, was resident at no charge.[19] This large property was presumably the Sommaia property that was willed by Girolamo to the nearby Casa della Pietà after the exile of his son and heir Giovanni for a vicious crime in 1559.[20] Given the convoluted case, with the recent death of Girolamo, a male heir in disgrace, and several female heirs in the family, this valuable property was still in a state of flux in the summer of 1561 and therefore was recorded by the *Decima* surveyor as the common possession of the *redi*.[21] As Table 4.2 shows, women who were landlords generally held less valuable property than individual men. The major exception was the Duchess herself, Eleanor of Toledo, whose portfolio included a mansion confiscated from Bindo Altoviti.[22] Yet even the average woman's property entailed a higher tax burden than the typical possession of an institutional landlord.

The contrast between the taxable value of institutional and private property is not the result of some discount for religious bodies. In the *Decima*, all property besides the buildings that actually housed institutions – hospitals, churches, convents – was assessed according to the same standard, since all parcels could be transferred from an institution to an individual or vice versa.[23] We see this in the footnotes jammed between many entries. As one example, some time after 1561 a *Decima* official amended the entry for a house in Via dell'Albero owned by the convent of San Donato in Polverosa, adding 'today [this is found] under [the name of] Giovanni Rapetti, [in the register of] Red Lion, [folio] 320'.[24] Additionally, taxpayers owed nothing for their primary residences, yet several thousand homes inhabited by their owners are present in the *ricerche* and given a *stima* as if they were leased or rented properties.[25] The values assigned to each structure had no specific bearing on how and when a tax would be exacted – they were only the basis upon which a levy *could* be assessed.

Shaping the streetscape 69

Rather than indicating a discount, then, the striking difference in tax assessment between institutional and private holdings corresponds directly to the kinds of properties owned by each group. When we divide the residential property market into the six categories of contracts described earlier, we can see that certain contract types were predominantly used for properties of a particular value; homes for lease or rent were, on average, less valuable than buildings that housed the property-owning class. Of course, a single entry could have multiple levels of tenancy within it; a house might be leased to a tenant (*Livello*) who then sublet part of it for rent (*Pigione*). Because of these complex cases, it is useful to isolate both the *primary* holding type and the *secondary* holding type; simple cases, in which a building was sublet only once or not at all, have identical *primary* and *secondary* holding types.[26] In some rare cases there are two or more types of direct holding recorded for the same parcel, such as a home owned by the Monastery of Santa Maria Novella in the eponymous piazza. The friars leased it (*Livello*) to a Simone Fabbrizi, who sublet part of it for rent (*Pigione*) to a Giovanni Franzese, while Tusino Baldesi lived in another part of it for free (*Free/Office*).[27] In these few cases, I have selected only one chain of primary and secondary holding types, so this home is registered as *Livello* and then *Pigione*.

The disparity in assessed property value between institutional and noninstitutional landlords also reflects a distinction between the holding types employed by each group. Table 4.3 presents the statistics derived from the division of *ricerche* entries by primary holding type.

The biggest source of imbalance in this chart is the high average value assigned to buildings that are home to their owners (*Owner/Res*). The Florentine super-rich, such as the Ridolfi, Antinori, and Capponi and Duke Cosimo I himself, can be found among the 2,700 heads of household who were wealthy enough to own their homes. As it happens, only 878 owners in this category had a tax burden above the 21.1 *scudi* average, whereas 1,814 owners fell below that level.[28] Additionally, the

Table 4.3 Instances of each primary holding type and their average value (in *scudi*)

	Institutional Owner			'Private' Owner			
	Instances	Total % of Cat.	Av. Value	Instances	% Total	Av. Value	Total % of City
Free/Office	156	6.7%	10.2	117	1.8%	17.4	3.1%
Linea/Lifelease	411	17.6%	10.7	138	2.2%	15.7	6.3%
Livello	422	18.0%	11.6	18	0.3%	12.1	5.1%
Own/Res				2,768	43.4%	21.1	31.8%
Pigione	1,241	53.0%	9.9	3,020	47.3%	13.9	48.9%
Unocc./Other	110	4.7%	10.3	318	5.0%	17.7	4.9%
Total/Av	2,340	100%	10.4	6,379	100%	17.3	15.5

mean tax assessment in the *Owner/Res* category was actually a third higher than the median assessment, 16 *scudi*. In other words, most people who owned their own homes did not live in the mansions that occupied the extreme end of the property market. But even the modest homes clustered around the median would have been more valuable than the average dwellings available for lease or rent in the city – worth around 50 per cent more at the median and twice as expensive on average.

All of the buildings that physically housed religious institutions, such as convents, hospitals, and churches, were not subject to taxation and therefore appear without an assessed value in the *Decima*. Much of the 7-*scudi* price difference between the average private and average institutional assessment can thus be chalked up to the fact that institutions did not own the kinds of homes that members of the propertied class sought for their own dwellings. The disparate values in the *Free/Office* category, which nearly match the overall trend, can also be explained. Institutional *Free/Office* properties were by and large handed out to men and women who worked for the institution in question, such as bakers, gardeners, and even confessors, while privately owned *Free/Office* properties were generally home to the owner's extended family members; the latter naturally reflects the values seen in the *Owner/Res* category. If these institutions received valuable property in bequests, they appear to have divested themselves of most of it in favour of less expensive homes. There was a charitable tradition of religious institutions selling homes they had been given and distributing the proceeds, but this was clearly no longer the case for many, and institutions were likely influenced more by the fact that Florentines looking for temporary tenancy arrangements were not, by and large, interested in more expensive leases. Even so, institutional landlords held leased and rented properties (*Livello, Linea/Lifelease*, and *Pigione*) that were cheaper on average than the same kinds of properties owned by private landlords.

When we look at secondary holding types, we can see a further distinction within the category of leased properties (Table 4.4).

Table 4.4 Secondary holding types for properties under lease

Prim. Type	Sec. Type	Institutional Owner			'Private' Owner		
		Instances	% Total	Av. Value	Instances	% Total	Av. Value
Linea/ Lifelease	Free/Office	1	>1%	13			
	Linea/ Lifelease	274	66.7%	10.6	97	70.3%	16.9
	Livello	2	>1%	18			
	Pigione	133	32.3%	10.9	41	29.7%	13.1
	Uninhabited/ Other	1	>1%	8			
Livello	Linea/ Lifelease	1	>1%	12			
	Livello	192	45.0%	13.5	10	55%	11.9
	Pigione	229	54.2%	10.0	8	45%	12.3

Institutional properties let out under hereditary or perpetual leases differed little in terms of value whether or not they were sublet by the leaseholder. This may reflect the fact that, unlike *Livello* properties, these perpetual holdings remained in a family for an extended period of time, during which the holders' need for them would have changed. It is difficult to imagine that hereditary leases, functioning like annuities, were undertaken as part of a long-term monetization strategy, that is, for the sole purpose of subleasing, which does seem to be the trend for the more temporary *Livello* leases. Leaseholders in the latter category appear to have contracted more valuable property when seeking a residence for themselves and less valuable dwellings for sublet to renters. A similar phenomenon is evident among the perpetual and lineal leases offered by private landlords, but this is probably just a fluke of the small sample size.[29]

Taken together, these statistics reveal the roughly tripartite division of residential property in 1561 Florence. On average, men and women wealthy enough to own urban land lived in the most valuable homes, the top third of the whole market. Leaseholders, who were able to afford the large lump payments and long terms of *livello* contracts, resided in less expensive buildings, as did people who held property in nonmonetary arrangements. The cheapest kind of dwellings served as homes to people who paid a regular rent (*Pigione*), and around half of the city's property was monetized in this way. Nevertheless, while these contract types are useful in dividing residential housing along the lines of value, in each of the latter two categories there exists a further division between cheaper property held by institutions and more expensive property belonging to individuals. Lacking property of their own, many Florentines made do with leases and short-term rental contracts, and institutions catered to the least affluent among these.

*

By the *Decima*'s account, Duke Cosimo I owned twenty different residential properties in the city of Florence in 1561, the annual income from which was estimated at 872 *scudi*. His nearest rival in total holdings was Giulio di Giuliano Scali, with eleven parcels; his nearest rival in terms of portfolio value was the Marquis of Cetona, Chiappino Vitelli, whose urban income was estimated at around 350 *scudi*. The duke and Scali were the only individuals in town with more than ten properties apiece, excepting Puccio Ugolini, who held a remarkable portfolio of twenty-nine parcels. But Ugolini is listed as owner only in his capacity as chancellor of Santa Maria del Fiore, and these residences most likely were among the holdings of the cathedral chapter itself.[30]

Even excepting the property managed by Puccio Ugolini, the Congregazione di Santa Maria del Fiore had many more holdings than the duke himself, and similarly the portfolios of even smaller institutions outstripped in size and complexity the holdings of most individuals. Bearing in mind the difficulty of identifying unique people in the document, we have around 5,000 'private' owners and exactly 361 institutional owners in the 1561 *Decima*. Table 4.5 indicates the distribution of property and value among these different owners.

The division of property among private landlords in Florence forms a fairly flat pyramid, which is why the average number of properties per unique name is only

72 Daniel Jamison

Table 4.5 Owner count and assessments in *scudi* by holding size

#Holdings		1	2–5	6–10	11–20	Over 20	Total
Owner Count	Individuals	4,407 (85%)	758 (14%)	15 (<1%)	3 (<1%)	1 (<1%)	5,184 owners
	Institutions	182 (50%)	103 (28%)	27 (8%)	29 (8%)	21 (6%)	361
Total Holdings	Individuals	4,407 (69%)	1,791 (28%)	103 (2%)	48 (<1%)	29 (<1%)	6,378 entries
	Institutions	182 (8%)	302 (13%)	194 (9%)	432 (18%)	1,230 (52%)	2,341

about one and a quarter. Conversely, institutions held a higher average of six and a half properties apiece, but the sum of these parcels was distributed in an *inverse* pyramid, such that the twenty wealthiest institutions held a bare majority of all institutionally owned property in 1561 Florence. Naturally, only certain kinds of institutions could handle urban estates of this magnitude. What kinds of organizations were present on the property market, and what features distinguished them from one another?

To determine this, I have subdivided the Institutions category into six broad types: *Chapels and Churches, Monasteries and Convents, Confraternities and Guilds, Congregations of Priests, Hospitals,* and *State Offices*. In some cases, these are very tenuous distinctions. For example, all organizations identified by the document or identifiable from external sources are listed as *spedali* in the *Hospitals* category, even though some of these were connected to other institutions listed under *Confraternities and Guilds*; I chose in these cases to follow the distinctions employed by the *Decima* scribes.[31] *Chapels and Churches* contain properties owned by churches themselves or their building committees (e.g. *opere*), while *Congregations* are those institutions that are identified as collectives of priests, such as the cathedral canons. Yet this latter distinction may rely too heavily on the scribes' vexing tendency, mentioned earlier, to overspecify while simultaneously oversimplifying. In sum, the six categories employed here may elide or create distinctions as they follow the descriptions in the *Decima*, though it would require a far more extensive interrogation of the census manuscripts to address the issue.

Nonetheless, this scheme does help us to appreciate the different weight that monastic and parochial endowments had in the urban property market. Table 4.6 presents the same statistics as Table 4.5, but divided by institution type. I have excluded the *State Offices* category, which accounts for only twenty-four entries in the *Decima*, and these are mostly confiscated estates that ended up in the hands of the fisc rather than those of the Duchess.

Less than 10 per cent of institutions held only a single property, but around half of these belonged to the *Chapels and Churches* category. The property of these small endowments is distributed in a manner similar to the distribution in the

Table 4.6 Number of institutions and total portfolio by holding size

#Holdings		1	2–5	6–10	11–20	Over 20	Totals
Owner Count	Chap/Church	85	33	2	2	1	124 owners
	Mon/Convent	44	29	18	19	10	120
	Confrat/Guild	35	29	4	2	4	74
	Congregation	4	4	1	2	2	13
	Hospital	8	6	1	2	4	21
Total Holdings	Chap/Church	85	82	13	24	24	227 entries
	Mon/Convent	44	97	126	298	441	1,006
	Confrat/Guild	35	87	29	37	306	494
	Congregation	4	13	8	30	207	262
	Hospital	8	19	6	34	252	319

'private' owner category, and only the churches of San Apollinare, Sant'Apostolo, San Romolo, San Niccolò Oltrarno, and San Piero Scheraggio held more than four pieces of property. A similar distribution results even when the totals for chapels are added to the churches that housed them, as the smallest church endowments had no chapels endowed with urban property.[32] Another feature that distinguishes these institutions is that the *Decima* scribes frequently named their rectors (*rettori*); these rectors may or may not have held other duties in the churches in question, and some of them appear to have been the priests. It seems likely that these rectors served in lieu of a separate in-house administration for institutions that held little property in the city.

In every other category, however, we see the inverse pyramid of property distribution that distinguished institutional from private landlords in Table 4.5, albeit with differing degrees in each category. Among confraternities, monasteries, and convents, well-endowed organizations appear alongside an equal number of smaller portfolios. On the other hand, the only small hospitals that appear, such as the Spedale del Bigallo, Spedale del Tempio, and Spedale di San Lorenzo dei Maniscalchi, were not actually at all small; rather, they were branches of larger organizations present in the *Confraternities and Guilds* category, sectioned off by the *Decima* scribes under their own names.[33] Regardless of these differences at the lower end, the majority of property in each category belonged to institutions with more than twenty parcels apiece; joined by the Church of San Romolo, these twenty-one super-sized landlords owned a total of 1,230 buildings, around 14 per cent of all residential property in the city, and housed more than 7,500 people – a seventh of the total population. These organizations acted differently in the market as a consequence of their size.

Looking at each of these very large landlords in turn, we can see a definite trend in their property management strategies.

74 Daniel Jamison

Table 4.7 Contract types used by the wealthiest institutional landlords

	Free/ Office	Linea/ Life	Livello	Pigione	Other	Total Holdings	Total (scudi)
Congrega di S. Maria del Fiore	3	13	64	78	5	163	1,880
Cavalieri e Religione di S. Jacopo	1	5	65	60	3	134	1,024
Spedale degl'Innocenti		24	24	54	3	105	1,226
Convento dei Camaldoli		94	1	1	2	98	805
Spedale di S. Maria Nuova		14	13	56	5	88	1,230
Arte dei Mercatanti	2	9	31	30	1	73	1,117
Monasterio di S. Ambrogio	1	19	2	36	4	62	599
Convento d'Ognisanti		11	38	9	1	59	457
Offizio del Bigallo	1	5	4	40	3	53	487
Arte della Lana	8	7		28	3	46	620
Congrega di S. Lorenzo	1	5	7	29	2	44	656
Monasterio di S. Piero Maggiore		2		41	1	44	345
Convento di S. Maria Novella	1	12	19	9		41	408
Monasterio di S. Apollonia	2	4	4	26		36	335
Spedale di S. Paulo	2	8	7	18	1	36	332
Convento di S. Antonio	2	5	9	14		30	232
Monasterio di S. Niccolo di Cafaggio	1	6		17	2	26	338
Chiesa di S. Romolo	2	2		18	2	24	240
Convento della Nuntiata	1	6	9	5	2	23	358
Spedale della Trinita degl'Incurabili	2	2		19		23	298
Convento del Carmine		11	4	7		22	218
Grand Total	**30**	**264**	**301**	**595**	**40**	**1,230**	**13,205**

First, none of these disposed of significant portions of their property *gratis* besides the Arte della Lana, which parceled out eight properties to the headmen and employees of its fulling mills (*tiratoi*). Second, both categories of leases (*Livello* and *Linea/Lifelease*) are markedly more common among these institutions than in the portfolios of other institutional landlords. Half of the top ten institutions on this table, moreover, disposed of the majority of their properties with this contract type, whereas only one landlord (Convento di Santa Maria Novella) in the lower eleven let more than 50 per cent of its estate *a livello* or *a linea*. This affinity between larger portfolios and the long-term lease is unsurprising. On the one hand, collecting regular rent from more than fifty, let alone one hundred, tenants on a regular basis would most likely have been inefficient, although admittedly the *ricerche* do nothing to illuminate the logistics of the *pigione* contract. On the other hand, the long-term lease offered a number of ways for the institution to divert maintenance costs onto the lessee; Nicholas Eckstein noted one such contract from the fifteenth century for the Compagnia di Santa Agata (the Brucciata), which contains the stipulation that the lineal tenant must contribute 100 *lire* towards the repair of the property within the first few years.[34] The pressure to alleviate carrying costs would have been proportional to the size of the estate, and this pressure, alongside tradition, would have affected the choice of contract for larger landlords.

Leaving aside contract types for the moment, another behaviour that distinguishes larger institutional entities from smaller ones in the *ricerche* is a tendency towards consolidation. Whether received directly through bequests or purchased with other endowments, the various buildings owned by institutional landlords would presumably have been scattered at the outset – throughout a parish, a quarter, or even the whole city. Combining these individual pieces into a contiguous whole could reduce maintenance and supervision costs and curb disputes with neighbours. But consolidation itself was surely a drawn-out process entailing numerous transactions and careful attention to the property market, and we should expect to find wealthier institutions with larger portfolios – and thus higher overhead costs – leading the way. The converse is also true: institutions that held only a few properties had much less incentive to consolidate them as heavily as those with large portfolios. With the data provided by the *ricerche*, DECIMA allows us to see whether institutions did indeed work to consolidate a unified urban portfolio.

Consolidation can be measured by looking at rates of contiguity. A property can be said to be contiguous relative to a single entity's estate if it is bounded on at least one side by another parcel belonging to that owner.

Looking at institutional estates with more than one property, it is clear that consolidation in 1561 Florence reflects an expected distribution: the larger the estate, the more streamlined. The twenty-one biggest landlords had, on average, brought two-thirds of their properties into connection with one another. Because the *Decima* provides a single snapshot of the urban property market, it sheds no light on the diachronic processes at work behind these statistics.

*

Measuring contiguity leads us to look more closely at specific institutions. Because the DECIMA project joins census data to the Buonsignori map, the physical

Table 4.8 Rates of contiguity among institutional owners by holding size

# Holdings	2–5 Holdings	6–10 Holdings	11–20 Holdings	>20 Holdings
Contiguity	41.3%	51.0%	63.2%	66.8%

layout of large holdings can be viewed from above. The twenty-one largest portfolios light up the entire map, their thousand-odd properties spreading around the city. Given the rate of contiguity within this group, a number of clusters are also visible.

To investigate these clusters more closely, we look briefly at concentrated holdings owned by the four largest institutions (the foundling Ospedale degli Innocenti, the Camaldolese monastery of Santa Maria degli Angeli, the cathedral chapter of S. Maria del Fiore, and the Order of S. Jacopo).

In 1561, the Ospedale degli Innocenti was the third largest landlord in Florence. However, its holdings were comparatively scattered, such that only 47 of its 103 properties were contiguous to other Innocenti property. Its holdings were found in all four quarters, but the largest concentration were located in San Giovanni and close to the institution itself: twenty-two properties on the southern side of Via Guelfa as it meets Via Tedesca (the modern Via Nazionale).[35]

This cluster was not particularly valuable. Each parcel was valued at an average of 8 *scudi*, which was below Innocenti's overall average of around 11.5 scudi. Fourteen were being rented out and eight were under lease, but five of the leaseholders were nonresidents who sublet the properties to others. And, although each Innocenti building in this line was contiguous with another, three other landlords owned a property in between the hospital's clusters: two private individuals and the Ospedale degli Incurabili. Even here, where it was put together best, the estate of the Innocenti was not in complete control of the block. Across the street to the

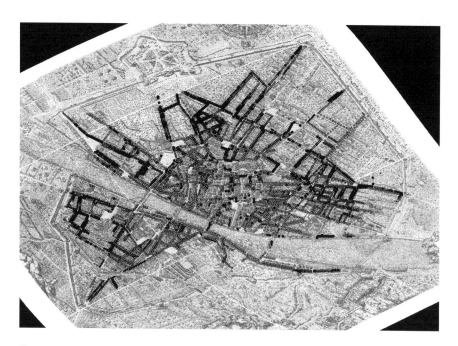

Figure 4.1 Institutional properties in ducal Florence, 1561.

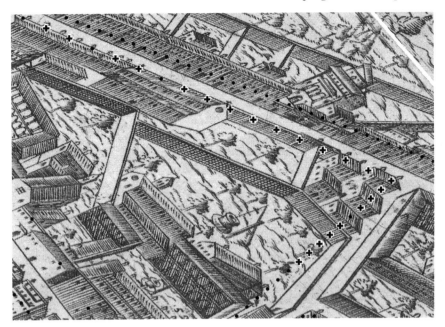

Figure 4.2 Innocenti properties (x) on the corner of Via Guelfa and Via Tedesca.

north, the cathedral canons of Santa Maria del Fiore were in a similar position: they, too, held a number of contiguous strips along this length of Via Guelfa, interspersed with the holdings of other owners.

The Congregazione or Capitolo di Santa Maria del Fiore was in a similar situation elsewhere, in the warren of streets around San Paolo in the quarter of Santa Maria Novella.

The Chiasso di Coda Rimessa, or Droop-Tail Alley (modern Via di San Paolino), ran from the Piazza San Paolo down to Via Nuova (modern Via del Porcellana), slicing off a thin block of the otherwise intact Borgognissanti-Fossi-Palazzuolo-Porcellana mass. Twenty-two of the cathedral chapter's 163 total holdings (73 per cent contiguous) were in this area, running along both sides of the block as well as along the eastern side of the alley. Many of the residents here, including twenty of the chapter's tenants, are described as prostitutes (*meretrici*) in the *Decima*, but the alley was also home to a number of women described only as widows (*vedove*). The chapter's most valuable property here was the mansion leased to one of its own canons, Messer Alessandro Strozzi; excluding this 80-*scudi* outlier, the average assessment was below 9 *scudi*. As on Via Guelfa, though, a high level of contiguity here belies the fact that the chapter did not hold a single unbroken string of properties. The distribution seen here suggests a middle point in a process – whether of investment or divestment is unclear. The synchronic image provided by the *ricerche* must be supplemented by further study to pose a solution here.

78 *Daniel Jamison*

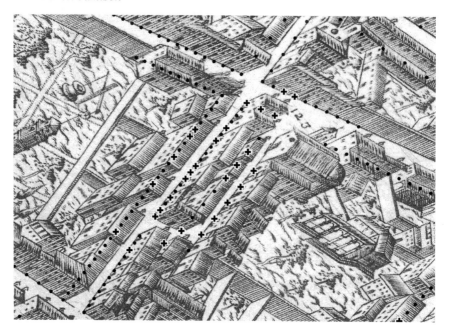

Figure 4.3 Congregazione Santa Maria del Fiore properties (x) around San Paolo.

Even when these larger institutions did not own an entire neighbourhood, they could have a preponderant share in it. The Camaldolese monastery in southwestern Santo Spirito owned ninety-eight parcels in the city (79 per cent contiguous) but only a single holding outside its home quarter. Most of these were concentrated in the neighbourhood just northeast of the Camaldolese themselves.

Our focus here is the block between Via dell'Orto in the north, Via del Leone in the east, Via San Salvatore (modern Via Torquato Tasso) in the south, and Via del Fiore (modern Via dei Camaldoli) in the west.[36] There were eighty-three separate properties ringing this block in 1561, of which the Camaldolese owned forty-five. Although there were many private landlords in between the Camaldolese holdings, the monks and their representatives would have been administering a largely unified estate in their midst. All of these, which were worth an average of 8.5 *scudi*, were leased out *a linea*, the heritable form of perpetual leasehold discussed earlier. Nicholas Eckstein noted that these same hereditary leases (*per linea masculina*) were the predominant contract form for Camaldolese properties in the fifteenth century, and it appears that the passage of a century did not change how this institution managed its properties in the district of the Green Dragon.[37]

The most completely unified estate in Florence belonged to the Order of S. Jacopo (Religione e Cavallieri di San Jacopo), which held 134 parcels (92 per cent contiguous) concentrated in an area just north of the Piazza di Santa Maria Novella, near the modern train station.

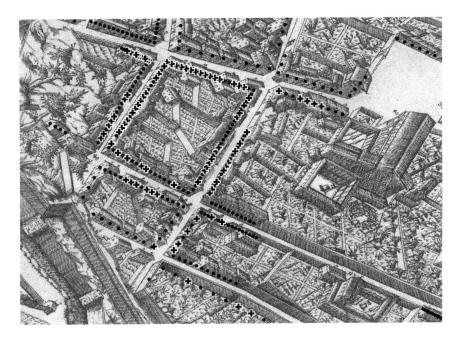

Figure 4.4 Camaldolesi properties (x) in Santo Spirito.

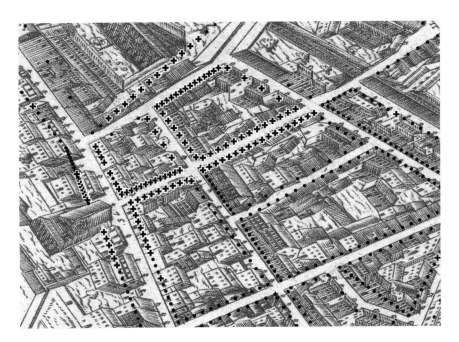

Figure 4.5 Order of San Jacopo properties (x) near Piazza Santa Maria Novella.

The Order's holdings were not merely a significant chunk of this neighbourhood – they *were* the neighbourhood, comprising two entire blocks and all property across the street from these. The spaces between these holdings or around the corner from them would have been characterized by the manner in which the Order maintained its façades and cisterns, the tenancy arrangements under which it administered the property, and consequently what kinds of tenants it selected or was able to court. In 1561, half of the neighbourhood was leased out (*Livello*) and half was rented (*Pigione*); all of these homes were assessed an average *stima* of 7.5 *scudi*. At least some of these homes bore numbers above their doors, an unusual detail recorded by the census takers for a number of the Order's properties here but nowhere else in the city.[38] At some point before 1561, this neighbourhood had been consolidated into a single block and marked out for easy management.

*

'Who owned the streets of Florence in the summer of 1559?' asks David Rosenthal in a recent essay on the yearly wars of the city's neighbourhood brigades.[39] If his reveller-warriors sought to create an 'alternative geography' of the city, mapped in their own favour, the normative geography against which they revolted was the city as seen in this chapter: divided into tracts controlled by powerful institutions. While Nicholas Eckstein was quite right to point out that the relations between tenants and institutional landlords in the neighbourhood of the Green Dragon were more complicated than a rental contract could ever encapsulate, it is nonetheless very useful to have the complete picture of those property relations.[40] With the DECIMA database, it is a relatively straightforward task to assess and locate a given entity's landed assets, which is an aid to anyone intending to begin a thorough investigation or hoping to clarify the findings of a completed study. This total view is what the DECIMA project offers: the ability to look behind the façade of every building in the city, to tabulate and compare the statistical realities of each household, and to visualize property values, densities, and ownership patterns. Every institution and every individual in the city can be securely localized to the neighbourhoods that affected them and that they themselves helped shape.

The experience of street life in early modern Florence certainly cannot be inferred from estate assessments alone. Yet the institutions of Renaissance Florence administered much of the property that faced onto the street, collected rent from its people, and engaged in tenancy arrangements that built neighbourhoods into contractually bound communities. Some of these institutional landlords evidently pursued strategies of agglomeration and standardization that would have had an impact on entire neighbourhoods. The statistics presented in this chapter suggest avenues for further research into how these institutions managed their urban property and how the processes of consolidation and standardization evident in the *Decima* impacted the large class of Florentine renters. The DECIMA project provides a tool with which to *visualize* the influence of these institutional landlords as contemporaries would have *felt* it: coalescing thickly in certain neighbourhoods, absent entirely in others.

Notes

1 L. Faibisoff identifies '*ricerca*' as the contemporary term describing ASF, *Decima Granducale*, 3780–84; in her chapter in this volume, she clarifies the distinction between the registers of the *Magistrato* (organized by *gonfalone*) and the *ricerche* (organized along a route).
2 In his chapter in this volume, E. Fabbro outlines not only the palaeographic deviations among the *ricerche* hands but also the differing levels of detail provided by each scribe.
3 This may seem like an exhausting task, but regular notes in the *ricerca* indicate that the document was crosschecked against the *campioni* in later years; in her chapter, L. Faibisoff describes the complex systems of reference between taxpayers and properties already in use by *Decima* officials before 1561. A systematic comparison of the 1561 *ricerca* and the contemporary *Decima campioni* has yet to be undertaken.
4 For a more complete discussion of standardization, see C. Rose's chapter in this volume.
5 The case of the cathedral chapter does present some ambiguity: the term *capitolo* certainly refers to the canonry, but the scribes also use *congrega* or *congrega di preti* [*sic*] with some regularity. These may have been different organizations within the chapter, but the *Decima* scribes were far from clear about the separation between them: see, for example, ASF, *Decima Granducale*, 3782, f. 41r (SM.704–7), where the owner is given as interchangeably *capitolo* and *congrega di santa maria del fiore* and is described in the building description as *detto capitolo, ò congrega*. If these were different bodies, then, they must have been operating as a single institution for the purpose of land management, or else the tenants interviewed for the *Decima* would certainly have known and clearly declared the body to which they paid their rent.
6 ASF, *Decima Granducale*, 3783, f. 181v (SG.2814); f. 218r (SG.3372); f. 43v (SG.673).
7 Ibid., f. 10r (SG.119).
8 ASF, *Decima Granducale*, 3781, f. 110r (SC.528).
9 G. Canestrini describes a separate rate used by the *Magistrato della Decima* to factor returns from leased (*livello*) property into a subject's total tax burden: G. Canestrini, *La scienza e l'arte di stato desunta dagli atti officiali della repubblica fiorentina e dei medici*, vol. 1, Florence, Italy: Le Monnier, 1862, 391–92.
10 In the case of the 1427 *Catasto*, this was assumed to be 7 per cent of the value of the property (D. Herlihy and C. Klapisch-Zuber, *Tuscans and Their Families*, New Haven, CT: Yale University Press, 1985, 14–15; see also Canestrini, *La scienza e l'arte*, 110–1). For the *Decima*, each taxpayer's declaration (*portata*) had to include all rents; see the overview from a more contemporary perspective provided by G.F. Pagnini della Ventura, *Della decima e di varie altre gravezze imposte dal comune di Firenze*, vol. 1, Florence, Italy: G. Bouchard, 1766, 37–108.
11 Pagnini della Ventura, *Della decima*, 47–48.
12 Rent was reported for most properties in the *Pigione* category, but only rarely is the annual rent recorded for leased properties; owners of property leased *a livello* were assessed based on the total income from the property, including the lump sums paid on entry into the contract: see Pagnini della Ventura, *Della decima*, 69–70.
13 The *botteghe* were recorded by *Decima* scribes in another document, *Decima Granducale*, 3784, which unfortunately but unavoidably, cannot be superimposed on the Buonsignori map in contiguous lines as have the other *ricerche* entries. It is to be hoped that it will be added in a future release.
14 ASF, *Decima Granducale*, 3783, f. 175r (SG.2708).
15 A total of 1,192 out of 3,949 properties surveyed; a much smaller proportion of these properties (207/3,949 or around 5 per cent) earned rent above 110 per cent of their estimated value. The entries examined for these statistics were 'pure' *Pigione* properties as described later (i.e. no leaseholders or owners enjoyed right of residence in part of the holding), and there is therefore no clear reason why the rents would be so much lower.

82 *Daniel Jamison*

Leases (the *Livello* and *Linea/Lifelease* categories) very rarely include any description of rent.
16 For a more thorough description of the currencies used by the *Decima* office, see L. Faibisoff's chapter in this volume; see also the currencies described in Pagnini della Ventura, *Della decima*, 52–53.
17 Note that these categories have not been used to standardize the records currently available, so a researcher can use the DECIMA interface to access all the original 'Holding Types'. These categories of holding type are also distinct from the five categories described by C. Rose in this volume, which concern the categorization of individuals within an entry rather than the exact property relations between them.
18 Percentages from Table 4.2 can be combined with the grand totals from Table 4.1 for the exact sums.
19 ASF, *Decima Granducale*, 3782, f. 193r (SMN.756).
20 See N. Terpstra, *Lost Girls: Sex and Death in Renaissance Florence*, Baltimore, MD: Johns Hopkins University Press, 2010, 103–4, 174–76.
21 This situation would certainly contradict the conditions of Girolamo's will as laid out by N. Terpstra; Girolamo died in May 1561, and the Casa della Pietà had legal possession when it sold the house in 1564: Terpstra, *Lost Girls,* 205, n.43, 217, n.8.
22 ASF, *Decima Granducale*, 3782, f. 78v (SMN.1335–38).
23 According to Canestrini, the same assessment standards were applied to both ecclesiastical property and the holdings of other Florentines; what differed between owner type were the formulas applied to these assessments to determine the tax actually paid: (1886), 381–83; additionally, Pagnini della Ventura, eighteenth-century historian of the Florentine tax code, reports that four hospitals (Innocenti, S. Maria Nuova, S. Matteo, Ospedale di Bonifazio) had their exemptions from the *Decima* confirmed by Duke Cosimo I in 1548, but their properties are all listed: Pagnini della Ventura, *Della decima*, 97–98.
24 ASF, *Decima Granducale*, 3782, f. 13r (SMN.190), below the entry *hoggi in giovanni rapetti lione rosso* 320.
25 The exemption for a taxpayer's primary dwelling was a commonplace in Florentine fiscal policy; for the *Decima* in particular, see Pagnini della Ventura, *Della decima*, 79–80.
26 I have found no entries in which this would be ambiguous, that is, no one let *a livello* a property that he himself leased *a livello*; such subleases may not have been permitted under the terms of the normal *livello* contract.
27 ASF, *Decima Granducale*, 3782, f. 45v (SMN.778).
28 Several owners, especially those at the upper end of the economic spectrum, were reported to be 'resident' at multiple properties; only 2,700 individual private owners can be found in the *Owner/Res* category, and 8 entries in this category are missing tax assessments.
29 The kinds of perpetual leases offered by private landlords are more complex than those extended by institutional landlords, which, along with shorter-term *livello* contracts, are probably related to the relatively familiar phenomenon of institutional annuities. 'Private' perpetual leases and lineal leases are probably related to dotal property and inheritance strategies and fall outside the focus of this chapter.
30 Many institutional properties, especially those belonging to parish churches, were listed under the names of their rectors. Puccio Ugolini's case is less clear, and it is possible, though unlikely, that such an enormous collection of urban property was his personal portfolio. In any case, Ugolini was a well-established canon with benefices throughout Tuscany; he was described in Salvino Salvini's 1751 catalogue of the cathedral chapter: S. Salvini, *Catalogo cronologico de' canonici della chiesa metropolitana fiorentina*, Florence, Italy: G. Cambiagi, 1782, 86–87.
31 J. Henderson's work on Florentine confraternities includes a key to the confraternities active up to the end of the fifteenth-century; this is reliable enough for the 1500s, and

it helpfully highlights the other institutions (churches and hospitals) to which these groups were attached: J. Henderson, *Piety and Charity in Late Medieval Florence*, Oxford, UK: Clarendon Press, 1994, 443–74.
32 Although evidence from the *ricerche* cautions us against uniting what may have been administratively distinct institutions. For example, the document indicates ser Andrea di Giovanni da San Miniato al Tedesco was rector (and rent collector) for the chapel of the Conception in San Niccolò Oltrarno while the rector of San Niccolò proper was Messer Lionardo Renci: ASF, *Decima Granducale*, 3780, f. 8r (SS.126), f. 7r (SS.107). No further description of either man is provided, such that it seems possible that the chapel's endowment was administered separately from other parish holdings.
33 Indeed, these may not need to be distinguished at all from their parent companies, and, as with the congregations and churches, the two names might be the result of scribal overcomplication.
34 N. Eckstein, *The District of the Green Dragon: Neighbourhood Life and Social Change in Renaissance Florence*, Florence, Italy: Leo S. Olschki, 1995, 36–37.
35 ASF, *Decima Granducale*, 3783, ff. 27v-28v (SG.393–417).
36 ASF, *Decima Granducale*, 3780, ff. 112r-117v (SS.1747–830).
37 Eckstein, *The District of the Green Dragon*, 33.
38 E.g. ASF, *Decima Granducale*, 3783, f. 42v (SG.654): ' . . . in un canto dirimpetto a un crocifisso dipinto in un'altro canto, contigua d'ogn'intorno a detta religione, sopra e numero 42'.
39 D. Rosenthal, 'Owning the Corners: The "Powers" of Florence and the Question of Agency', *I Tatti: Studies in the Italian Renaissance* 16, 2013, 181.
40 Eckstein, *The District of the Green Dragon*, 37.

Bibliography

Manuscript sources

Archivio di Stato di Firenze (ASF), *Decima Granducale*, 3780–3783.

Print sources

Canestrini, G., *La scienza e l'arte di stato desunta dagli atti officiali della repubblica fiorentina e dei medici*, Florence, Italy: Le Monnier, 1862.
Eckstein, N., *The District of the Green Dragon: Neighbourhood Life and Social Change in Renaissance Florence*, Florence, Italy: Leo S. Olschki, 1995.
Henderson, J., *Piety and Charity in Late Medieval Florence*, Oxford, UK: Clarendon Press, 1994.
Herlihy, D., and Klapisch-Zuber, C. *Tuscans and Their Families,* New Haven, CT: Yale University Press, 1985.
Pagnini della Ventura, G.F., *Della decima e di varie altre gravezze imposte dal comune di Firenze*, 4 vols, Florence, Italy: G. Bouchard, 1766.
Rosenthal, D., 'Owning the Corners: The "Powers" of Florence and the Question of Agency', *I Tatti: Studies in the Italian Renaissance* 16, 2013, 181–96.
Salvini, S., *Catalogo cronologico de' canonici della chiesa metropolitana fiorentina*, Florence, Italy: G. Cambiagi, 1782.
Terpstra, N., *Lost Girls: Sex and Death in Renaissance Florence*, Baltimore, MD: Johns Hopkins University Press, 2010.

Part 2
Using digital mapping to unlock spatial and social relations

5 Women behind walls

Tracking nuns and socio-spatial networks in sixteenth-century Florence

Sharon Strocchia and Julia Rombough

In 1548, Cosimo I de' Medici commissioned a census of Florentine convents. The census required every convent in the city to supply a list recording the full names of the convent's nuns in descending order of rank and seniority, beginning with the abbess and ending with the novices. In the absence of a formal protocol like the ones guiding episcopal visitations, some female religious houses provided more information than others, listing their confessors, young female boarders, and convent servants. Others provided incomplete lists that appear hurried and perfunctory. Some lists were recorded by ducal administrators, who apparently compiled their rosters while sitting in the convent parlour, while other lists were self-generated by nuns who provided information on their own terms and inscribed it in their own hands. Consequently, the census is marked by great variations in script, form, and level of detail, as illustrated by the two contrasting rosters shown in Figure 5.1. Despite these variations, the lists, composed between 1548 and 1552 and later compiled into a large volume, provide a fairly complete record of Florentine nunneries during this period.[1] The ducal census records the names of 2,658 professed nuns who represented approximately 4.5 per cent of the overall Florentine population and roughly 11 per cent of the city's female residents at the time.[2] These census records provide valuable resources for examining the identities and social relationships of Florentine religious women in the mid-sixteenth century. They are also unique in that the Medici duke did not commission a comparable census of male monastic personnel.

A particularly valuable element of the convent census is its inclusion of patronymics, which allows us to trace individual nuns' relationships to their households and immediate families. Florentines placed great store in personal names as markers of identity; by the mid-sixteenth century, repeated chains of patronymics became a common way for local elites to encode a cherished genealogy.[3] The inclusion of patronymics in the convent census reflects the deep connections Florentine nuns sustained with their natal kin as daughters, sisters, aunts, nieces, and cousins, despite living cloistered lives. It was primarily through their households and extended families that religious women participated in the larger social and political networks undergirding urban life.

This essay uses digital mapping to visualize the social and spatial connectivity of sixteenth-century Florence created by monastic placement patterns, which

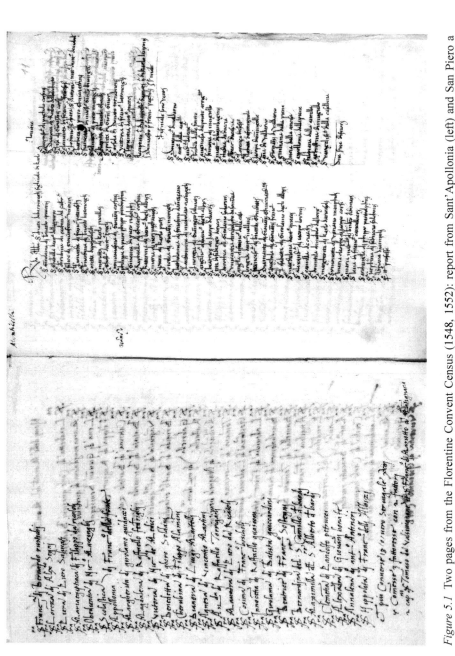

Figure 5.1 Two pages from the Florentine Convent Census (1548, 1552): report from Sant'Apollonia (left) and San Piero a Monticelli (right). Archivio di Stato, Florence. *Auditore dei benefici ecclesiastici*, vol. 4892, fols. 10v–11r. Image used by permission of the Ministero dei Beni e delle Attività Culturale e del Turismo.

both reflected and were reinforced by nuns' familial networks and property holdings. The stunning growth of female monasticism as a defining feature of late Renaissance Italy has become a staple of recent historiography.[4] Yet the convent has rarely been utilized as the main lens through which to view how Italians constituted social networks, distributed religious patronage, and strengthened ties to other people and places within the early modern city. As both the size and number of female religious communities exploded after 1500, familial decisions about where to place young girls as nuns reflected a complex social calculus. Selecting a religious community for girls – who rarely chose for themselves – can be considered a form of transactional patronage expressing familial loyalty, respect, and affiliation, whether current or hoped for. Impacting these deliberations were the size of the monastic dowry each convent required; the civic status and political reach of a religious house; the extent to which monastic lifestyle aligned with pious preferences; the presence of other kinswomen in the convent; the community's geographical proximity to established family neighbourhoods; and aspirations to exercise power and influence in far-flung locales.

By correlating two substantial data sets – the 1548–52 convent census and the 1561–62 *Decima* census – our project maps the outcomes of these complicated placement decisions on the macro-level of the city as well as on more intimate micro-scales. Cross-referencing the nuns recorded in the convent census with the more general *Decima* census reveals that, by the mid-sixteenth century, the majority of nuns born into elite families no longer lived in proximity to their family homes. Nor were their familial property holdings restricted to the customary neighbourhood enclaves surrounding their family palaces and principal residential sites. This geographical dispersal marks a shift away from placement strategies used in the fourteenth and early fifteenth centuries, when elite Florentine families tended to enrol female kin in convents close to home, where the majority of their property holdings were also located. Members of the Florentine ruling class tended to reside in the same parish, neighbourhood, and quarter for decades, often filing their tax returns in the same administrative ward throughout the fifteenth century. Monastic placements mirrored these localized practices until the 1470s and '80s, when the spatial field for convent enrolments dramatically expanded to encompass the entire city. By 1500, monastic placements more closely resembled the geographical mobility seen in elite marriage alliances, where members of the propertied classes chose marriage partners from across the city in order to cement elite partnerships and extend their influence into new districts.[5] These new placement strategies resulted in a more spatially diffused patronage of local convents by urban elites, which enabled top-tier families to control these rich social resources to an unprecedented degree, in concert with the Medici dukes.

Thanks to GIS mapping, we have been able to visualize the results of this new pattern on several different scales and to consider its potential role in the distribution of ecclesiastical patronage and other aspects of urban life under the Medici dukes. Our inquiry also allows us to conceptualize the early modern city in ways that raise intriguing questions about the everyday kinetic experiences of inhabitants who moved across Florence with different levels of ease and purpose.

Understanding the convent census

Duke Cosimo's census of Florentine convents was part of a larger project of taking stock of local institutions following his ascendance to the ducal throne in 1537. Keen to assert his power and influence over the city, Cosimo I founded various magistracies designed to oversee the affairs and governance of Florentine religious and charitable institutions, thereby bringing them under the control of a more centralized state.[6] The newly formed office of the Magistrato sopra i monasteri (founded 1545) consisted of three deputies appointed by the duke; they were granted authority to conduct visitations of convents, select four lay supervisors for each house, mitigate conflicts within institutions, oversee budgets and building projects, and conduct the 1548 census.[7] Couching the magistracy's remit as a 'reform' of local nunneries gave this effort greater legitimacy among laity and deflected concerns about state intrusion into ecclesiastical affairs.

Both the establishment of the magistracy and the census itself were highly gendered initiatives focused solely on female religious. The magistrates exercised no purview over male clerics or monastic houses; nor were monks and friars included in the convent census, in contrast to fifteenth-century civic attempts to inventory monastic personnel and property driven by fiscal needs.[8] Instead, the young Medici duke limited his inquiry to nuns' identities, leaving aside any stated interest in their income or property holdings. Nevertheless, this personnel inventory gave Duke Cosimo a baseline against which to gauge later convent requests for special tax concessions or exemptions; an equally important result was the ability to judge the political attachments and numerical strength of specific houses. Knowing nuns' family affiliations also helped ducal magistrates in selecting appropriate male supervisors for each convent, in keeping with the new legislation.

The formation of the magistracy, which aimed to bring Florentine convents under direct ducal supervision, brought Cosimo I into conflict with Church authorities, who were unwilling to cede traditional jurisdiction to a secular authority so easily. In fact, much of Duke Cosimo I's reign (1537–74) was marked by ongoing power struggles with local archbishops, in which he often held the upper hand. The Florentine see was ruled by weak or absentee bishops during the first decade of his reign. That situation changed dramatically in June 1548 with the appointment of Archbishop Antonio Altoviti by Paul III, who chose this young churchman specifically to spite the Medici. Locked in an ongoing battle with Altoviti's father – the fabulously wealthy banker Bindo, who opposed the Medici principate on political grounds – Duke Cosimo blocked the younger Altoviti from formally claiming the see until 1567.[9] Initiating the convent census soon after Altoviti's appointment thus offered Duke Cosimo a way to strike back at his personal enemies while asserting new state prerogatives. Although the duke surveyed other pious institutions and created various innovative political tools to advance his centralizing ambitions in these same years, a sense of deep personal animosity underlay the timing of the convent census. Reflecting the heated political moment as well as cooler long-term strategies, the convent census marked a bold gesture towards ducal control of local convents.

Ducal incursion into religious affairs also threatened potential conflict with the city's religious women, who were often wary of external challenges to their traditional privileges and modes of self-governance. In the census's hurried script and sometimes half-completed recording of demographic information, we can perhaps glimpse nuns' resistance to outside interference in their affairs; by the same token, the fact that numerous rosters were recorded by nuns themselves speaks to their interest in shaping what information was delivered. Many scholars have noted the complex manner in which nuns regularly negotiated power, carefully exploiting tensions between secular and religious authorities in an attempt to sway decision making in their favor without appearing too aggressive.[10] While virtually all convents complied with the census, the great variations in script and detail gesture towards some of the nuanced power relationships at work. While convents could not ignore the demands of the census outright, they could delay their response and obscure certain information, much as hospitals and other charitable communities had done when brought under ducal oversight in 1542.[11]

The web of competing interests – ducal, papal, monastic – that typified the sixteenth-century religious landscape meant that all parties positioned themselves with great care and deliberation. Hence it seems appropriate to characterize the convent census as both bold and careful in its approach. On the one hand, Cosimo I was clearly interested in extending control over the city's convents, which had become increasingly valuable civic resources by his day. In particular, the recording of patronymics suggests an interest in tracking how several thousand religious women were connected to the broader family politics of the city. On the other hand, the haphazard manner in which much of the census information was collected, the five-year lag in completing the project, and the unstandardized methods of recording material indicate the duke's reluctance to overreach.

Methods

Our goal in bringing together the 1548 convent census and the *Decima* census was to examine the socio-spatial networks linking nuns and their families, especially those evidenced by residential and property holding patterns. Cross-referencing the patronymics and surnames in the convent census with names in the *Decima* census allowed us to trace the links among the convents in which nuns lived, the homes in which their relatives resided, and the properties their families owned throughout the city. Mapping these links shows how the built environment, social groups, politics, and economics coalesced and were expressed spatially in the sixteenth-century city. These themes have occupied historians of Florence since the 1980s, but the advent of digital mapping tools makes it possible to see how urban spaces were connected to layers of social experience in more nuanced ways.

To explore these themes, we mapped placement strategies and property holdings related to four convents, one from each quarter of the city, which represent a cross section of the city's districts, religious orders, and parishes. The location of sample convents is shown in Figure 5.2. All four convents were founded before 1400, giving us a long time line against which to read the ducal census

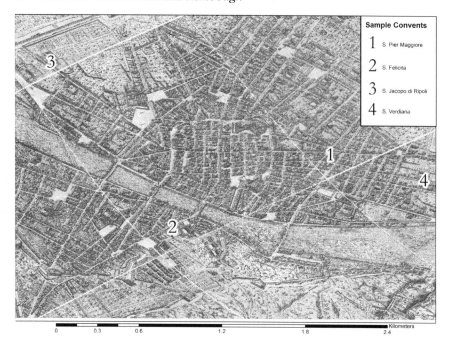

Figure 5.2 Location of four sample convents.

data. In addition, all four institutions enjoy ample supplementary documentation that permits future inquiries. Ranging from traditional Benedictines to Observant Dominicans, from locations on the fringes of the city to sites in its densely packed centre, these four convents housed a total of 156 nuns hailing from 107 different lineages; three nuns in this group did not have surnames. We did not include novices, boarders, or serving sisters in our sample.

Our first pair of convents – San Pier Maggiore and Santa Felicita – form a north/south axis cutting through the core of the medieval city and its traditional centres of power. Founded around the year 1000, they exemplify the traditional, highly prestigious religious institutions that housed women from the top tier of Florentine society. San Pier Maggiore [Figure 5.2, no. 1], a Benedictine parish convent located in the wealthy San Giovanni quarter, recorded twenty-seven nuns in the convent census. Since the late thirteenth century, this house had occupied a special place in Florentine religious topography and civic ritual because of its key role in the investiture ceremonies of local bishops. At the heart of these ceremonies was the fictive marriage rite enacted between the incoming bishop and the abbess of San Pier Maggiore, which symbolically bound the bishop to his see.[12] Santa Felicita [Figure 5.2, no. 2] was also a Benedictine parish convent with deep roots in the medieval city. Situated on the south bank of the Arno in the quarter of Santo Spirito, this influential convent housed thirty-one professed nuns. The precincts of the convent church, as well as areas of the cloister itself, were packed with the tombs of celebrated local families, such as the Guicciardini, Pitti, and Capponi. Both communities benefitted from the largesse of powerful families and enjoyed large endowments; they ranked as the two wealthiest convents sited inside the walls in the 1427 Florentine tax survey.[13] Throughout the fourteenth and early fifteenth centuries, admission to these convents was largely restricted to girls from families clustered in the neighbourhood surrounding the convent and parish. This strategy of localism, which further contributed to patrician control and dominance of specific wards, began to change by the 1470s, as recruits from areas beyond the immediate vicinity gained admittance in greater numbers.[14] The ability to expand both physically and numerically, however, was always constrained by site considerations.

Our second set of convents – San Jacopo di Ripoli and Santa Verdiana – form an east/west axis running through the urban peripheries, where the relative isolation and greater availability of space attracted new convent foundations before the final set of city walls was completed in the 1330s.[15] In the Santa Maria Novella quarter on the western side of Florence, the Dominican convent of San Jacopo di Ripoli on Via della Scala recorded fifty-six nuns in the census [Figure 5.2, no. 3]. Founded before 1292, the convent was home to a renowned scriptorium and an early printing press where many literate nuns produced valuable books that sustained its strong sense of corporate identity throughout the fifteenth and sixteenth centuries.[16] One of its inhabitants at the time of the ducal census, Sister Fiammetta Frescobaldi (1523–86), was a polymath who kept a personal diary, penned a lengthy chronicle of the Dominican order, translated and compiled works of history, geography, and natural history, and even wrote a short Spanish grammar with phrases for use by other nuns.[17] The fourth convent selected was located in the eastern quarter of Santa Croce. Housing forty-two nuns, the Vallombrosan convent of Santa Verdiana on Via dell'Agnolo opened its doors in 1400 [Figure 5.2, no. 4]. This comparatively new convent emerged as a site of Medici patronage by the mid-fifteenth century, largely due to the efforts of Abbess Piera de' Medici (abbess 1451–82).[18] By the turn of the sixteenth century, the community had accumulated valuable relics, reliquaries, and other liturgical furnishings that augmented its status and established it as an important devotional site. Taken together, these four convents present a sampling of the sixteenth-century Florentine conventional experience, exhibiting shared and unique experiences across the urban spatial field.

We began by entering the complete convent census data into the ArcGIS map created by the DECIMA team, allowing all 2,658 names recorded in the census to interact with the *Decima* data. Because the *Decima* census did not record information on nuns, who were bypassed as nontaxable subjects, adding nuns to the map also creates a more complete portrait of the city's population. Using the patronymics and surnames recorded in the convent census, we were able to connect the two data sets and produce a series of queries linking individual nuns to the taxable property holdings of their immediate and extended families of origin. From these data, we produced a range of maps illustrating different expressions of these relationships that gesture towards the socioeconomic strategies linking property ownership and convent placement.

Our original research questions sought to explore three types of socio-spatial relations in widening concentric circles: first, the geospatial relationship of convents to their inhabitants' natal homes; second, the geospatial relationship of nuns to familial property holdings within the same patriline; and finally, nuns' geospatial relationship to the property holdings belonging to their lineages. In this way we sought to consider how three major nodes within the urban network – residences, convents, and family properties – interacted and influenced one another socially and spatially.

However, joining two distinct sixteenth-century data sets compiled under different circumstances and for different purposes into a digital format produced methodological and theoretical problems that must be accounted for. Initially we anticipated that linking nuns to their natal homes by way of patronymics would produce strong results. We were curious to see whether digitally mapping this relationship would reveal new insights into the residential patterns that linked religious and domestic residences. Test runs of this map, however, revealed scant results. The fourteen-year gap between the earliest convent rosters (1548) and the last *Decima* recordings (1562) meant that by the time *Decima* magistrates were collecting information about urban residents, many of the fathers named in the convent census had died, moved out of the city, or relinquished property or for some other reason were not recorded in the *Decima*. The sequence of the two censuses works in direct opposition to the natural flow of generations and the sociocultural values that dictated life stages in Renaissance Italy. It is well known that Florentine men married late, generally when they were in their early thirties; hence many fathers were already somewhat elderly when they enrolled their daughters in religious communities. Moreover, many Florentine nuns lived exceptionally long lives, since they escaped the dangers associated with epidemic diseases and childbirth.[19] Consequently, older nuns recorded in the convent census had likely long outlived their fathers, along with other members of their natal households, making these intimate kin relationships extremely difficult to track.

In view of these challenges, we shifted our analysis from household residential patterns to the socio-spatial networks linking nuns to familial properties. Here family surname rather than patronymics provided the key connection. Returns on these data queries were much more robust. We created a collection of maps plotting family property holdings in relation to the four selected convents. Figure 5.3 illustrates our broadest results, in which we aggregated and mapped all traceable family property holdings related to the 156 nuns residing in the four convents. This approach allowed us to consider the relationship between nuns and lineal properties at the panoptic level, revealing citywide trends discussed later in this chapter. At the same time, we generated a smaller scale of analysis by creating individual maps displaying familial holdings associated with the four abbesses who headed our sample convents. These focused maps provided a micro-level comparison to the macro-level trends elucidated in Figure 5.3. Comparing and contrasting these two levels allowed us to look at both general and specific patterns and to view the city holistically and as discrete sectors. In this manner, we were able to emphasize textured variations within the data and avoid a sense of homogenization.

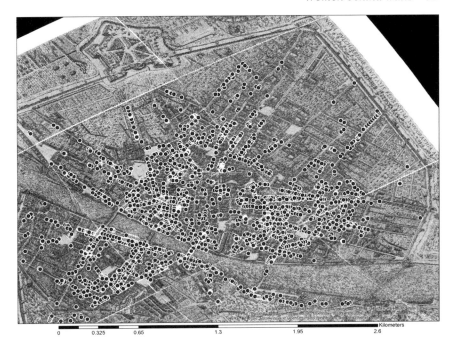

Figure 5.3 Property holdings of selected nuns' families by surname, 1562.

In the mapping process it became clear that the successful digital mapping of historical data requires scholars to experiment with an array of data combinations and queries, tying together different elements of the data in various ways and bringing multiple maps into conversation with one another. While the maps we generated were unable to display or answer all of our original research questions – forcing us to recognize the limitations of our data sets and digital mapping formats – continued experimentation ultimately revealed exciting information about how elite Florentine families strategized both their property acquisitions and the convents in which they placed their kinswomen.

Mapping convents as citywide institutions

Since our initial mapping exercise using patronymics yielded meagre results, we recalibrated our research strategy to use nuns' surnames instead as our key entry point into the data. We cross-referenced the 107 family names in our sample with the surnames listed in the *Decima* to track the spatial relationships linking nuns to their paternal kin, using property holdings as the means of plotting connectivity. Here we worked on the premise that property ownership not only represented some type of financial investment but also gave landlords an ongoing socioeconomic interest in the vicinity; property created relationships with other people and places throughout the city. We also worked from the premise that lineage was a fundamentally important aspect of Florentine identity and that elite Florentines were extremely conscious of their familial networks. Consequently, property holdings amassed under a shared surname were something that many members of the lineage would have understood as resources that augmented the power and presence of the family at large – even if, as individuals, they claimed no immediate stake as owners.

While aggregating the data by surname meant that we could not link nuns to specific residences, this query nevertheless yielded far more robust results, which are illustrated in Figure 5.3. To be clear, the map does not show the property holdings of convents themselves as institutional landlords. Rather, it plots the residences and property holdings of paternal kin listed in the *Decima* who, at some earlier point, had placed their female relatives in our sample convents – a group we call 'convent patrons' for short. Obviously the resulting snapshot does not capture a sense of temporal dynamics; it cannot show us with any precision when the 156 nuns had entered religious life or exactly what factors influenced specific familial choices.

Nor does Figure 5.3 illustrate spatial relationships linking convents to the property holdings of nuns' maternal kin or other female relations, since these women generally had different surnames. The convent census itself reflects contemporary social practices that privileged lineage over more extended forms of bilateral kinship. The names of nuns' mothers, sisters, aunts, and female cousins did not make their way into the convent census, although their identities often can be recovered through painstaking research in other civic and monastic records. Mapping these female networks would launch an exciting new research agenda, especially since the flexibility of the DECIMA tool makes it possible to add additional, interactive layers in future.

Regardless, the lineal bias of census evidence is especially significant in a convent context. Italian nunneries were crucial nodes of female sociability for elite women throughout their life cycle, from their youthful days as pupils to their mature years as patrons, when convents loomed large in women's choice of burial site.[20] Consequently, one of the great ironies of reconstructing nuns' socio-spatial networks using census data is that a substantial part of that connectivity is automatically lost because of the gendered nature of the evidence. The reliance on surname and patronymic as key social identifiers, even for cloistered religious women, speaks volumes about the prominence of lineage in sixteenth-century Florence, even as it obscures a fuller understanding of nuns' social relationships within the life of the city. The convent census is not a neutral document; nor are the maps it produces. That the nonlineal relationships so central to the patterning of daily life fall outside the purview of the maps is a reflection of the public and political identities Florentines cherished most and thus took the greatest care to record. In this sense, mapping the convent census constitutes a mapping of public ideals and social priorities to the neglect of many other facets that shaped urban experience. The maps present one perspective among many.

Despite these shortcomings, Figure 5.3 successfully establishes a macroscopic view of urban social geography as it was constituted by the collective placement strategies of patrilineal convent patrons. What is immediately apparent from this visualization is that elite Florentine families owned properties well beyond their traditional neighbourhood enclaves, where they had declared their tax homes since the early fifteenth century.[21] Geographical dispersion of interests across the city had become the norm by 1550, replacing earlier social and economic strategies based on localism. The breadth of property holdings recorded by convent patrons is impressive: they held properties stretching from the southernmost gate through the medieval urban core to more isolated areas near the eastern walls. This visualization of widely diffused property ownership by convent patrons allows us to appreciate the extent to which numerous prominent families 'owned' the city both physically and psychologically by 1550. Since these real estate holdings describe the spatial reach of families that opted to place girls in our sample religious communities, it seems reasonable to infer that acquiring properties outside traditional neighbourhoods was dynamically interwoven with strategies for convent placement. By the mid-sixteenth century Florentine elites had acquired real estate scattered throughout the city; at the same time they were enrolling their girls in more distant religious communities and marrying their daughters across urban territory.

Mapping one layer of these patterns illustrates some of the socio-spatial networks animating mid-sixteenth-century Florence. Figure 5.3 visually demonstrates that top-tier local families were able to consolidate their mastery over the city as a whole by distributing their property holdings as well as their daughters, sisters, nieces, and cousins across a wide spatial field, well beyond their customary tax homes. The kind of geographical mobility that characterized the matrimonial alliances of the Florentine elite also marked their patterns of property ownership and monastic placement. Visualizing familial real estate holdings in relation to nuns further augments our understanding of the social role that convents played in class formation. As important nodes within the cityscape, convents were convergence points that brought privileged families together in common spaces, common projects, and common institutional undertakings, ranging from the allocation of tomb sites to the defence of convent privileges jeopardized by religious reform. Exercising a common stake in convent affairs reinforced a sense of elite social identity within the city writ large.

Our visualization also suggests how convents themselves enjoyed a pervasive, citywide presence as a result of these strategies. In mid-sixteenth-century Florence, nuns enjoyed a capillary reach across the city not as institutional landlords but by virtue of familial property holdings. Because these socio-spatial networks permitted both people and information to flow into and out of the convent with both rapidity and regularity, cloistered religious women could stay abreast of neighbourhood news, keep tabs on local property values, grasp the dynamics of heated disputes, and participate in broader forms of civic discourse. Implicit in our map is a sense of knowledge in transit: it shows us how information may have flowed across the city by being mobilized and circulated from one site to another. Furthermore, the maps suggest that power and influence themselves were often products of the built environment.

At the same time, this map prompts other questions about the everyday kinetic experiences of convent patrons. It is well known that nuns' relatives – especially other women – came to visit them frequently to share news, pay boarding fees, obtain spiritual counsel, or deepen relationships on both sides of the parlor grate. It would be intriguing to trace the spatial routes and itineraries they followed (whether on foot or in carriages) when they visited nuns living at some distance from home. This information would give additional insights into the dynamic personal encounters that occurred within spatial networks. In the same vein, our visualization raises qualitative questions about the mental maps convent visitors created as they traversed squares and street corners, passed shrines and civic monuments, and encountered notorious zones of prostitution. The widespread spatial affiliations of convent patrons call attention to what humanistic geographers have called 'place making', that is, the ways in which people develop affective attachments to particular spaces or locales.[22] As nuns increasingly lived at a greater remove from their traditional neighbourhoods, how did they and their relatives create a new sense of place beyond the familiar zones that represented the accumulated product of thick social relations?[23] Thus, our visualization of socio-spatial networks invites us to interrogate the ways in which lived experience dynamically reshaped mental maps and social attachments.

Taking the micro-view

To obtain a more detailed visualization of the spatial relationships that linked convents, neighbourhood, and lineage, we mapped the familial property holdings of the four abbesses who headed our core convents, querying the *Decima* census by their surname. This method ensured a neutral approach to the data, since it did not involve any filter on our part. Focusing on the property distribution of abbesses' lineages allowed us to separate individual strands from the larger bundle of real estate holdings aggregated in Figure 5.3. The resulting four maps reveal more nuanced variations within general trends: while elite families were rapidly extending their influence into diverse areas of the city, they exercised noticeably different approaches to property holding and monastic placements.

The four maps plot a spectrum of strategies, ranging from a conservative localism to a far more aggressive spatial penetration into urban territories. These variations carry special significance because all four abbesses belonged to premier lineages bound by similar social values and practices. Three of the four lineages under consideration – the Altoviti, Canigiani, and Carducci – were considered 'high-status' families, whose political activity, social reputations, and wealth placed them at the very pinnacle of Florentine society well into the granducal period. The fourth lineage – the Del Giocondo family – did not rank quite as high as the other three but was still firmly entrenched in the Florentine ruling class.[24]

It is worth pausing here to introduce the four women who act as pivots around which our maps are constructed. Heading San Pier Maggiore from 1528 to 1548 was Paola di Lorenzo Carducci, who had been a nun for forty years before her election as abbess. The eldest of the four officers considered here, Abbess

Women behind walls 99

Paola embodied the haughtiness and sense of privilege for which her convent was renowned. The Carducci had had their tax home in the Vipera ward of Santa Maria Novella since the early fifteenth century.[25] Paola Carducci's counterpart across the river at Santa Felicita was Lena di Francesco Canigiani, a member of a powerful fourteenth-century lineage who became a nun around 1501. Her tenure as abbess from 1543 to 1564 coincided with the most intense period of monastic reform; she often turned to her kinfolk to help navigate uncharted waters. The Canigiani tax home stood in proximity to the convent, in the Scala ward of Santo Spirito.[26] Filippa di Gentile Altoviti, who belonged to a different patriline from her younger cousin Archbishop Antonio Altoviti, served as abbess of Santa Verdiana from 1537 to 1551, following in the footsteps of another Altoviti abbess a few decades earlier. As discussed later, this lineage did not hesitate to venture beyond its tax home in the Vipera ward, either when purchasing property or when placing nuns.[27] Serving three terms as prioress of San Jacopo di Ripoli was Caterina di Amadeo Del Giocondo, a pious, esteemed administrator related by marriage to the famed sitter in Leonardo's *Mona Lisa* portrait. This upwardly mobile lineage customarily resided in the populous ward of Lion d'oro, a quarter of San Giovanni.[28]

At one end of the spectrum described by these micro-views stand the Canigiani, affiliated with Santa Felicita, whose holdings illustrate the most traditional, localized property distribution pattern of the four lineages queried (Figure 5.4).

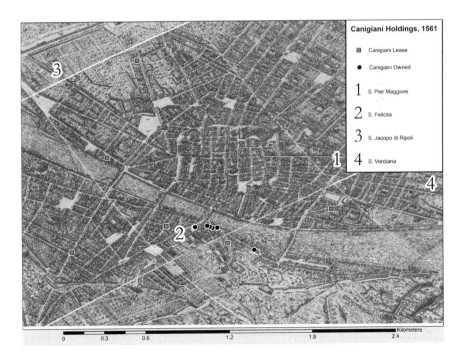

Figure 5.4 Property holdings of Canigiani family, 1562.

100 *Sharon Strocchia and Julia Rombough*

While some Canigiani family members leased residential properties outside the Oltrarno, all of their titled holdings (nine of sixteen properties) were clustered on Via de' Bardi, running along the south bank of the river, just a stone's throw from the convent. Scholars have shown that the Oltrarno quarter of Santo Spirito exhibited a particularly strong sense of local identity, a sentiment reflected in the dense bundling of Canigiani properties.[29] This quarter remained a world unto itself in many respects, owing partly to the concentration of artisans and working poor living there, as shown in Daniel Jamison's discussion of density and property values across Florence's four quarters.

This pronounced localism reaped rewards in the Canigiani family's ability to influence parish and neighbourhood affairs. Because this old Benedictine convent headed an important parish, the nuns of Santa Felicita bore responsibility for aspects of parish decision making and liturgical life, such as appointing chaplains, allocating burial sites, and handling commemorative bequests. Surrounded by her powerful kinsmen, Abbess Lena Canigiani not only led chapter deliberations with an eye to neighbourhood interests; she also protected private lineal privileges, such as patronage rights to the convent sacristy, where the Canigiani coat of arms had been visible in the vault since 1473.[30] Given the overall spatial and ecclesiastical structure of the Oltrarno, it made good sense for the Canigiani to orient their energies towards the immediate locale.

At the other end of the spectrum stood the Altoviti, one of whose family members headed Santa Verdiana (Figure 5.5). The holdings of this great banking lineage

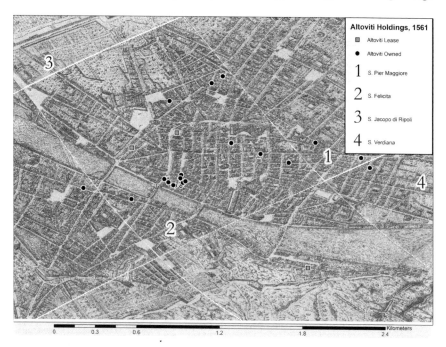

Figure 5.5 Property holdings of Altoviti family, 1562.

were far more dispersed than those of the Canigiani, sweeping out from their familial tax base in the western sector of the city, on Borgo Santi Apostoli near Ponte Santa Trinita, towards the city's east side, where the convent was located. Like the Canigiani, the Altoviti retained residential strength in its traditional ward well into the sixteenth century. Unlike the Canigiani, however, the Altoviti did not own any properties immediately around the community where two members of their lineage had occupied the top leadership post since 1500. Local property interests encircling Santa Verdiana cannot explain this strong familial presence at the convent.

Still, Altoviti property holdings provide indirect clues to their monastic placement strategies if we look instead at the thick cluster of residential holdings abutting the influential parish church of Santa Trinita, headed by Vallombrosan monks. This church continued to attract important patrons throughout the Quattrocento, especially those from the immediate vicinity. Like many of their neighbors, the Altoviti developed strong affiliations with that monastic order. By 1463 the respected cleric Francesco Altoviti had risen to the position of General of the Vallombrosan order, in which capacity he conducted a pastoral visitation of all local Vallombrosan communities, including Santa Verdiana.[31] Since this house was the only female Vallombrosan convent within the city, the Altoviti family's choice of community was almost certainly coloured by long-standing affiliations linked to residential and property-holding patterns on the opposite side of Florence. Through their pious affiliation with the Vallombrosans, the Altoviti participated in a religious network that carried them out of their traditional ward. The trail of properties extending east from their home base in the Vipera ward towards Santa Verdiana suggest a concerted effort on their part to cement their role as Vallombrosan patrons while extending their influence across the city. While we cannot establish a causal relationship here, both ambitions are captured through a simultaneous examination of Altoviti property holdings and convent placements.

Considered together, these micro-views have important implications for understanding how elite families made choices when placing girls in religious life. Spatializing data helps us see more clearly why the Canigiani may have opted for the parish convent down the street, while the Altoviti selected a community on the opposite side of the city. These visualizations offer concrete evidence for property holdings that at the same time complicates our understanding of ecclesiastical patronage. When used to read visual evidence 'against the grain', digital mapping serves as an auxiliary tool for investigating connections between spatial fields and spiritual allegiances.

While these lineage-specific maps visualize contrasting strategies of localism and expansion, they also corroborate the broad trends seen in Figure 5.3. Both the Canigiani and the Altoviti used convents as extensions of household and lineage, transforming these communities into civic institutions that bolstered familial presence in the city. Despite employing different strategies, both families worked on the understanding that convent placements solidified connections among family name, civic piety, and institutional prestige. Here lineage, property holding, and convent placement coalesced to form a feedback loop that created and compounded social capital.

Conclusions and reflections

Our research considers how convents, lineages, neighbourhoods, and family property holdings layered on top of each other in sixteenth-century Florence to produce specific types of socio-spatial connectivity with nuns at the centre. Our maps provide a filter for examining the early modern city that, taken together with the diverse digital perspectives offered by the larger DECIMA tool, explore how meaning and experience were attached to different spaces and locales in the historical city.

Mapping the links connecting the 1548 convent census to the 1561 *Decima* census reveals that convents were important nodes in the socio-spatial field of sixteenth-century Florence. As Florentine families placed their girls in convents throughout the city, they stretched their influence into surrounding neighbourhoods. At the same time, they used property ownership to augment their presence in specific wards and districts. Information, influence, and money flowed in and out of convents, marking them as important sites of exchange and tying them to their surroundings and to the families who patronized them. By the mid-sixteenth century, elite Florentine families had developed monastic placement strategies that largely mirrored those underlying marital alliances. Like convent patrons, Duke Cosimo was aware of the important role that convents played in local power politics and sought to assert control over the city's religious institutions for his own uses. The convent census stands as testament to this aim.

Thanks to digital mapping, we were able to plot and conceptualize aspects of the social strategies linking convent placement and property ownership. Specifically, we teased out individual threads of the data and opened them up for inquiry, foregrounding nuances while at the same time maintaining a bird's-eye view of the city at large. We learned that digital mapping can consider a range of experiences and how they interact in shared space – in our case, the Florentine cityscape. These are subtleties and variations that might be lost if we were to rely solely on text. Translating written sources into a visual format allows us to see both the city and the sources anew, prompting a creative exploration of the data at hand. Thus, while the maps we produced are a snapshot of the city at a fixed point in time and in this sense are static, they nevertheless display a unique type of dynamism, visually documenting variation and range within the city.

Just as digital mapping highlights certain features, however, it inevitably obscures others. The maps are limited by what we ask them to display; as a result there will always be information, patterns, and realities that are bypassed because of the nature of the selective process required to produce maps. GIS mapping does not discriminate among the data, treating each data point with equal weight. This is both a strength and a weakness of the mapping process. On the one hand, it allows us to observe patterns we might have otherwise overlooked, inviting us to look beyond the original research questions, consider what the maps reveal, and ask new questions. On the other, important distinctions and unique circumstances can be concealed by the maps, drawing us away from the richness and complexity that marked everyday life. In the face of these digital silences, we must return

Women behind walls 103

to the historical sources from which our inquiry began in order to round out our analyses and further explore the questions prompted by the mapping project.

Notes

1 Archivio di Stato, Florence. All archival references are to this repository. *Auditore dei benefici ecclesiastici poi segretario del regio diritto*, 4892.
2 Census figures for Italian convents are imprecise owing to organizational volatility and inherent difficulties in determining monastic status. R.C. Trexler, 'Celibacy in the Renaissance: The Nuns of Florence', in his *The Women of Renaissance Florence*, Binghamton, NY: Medieval & Renaissance Texts & Studies, 1993, 6–30, tallied 3,410 nuns in Florentine convents in 1552, representing 11.5 per cent of the city's female population. By contrast, P. Batarra, *La popolazione di Firenze alla metà del '500*, Florence, Italy: Rinascimento del libro, 1935, 9, put the urban convent population at 2,826 nuns in the same year.
3 C. Klapisch-Zuber, 'The Name "Remade": The Transmission of Given Names in Florence in the Fourteenth and Fifteenth Centuries', in her *Women, Family, and Ritual in Renaissance Italy*, trans. L. Cochrane, Chicago, IL, and London, UK: University of Chicago Press, 1985, 283–309.
4 G. Zarri, *Recinti: Donne, clausura e matrimonio nella prima età moderna*, Bologna, Italy: Il Mulino, 2000; J.C. Sperling, *Convents and the Body Politic in Late Renaissance Venice*, Chicago, IL: University of Chicago Press, 1999; and S.T. Strocchia, *Nuns and Nunneries in Renaissance Florence*, Baltimore, MD: Johns Hopkins University Press, 2009, 1, who notes the ratio of one nun per nineteen urban residents in 1552.
5 A. Molho, *Marriage Alliance in Late Medieval Florence*, Cambridge, MA: Harvard University Press, 1994, 250–56.
6 N. Terpstra, 'Competing Visions of the State and Social Welfare: The Medici Dukes, the Bigallo Magistrates, and Local Hospitals in Sixteenth-Century Tuscany', *Renaissance Quarterly* 54, 2001, 1319–55.
7 L. Cantini, *Legislazione Toscana*, vol. 1. Florence, Italy: Albizziniana, 1800, 260–64. See also S. Evangelisti, 'Art and the Advent of Clausura: The Convent of Saint Catherine of Siena in Tridentine Florence', in J. Nelson (ed.), *Suor Plautilla Nelli (1523–1588): The First Woman Painter of Florence*, Florence, Italy: Cadmo, 2000, 67–82.
8 G. Brucker, 'Monasteries, Friaries, and Nunneries in Quattrocento Florence', in T.J. Verdon and J. Henderson (eds), *Christianity and the Renaissance: Image and Religious Imagination in the Quattrocento*, Syracuse, NY: Syracuse University Press, 1990, 41–62.
9 G. Aranci, *Formazione religiosa e santità laicale a Firenze tra Cinque e Seicento*, Florence, Italy: G. Pagnini, 1997, 29–44; L. Passerini, *Genealogia e storia della famiglia Altoviti*, Florence, Italy: M. Cellini, 1871, 55–62.
10 S. Evangelisti, '"We Do Not Have It, and We Do Not Want It": Women, Power, and Convent Reform in Florence', *Sixteenth Century Journal* 34, 2003, 677–700; M. Laven, *Virgins of Venice: Broken Vows and Cloistered Lives in the Renaissance Convent*, London, UK: Viking, 2002; K. Lowe, *Nuns' Chronicles and Convent Culture in Renaissance and Counter-Reformation Italy*, Cambridge, UK: Cambridge University Press, 2003.
11 Terpstra, 'Competing Visions'.
12 S. Strocchia, 'When the Bishop Married the Abbess: Masculinity and Power in Florentine Episcopal Entry Rites, 1300–1600', *Gender & History* 19, 2007, 346–68; M. Miller, 'Why the Bishop of Florence Had to Get Married', *Speculum* 81, 2006, 1055–91.
13 Strocchia, *Nuns and Nunneries*, 76.
14 Ibid., 40–57.

15 S. Weddle, 'Identity and Alliance: Urban Presence, Spatial Privilege, and Florentine Renaissance Convents', in R. Crum and J. Paoletti (eds), *Renaissance Florence: A Social History*, Cambridge, UK: Cambridge University Press, 2006, 394–412.
16 M. Conway, *The Diario of the Printing Press of San Jacopo di Ripoli (1476–1484)*, Florence, Italy: Olschki, 1999.
17 E. Weaver, 'Frescobaldi, Fiammetta (1523–1586)'. Online. Available <www.lib.uchicago.edu/efts/IWW/BIOS/A0160.html> (accessed 24 June 2015).
18 S. Strocchia, 'Abbess Piera de' Medici and Her Kin: Gender, Gifts and Patronage in Renaissance Florence', *Renaissance Studies* 28, 2014, 695–713.
19 D. Herlihy and C. Klapisch-Zuber, *Les toscans et leurs familles: Une étude du 'catasto' florentin de 1427*, Paris, France: École des hautes études en sciences sociales, 1978; J.C. Brown, 'Monache a Firenze all'inizio dell'età moderna: Un analisi demografica', *Quaderni storici* 85, 1994, 117–52.
20 Strocchia, *Nuns and Nunneries*, 49–50; S. Chojnacki, 'The Patronage of the Body: Burial Sites, Identity, and Gender in Fifteenth-Century Venice', *Journal of Medieval and Early Modern Studies* 45, 2015, 79–101.
21 D. Jamison, 'Shaping the Streetscape', in this volume.
22 C.W.J. Withers, 'Place and the "Spatial Turn" in Geography and in History', *Journal of the History of Ideas* 70, 2009, 637–65.
23 As described by D.V. Kent and F.W. Kent, *Neighbours and Neighbourhood in Renaissance Florence: The District of the Red Lion in the Fifteenth Century*, Locust Valley, NY: J.J. Augustin, 1982.
24 A. Molho, *Marriage Alliance*, 365–75. Molho defined the fifteenth-century Florentine ruling class as composed of 417 lineages grouped into three categories, from high-status lineages at the top to low-status ones at the bottom. Molho assigned the Altoviti, Canigiani, and Carducci to the 'high-status' group; the Del Giocondo belonged to the middle tier, the 'status' category.
25 Carducci entered the convent around 1488 and professed by 1491; San Pier Maggiore, vol. 4, tomo 1, under 29 January 1491. Carducci tax home in Molho, *Marriage Alliance*, 367.
26 *Corporazioni Religiose Soppresse dal Governo Francese* (hereafter *CRSGF*), 83, vol. 239, 39; Molho, *Marriage Alliance*, 367.
27 *CRSGF*, 90, vol. 67, fols 76v-77r. Her older cousin Lodovica di Zanobi Altoviti, from yet a different patriline than the archbishop, had served as abbess from 1500 to 1516 (fols 74v, 85r). See Passerini, *Genealogia*, 59–63, 66, 76–77, for these relationships; tax home in Molho, *Marriage Alliance*, 365.
28 San Jacopo di Ripoli, vol. 23, fol. 127v. R. Hatfield, *The Three Mona Lisas*, Milan: Officina Libraria, 2014, 10–12; tax home in Molho, *Marriage Alliance*, 369.
29 N. Eckstein, *The District of the Green Dragon: Neighbourhood Life and Social Change in Renaissance Florence*, Florence, Italy: Olschki, 1995; J. Burke, 'Visualizing Neighborhood in Renaissance Florence, Italy: Santo Spirito and Santa Maria del Carmine', *Journal of Urban History* 32, 2006, 693–710.
30 F. Fiorelli Malesci, *La Chiesa di Santa Felicita*, Florence, Italy: Giunti, 1986, 258–59, 261.
31 *CRSGF*, 260, vol. 217, fols 80r-85v for Santa Verdiana.

Bibliography

Manuscript sources

Archivio di Stato di Firenze (ASF), *Auditore dei benefici ecclesiastici poi segretario del regio diritto*, 4892.

——— *Corporazioni Religiose Soppresse dal Governo Francese* (hereafter *CRSGF*), 83, 90, 260.

Print sources

Aranci, G., *Formazione religiosa e santità laicale a Firenze tra Cinque e Seicento*, Florence, Italy: G. Pagnini, 1997.

Batarra, P., *La popolazione di Firenze alla metà del '500*, Florence, Italy: Rinascimento del libro, 1935.

Brown, J.C., 'Monache a Firenze all'inizio dell'età moderna: Un analisi demografica', *Quaderni storici* 85, 1994.

Brucker, G., 'Monasteries, Friaries, and Nunneries in Quattrocento Florence', in T.J. Verdon and J. Henderson (eds), *Christianity and the Renaissance: Image and Religious Imagination in the Quattrocento*, Syracuse, NY: Syracuse University Press, 1990, 41–62.

Burke, J., 'Visualizing Neighborhood in Renaissance Florence: Santo Spirito and Santa Maria del Carmine', *Journal of Urban History* 32, 2006.

Cantini, L., *Legislazione Toscana*, Florence, Italy: Albizziniana, 1800.

Chojnacki, S., 'The Patronage of the Body: Burial Sites, Identity, and Gender in Fifteenth-Century Venice', *Journal of Medieval and Early Modern Studies* 45, 2015, 79–101.

Conway, M., *The Diario of the Printing Press of San Jacopo di Ripoli (1476–1484)*, Florence, Italy: Olschki, 1999.

Eckstein, N., *The District of the Green Dragon: Neighbourhood Life and Social Change in Renaissance Florence*, Florence, Italy: Olschki, 1995.

Evangelisti, S., 'Art and the Advent of Clausura: The Convent of Saint Catherine of Siena in Tridentine Florence', in J. Nelson (ed.), *Suor Plautilla Nelli (1523–1588): The First Woman Painter of Florence*, Florence, Italy: Cadmo, 2000, 67–82.

——— '"We Do Not Have It, and We Do Not Want It": Women, Power, and Convent Reform in Florence', *Sixteenth Century Journal* 34, 2003.

Fiorelli Malesci, F., *La Chiesa di Santa Felicita*, Florence, Italy: Giunti, 1986.

Hatfield, R., *The Three Mona Lisas*, Milan, Italy: Officina Libraria, 2014.

Herlihy, D., and Klapisch-Zuber, C., *Les toscans et leurs familles: Une étude du 'catasto' florentin de 1427*, Paris, France: École des hautes études en sciences sociales, 1978.

Kent, D.V., and Kent, F.W., *Neighbours and Neighbourhood in Renaissance Florence: The District of the Red Lion in the Fifteenth Century*, Locust Valley, NY: J.J. Augustin, 1982.

Klapisch-Zuber, C., *Women, Family, and Ritual in Renaissance Italy*, Chicago, IL: University of Chicago Press, 1985.

Laven, M., *Virgins of Venice: Broken Vows and Cloistered Lives in the Renaissance Convent*, London, UK: Viking, 2002.

Lowe, K., *Nuns' Chronicles and Convent Culture in Renaissance and Counter-Reformation Italy*, Cambridge, UK: Cambridge University Press, 2003.

Miller, M., 'Why the Bishop of Florence Had to Get Married', *Speculum* 81, 2006, 1055–1091.

Molho, A., *Marriage Alliance in Late Medieval Florence*, Cambridge, MA: Harvard University Press, 1994.

Passerini, L., *Genealogia e storia della famiglia Altoviti*, Florence, Italy: M. Cellini, 1871.

Sperling, J.C., *Convents and the Body Politic in Late Renaissance Venice*, Chicago, IL: University of Chicago Press, 1999.

Strocchia, S.T., 'When the Bishop Married the Abbess: Masculinity and Power in Florentine Episcopal Entry Rites, 1300–1600', *Gender & History* 19, 2007, 346–68.

——— *Nuns and Nunneries in Renaissance Florence*, Baltimore, MD: Johns Hopkins University Press, 2009.

———'Abbess Piera de' Medici and Her Kin: Gender, Gifts and Patronage in Renaissance Florence', *Renaissance Studies* 28, 2014.

Terpstra, N., 'Competing Visions of the State and Social Welfare: The Medici Dukes, the Bigallo Magistrates, and Local Hospitals in Sixteenth-Century Tuscany', *Renaissance Quarterly* 54, 2001, 1319–55.

Trexler, R.C., *The Women of Renaissance Florence*, Binghamton, NY: Medieval & Renaissance Texts & Studies, 1993.

Weaver, E., 'Frescobaldi, Fiammetta (1523–1586)', 2001. Online. Available <www.lib.uchicago.edu/efts/IWW/BIOS/A0160.html> (accessed 24 June 2015).

Weddle, S., 'Identity and Alliance: Urban Presence, Spatial Privilege, and Florentine Renaissance Convents', in R. Crum and J. Paoletti (eds), *Renaissance Florence: A Social History*, Cambridge, UK: Cambridge University Press, 2006, 394–412.

Withers, C.W.J., 'Place and the "Spatial Turn" in Geography and in History', *Journal of the History of Ideas* 70, 2009.

Zarri, G., *Recinti: donne, clausura e matrimonio nella prima età moderna*, Bologna, Italy: Il Mulino, 2000.

6 Locating the sex trade in the early modern city
Space, sense, and regulation in sixteenth-century Florence

Nicholas Terpstra

In 1547, the Florentine magistrates of the Onestà (or Office of Decency), charged with regulating and policing prostitution, devised a list of eighteen streets where prostitutes could register to live and work. They identified some by street name, such as Via Palazzuola, and others by a set of landmarks, such as: 'From the corner of Monteloro beginning below the bakers' ovens of the Orbatello for 40 *braccia* to the convent of S. Maria di Candeli, and then around the corner to Via Fiesolana and on for 40 *braccia* to the house of Bettina Strozzina, and including within this boundary the house where the two prostitutes are'.[1] The first leg of this 'L'-shaped zone was the well-known Via dei Pilastri, though the officials never gave the name. Their referents were all spatial and social, starting from a large shelter for widows and old women (the Orbatello), turning at a corner marked by an Augustinian convent, and then continuing down to a private home owned by the well-known courtesan Bettina Strozzina. Whether using street names or a shorthand set of relational referents, the magistrates assumed close knowledge of the city, its institutions, and its inhabitants. The Onestà described the city as a Florentine might walk it and pegged the coordinates of the prostitutes' zone by reference to some familiar uses. In the example, these are all female: a widows' shelter, a convent, and a courtesan's house. With other zones the landmarks included 'the tavern of the Marmerucola', 'the bakery of San Paulo', and 'the fortress of his Excellency'. In fact, relatively few of the zones licensed for prostitution were identified by street name alone.

The Onestà magistrates' efforts were yet another in a series of quixotic moves by which the administration of Duke Cosimo I aimed to control the activities of prostitutes. These efforts had a long history, extending back to the origins of the Onestà in 1403.[2] Cosimo I actually removed the dogleg of Via dei Pilastri and Via Fiesolana from the Onestà's proposed list of approved zones, but it went on to become one of the city's key red-light districts nonetheless. The courtesan Bettina Strozzina may have been sufficiently notorious to become a bureaucratic boundary line, but she herself never bought one of the licenses that would authorize her to carry on her occupation.

Cosimo I and the Onestà sometimes cooperated with each other but often were at odds about who to target and how to enforce regulations. The duke's regulatory efforts were undermined by the fact that the Onestà was one of those

108 *Nicholas Terpstra*

civic magistracies that held to the old practice of rotating membership every four months. Its members' names were drawn from the old voting bags that had been the pride of the former republican regime, meaning that its composition could vary widely through the year, depending on which eight names were drawn out of the bags for terms beginning in February, June, and October. Little was predictable save that most Onestà magistrates worked assiduously through their short terms to exploit their powers of licensing and fining in order to generate funds and favours from the prostitutes under their control. Cosimo I wanted to clean up the Onestà as much as he wanted to clean up prostitution, but the magistrates were remarkably resistant to reform: Cosimo I first proposed reducing their numbers from eight to four in 1549 and approved legislation to this effect, but the change did not come into effect until 1578, four years after his death. This should keep us from assuming too much about using the activities of the Onestà to plot either the shifts in Florence's moral climate or the effectiveness of ducal administration.

Even if these issues limit the usefulness of the Onestà's activity as a guide to understanding prostitution in sixteenth-century Florence, the shifting regulations and their uneven enforcement can give us a broader understanding of how Florentines approached their urban fabric, particularly social space and the senses. This is particularly the case when the Onestà's records are read in conjunction with the data generated by the *Decima* tax census and made accessible through the DECIMA digital tool. Other chapters in this book deal with occupational distribution, land values and property consolidation, convent enrolment, health concerns, and mobility and rely to greater or lesser extents on other sources found in the Florentine State Archives. Some cross-reference these other manuscript sources directly, and some read them tangentially or against the grain. In all cases, we learn that what sixteenth-century bureaucrats compiled for immediate and practical fiscal or demographic purposes can generate new readings and new questions when juxtaposed with other records. All of the authors here have emphasized the gap between the *Decima*'s systematic regularity and the way that Florentines actually visualized and experienced their city. More than that, the panoptic vision of those of Cosimo I's bureaucrats who were intent on measurement and regulation implied uses of and for the city that were very different from how most Florentines experienced and practiced their streets as pedestrians, workers, and neighbours. Does the juxtaposition of *Decima* records with those of other magistracies such as the Onestà and then with how Florentine lived in their streets and neighbourhoods allow us to better understand what kind of space Florentines took their city to be and how they negotiated it? Can we move from census to city and from digital mapping to spatial humanities?

The DECIMA project was born in the effort to do just that, with a particular focus on changes in how Florentines defined and negotiated the boundaries between sex and the sacred and an interest in how senses such as sight, hearing, and smell might play a part in the process.[3] Starting from the senses allows us to see different conceptions of urban space shining through the constantly shifting Florentine regulations on prostitution from the fourteenth through the sixteenth centuries. Florentines of the thirteenth and fourteenth centuries cast prostitution as a generally polluting moral miasma to be controlled by keeping prostitutes from living within the holy space marked by the city walls. Through the fifteenth century they became preoccupied with ensuring that honest women would not be mistaken for prostitutes and so marked prostitutes with visual signs including yellow veils and ribbons and ordered them to keep far out of sight of where honest women might gather. By the mid-sixteenth century, the noisy nuisance of songs, shouts, and insults that gathered around prostitutes became the target, and new regulations targeted this aural problem, particularly around convents and monasteries. The DECIMA project aimed initially to plot the conjunctions among Onestà magistrates, the daughters they were pushing into convents, and the prostitutes, pimps, and clients who filled some streets with the racket Florentines called 'baccano'. While the source limitations described by Sharon Strocchia and Julia Rombough in this volume have made it difficult to complete this particular project within the time frame of the research grant, the effort to bring together the tools to realize it sparked much else, as this volume demonstrates. If we take seriously Silicon Valley's mantra of 'fail early, fail often', this has been a decidedly creative failure, and perhaps only a temporary one. As more records are assembled on DECIMA through crowd-sourcing, it may well be possible to pursue the original project of tracking those conjunctions among prostitutes, nuns, and magistrates.

In its ambitions and setbacks, the DECIMA project's original goal of tracing how Florentines negotiated the boundaries between sex and the sacred shows how social, spatial, and sensory history can intertwine. In what follows, I track these three approaches to demonstrate how they can reinforce and build on one another. I first review how reading archival documents with an eye to spaces and senses allows us to identify three distinct stages in Florentine approaches to mediating the boundaries of sex and the sacred. I then turn to setting some of this manuscript material into the broader lens made possible by the DECIMA tool in order better to set the spatial and sensory contexts for how Florentines manipulated, ignored, exploited, and sometimes observed those boundaries in a period of significant political and social changes. We will see how digitally mapping social historical evidence generates questions that turn us towards the history of the senses and how these two together can then be taken as a model for spatial history. This will bring us back to Via dei Pilastri and Betta Strozzina and the questions of how best to read the records that name them. Reading the records together allows us to see different visions of the city intersecting—the more panoptic regulatory vision and the multiple visions of the city held by those who lived in it, used it, and realized it with their work and actions. Did those who joked with Bettina Strozzina on the street, visited an aunt in the Orbatello widow's shelter, or bought bread from its baker's oven pay much attention to either Cosimo I's tax surveyors or the magistrates sitting in the Onestà office near the Mercato Vecchio? Were they much affected by those magistrates' efforts to set boundaries to what was happening in their neighbourhood? They had a complicated relationship: the regulatory impulse built on and codified existing practice even as it tried to tame and channel it, and eventually it was swallowed up by the very thing that it aimed to control. As we use these records to understand sixteenth-century Florentines' preoccupations about space, the senses, and sex, we can come to a better understanding of their experience of the city and their movement through it.

Sex and the sacred: negotiating spatial and sensory boundaries

Florentine legislation on prostitution always had spatial and sensory elements to it.[4] The first laws of the 1280s and 1290s restricted prostitutes to a zone 1,000 *braccia*, or more than half a kilometre, outside the old city walls. They had to remain 400 *braccia* (230 metres) from suburban settlements.[5] Zones this wide and absolute suggested that legislators considered prostitutes to be inherently polluting agents – like Jews, lepers, and criminals – who had to be kept as far as possible from the sacred space within the city walls. Yet it also suggests that the law was intended to make a general religious or moral statement more than to achieve a practical legislative result. Prostitutes certainly continued entering the prohibited zone even though they risked heavy fines of 200 *lire*. Over the course of the fourteenth century, legislators added nuance to their decrees, allowing prostitutes to have a brothel outside the walls (apparently never built) and to enter the city itself on Mondays (1325, 1355). By 1378, magistrates dropped the pretence of keeping prostitutes out entirely and extended prohibited zones around churches, convents, monasteries, guildhalls, and major public buildings. If not quite a decriminalization, this marked a move towards accommodation and regulation. This was underscored by the fact that prosecution of prostitutes who violated the laws was taken out of the hands of the foreign judicial official known as the *podestà* and entrusted instead to a series of civic magistracies including the *Grascia* (a provisioning magistracy that also regulated the affairs of artisans and labourers who had no guild to represent them) and the *Otto di Guardia* (Eight on Public Safety, established in 1378).[6]

That move from criminal prosecution to civic business regulation was signalled most clearly when Florence opened a brothel in the centre of the city in 1403 and created the new magistracy of the Onestà to oversee it. With this step, Florence joined those cities that considered prostitution to be a public service and a commercial activity that was better regulated than eliminated. Each city did this with a degree of reluctance, seeing prostitution as the necessary evil that would keep young men from violating honest women. Florence added to this the hope that readily available prostitutes would also keep young men from turning to sodomitical relationships with other young men.[7] Florence's civic brothel was a collection of taverns and hostels ringed with a wall and located just off the main market. It was originally meant to be supplemented by two civic brothels in working-class areas – one in S. Croce to the east and other in S. Spirito across the Arno – though neither of these was ever built. And while the Onestà worked to make prostitution more orderly and available by licensing brothel keepers and prostitutes, the more powerful criminal magistracy of the *Otto di Guardia* moved in a more punitive direction, particularly through the 1470s and 1480s. It set spatial limits to prostitutes' activities, extended exclusion zones of 300 *braccia* (or roughly 175 metres) around all convents, monasteries, churches, and public buildings where prostitutes could neither live nor work, limited their ability to work at night, expelled pimps, and authorized yet another magistracy, the *Ufficiali di Notte e dei Monasteri* (Officials of the Night and of Convents), to enforce the new rules.[8]

The late fifteenth and early sixteenth centuries saw a series of regimes rise and fall as the local effects of the ongoing Wars of Italy. In May 1527 the Medici regime fell and was replaced by a new republican regime that had a strongly Savonarolan orientation. A month later, the first set of Onestà magistrates drawn in this new context adopted new rules that strengthened the visual and spatial boundaries around prostitutes. Their homes could be in only the handful of streets set out in earlier legislation, and they were not to leave them wearing clothes that might let them pass as either ordinary housewives (the simple unlined dress known as the *gamurra* and the outer garment known as the *cioppa* that women pulled on when leaving the house) or as patrician ladies (velvet vests and robes). They had to wear veils that marked them as prostitutes, in either yellow, red, or green, and they had to register with the Onestà within fifteen days or risk a fine of 3 florins.[9] The besieged republic collapsed by 1530, but the ducal regime that followed it retained the regulatory approach of combining registration with visual and spatial boundaries. Relatively few records concerning the Onestà or the regulation of prostitution remain from the period of Duke Alessandro I (1530–37), but they multiply after Cosimo I succeeded his assassinated distant cousin in 1537.

Cosimo I aimed to stir up the personnel and procedures of the Onestà magistracy, though he achieved only limited success. He first targeted the procedures by which magistrates extorted money from those who came before them, whether prostitutes themselves or those who had pimped, beaten, or insulted them. Magistrates had enjoyed wide latitude to set or reduce fines, to offer exemptions, and to suspend trials for a fee. They could do all of this in individual one-on-one sessions with defendants. In October 1544, addressing the 'avarice' of the Onestà magistrates explicitly, Cosimo established a table of fees to be charged for particular violations and a breakdown of how these were to be shared with the other functionaries of the Onestà office (the chancellor, administrator, and two enforcement officers) and with the warden of the Bargello prison, where violators were held while waiting for their case to be heard. Any excess funds generated by license fees and fines were to go to public coffers. Until this time, the Onestà magistrates had paid their employees a pittance while keeping the bulk of the income for themselves: a year before, they had pocketed 42 per cent of the almost 3,000 *lire* paid out in fees and fines. They carried on blithely, creaming off 54 per cent of income in 1547 and then 42 per cent in 1548. Cosimo I ordered a systematic audit and imposed a new set of rules with stricter limits on activities and fixed salaries for magistrates and employees alike. While not successful in cutting the number of Onestà magistrates in half, his procedural overhaul did reduce the worst of the abuses and even sped up payment of fines. Under the earlier system, defendants had either negotiated a reduced fine with individual magistrates or simply waited months or even years until they had the funds to pay. As a sign of how destitute many prostitutes were, most had waited to pay their fines until the early summer, possibly because this was when it was easiest to find casual piecework in the very seasonal silk trade and to clear up debts. Cosimo I's reforms included cutting the fine by half if it was paid within two weeks, and many prostitutes took up the offer.[10]

The reforms clarified the visual and spatial markers of prostitution in Florence. Prostitutes could now wear the *coppa* and *gamurra* of 'honest' women if they pinned on a yellow ribbon two fingers wide and at least half a *braccio* long (about a third of a metre).[11] When pressed, the Onestà came up with its list of eighteen streets, corners, and neighbourhoods where prostitutes had to live if they wished to register and practice legally; to some extent, this list simply wrote into law the places prostitutes already practiced the sex trade (Figure 6.1). Cosimo I personally removed or reduced five of these, and although four more had been added by 1558, the general push to reduce them continued, so that by 1577 only six remained.[12] As noted earlier, these were not normally whole streets but rather sections of a few blocks bounded by a tavern, a bakery, a gate, or an intersection. As with the rules adopted decades earlier, prostitutes were not allowed to live or work outside these specific zones. Any house they rented on a corner or at the boundary of an authorized zone could not even have windows looking out on to a prohibited area, so that these residents did not have to see prostitutes in the windows or hear the songs and shouting coming from them. Moreover, all the houses within the authorized areas were to be for prostitutes and their families only, and owners and agents could not charge more than the customary rents that had been levied before; Onestà officials were to police this. Prostitutes living outside the zones and those renting or selling these places to them paid a 25 *scudi* fine. The rules imposed by Cosimo in the 1540s made two significant changes

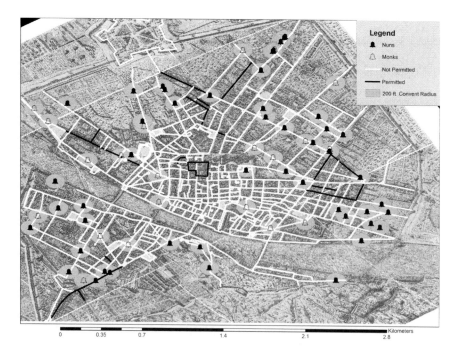

Figure 6.1 Prostitution zones (1547) with religious houses.

to the 300-*braccia* exclusion zones, established in the 1470 and 1480s, around churches, public buildings, convents, and monasteries. The new rules reduced the exclusion zones to 100 *braccia* (or about 60 metres), and they now 'protected' only convents and some monasteries.[13]

Under Cosimo I's new regime, a woman paid a license fee of 15 *lire* every three months to be registered as a prostitute with the Onestà. If she wanted to work at night as well, she had to pay 2 *lire* more for a *bollettino* that was good for fifteen days. This was at a time when that same woman would pay 2 *lire* to buy a flask of olive oil, 3 *lire* 6 *soldi* for a large basket (*staio*) of grain, and 2 *lire* 2 *soldi* for fourteen pounds of veal.[14] For impoverished women contemplating prostitution as they struggled to feed their families, the 15-*lire* fee was significant. With this extensive regulatory apparatus, Cosimo I and the Onestà were aiming to ensure that desperate women would not turn occasional tricks on the side somewhere outside their immediate neighbourhood but would be forced through bright visual markers, sharp geographical boundaries, and registration in the books of the Onestà to take on the identity of a professional prostitute. Many women ran foul of the regulations regardless. It is clear from the frequency with which the Onestà issued its regulations on clothing, licenses, and location that many women circumvented the rules.[15]

The new rules spread prostitution across the city and in this way made it more accessible to the young male labourers and apprentices who were the chief target group. The earlier exclusion zones of 300 *braccia* around all churches, chapels, and public buildings would have made it difficult to fit these zones into the city, and so reducing the zones to 100 *braccia* and extending them around fewer protected sites was a critical step in making the new system work. But did this also empty the rule of any effectiveness and meaning? The earlier zones had protected the sanctity of altars and the honour of those who worshipped at them; it had kept the hubs of civic life free from the moral pollution of the sex trade. Were these values no longer at play?

I have argued elsewhere that the earlier meaning of the exclusion zones was not eliminated but transformed and that we can see this more clearly when we bring together sensory and spatial history to look at how regulations had shifted from the thirteenth through the sixteenth centuries.[16] Negotiating the boundaries of sex and the sacred in Florence meant very different things for authorities from the late medieval and those in the early modern period. The successive magistracies, with their distinct sets of legislation and their different forms of prosecution, targeted different senses. We can distinguish three rough stages through the fourteenth, fifteenth, and sixteenth centuries. Communal legislators of the fourteenth century had aimed to keep the 'pollution' of prostitution entirely outside the city walls. Separating the spaces of sex and the sacred so completely would preserve the city's honour. In the fifteenth century, republican magistrates reversed this when building the brothel in the heart of the city and then extending the 300-*braccia* exclusion zones around religious and public buildings. The exclusion zones would be large enough to form a visual boundary keeping the sight and association of prostitution from these magistrates' own wives and daughters. In the expansive ducal regime of the mid-sixteenth century, when licensed prostitution spread out across the city, Cosimo I and his magistrates thought less about the view on the streets and more about the noises that prostitution generated. They thought of the daughters, nieces, and granddaughters whom they were sending in increasing numbers into convents, and they aimed to ensure that these female relatives would not have to endure the noises generated by a boisterous public life that was now lost to them. The new 100-*braccia* exclusion zone was sufficient to keep most of these noises from penetrating the convent cloister so long as it was well policed – as indeed it was. In short, if we look at the sequence of regulations from the point of view of the senses, it is clear that Florentine officials were changing what the boundaries between the spaces of sex and the sacred meant and how they functioned. In the fifteenth century these had been visual boundaries protecting the peace of laywomen outside convents and churches; in the sixteenth, they became aural boundaries protecting the peace of those women and men enclosed inside convents and monasteries.

Looking to the later sixteenth and seventeenth centuries, we can see that these sensory and spatial concerns continuing to preoccupy regulators as they faced new challenges. Coach travel exploded from the mid-sixteenth century, and the first proclamations prohibiting prostitutes from travelling in coaches emerged in 1550 and multiplied through the decades following until the 1630s.[17] These really affected only upper-class courtesans. On one level we can read them as an expression of the kind of anxiety that informed sumptuary legislation generally: these women should not use their wealth or patrons to disrupt class lines and pose as honest patrician ladies. Additional rules forbidding the courtesans from wearing brocades or pearls certainly reinforce this connection. Yet concerns about sound, secrecy, and particularly mobility – and who could exploit and impede it – also drove the new rules. Travel at night drew many complaints since carriages were extraordinarily noisy. These complaints and the laws they triggered frequently focused on the noisy coming and going when patrician clients visited a courtesan or sent their carriage to bring her to their urban palace or rural villa. They also singled out the problem of prostitutes wearing masks while in the carriages.[18] A society of orders that was obsessed with precedence found carriage blinds and prostitutes' masks disconcerting in part because it might not be clear who was travelling and hence who had the right of way. This was a serious concern since carriages and their trains of horses and groomsmen frequently clogged streets and made any motion at all difficult. Should a mere prostitute have a noble's power to halt traffic on Florence's city streets? One initial response was to order that prostitutes could mount a coach only when exiting Florence from one of the city gates, a faint ironic echo of the late thirteenth-century view that aimed to separate sharply those who lived and worked in the privileged space within the walls, and those whose noisome presence and activities were best kept outside.

Rules remained as difficult to enforce as ever. When we map the provisions and track the prosecutions, we can see that the magistrates were at least serious in making the effort. Yet Cosimo I, the Onestà, and Florence's prostitutes had a curious three-way relationship with constantly shifting alliances and with the duke

Locating the sex trade 115

and his magistrates often at odds with each other, making regulation less effective. Mapping the boundaries and spaces of prostitution, and tracking shifts in prosecution over the centuries allows us better to appreciate the shifts in how generations of legislators aimed to regulate the sights, the sounds, and, above all, the politics of sex and the sacred in Florence.[19] Experience in Florence and elsewhere reminds us that all such regulation was quixotic, yet if we can read the bureaucratic sources that set out regulatory ambitions together with other statistical sources that clarify socioeconomic contexts, we may gain a better understanding of why practice so often triumphed over prescription. This is where DECIMA can come in.

From digital mapping to spatial humanities

What do the *Decima* and DECIMA add to our efforts to use shifting controls around prostitution and the spatial and sensory registers they engaged to understand how Florentines lived in their city? There are at least three linked inquiries that we can undertake. DECIMA allows us to plot more accurately where prostitutes lived and worked and in what numbers. It also allows us to plot the prosecutions that the Onestà pursued and to assess how much spatial and sensory concerns may have driven them. Perhaps most ambitiously, it allows us to set this firmer spatial analysis of the sex trade into the broader contexts of occupation, density, and value that distinguished Florentine neighbourhoods from one another. In what follows, I focus on using data from the early 1560s.

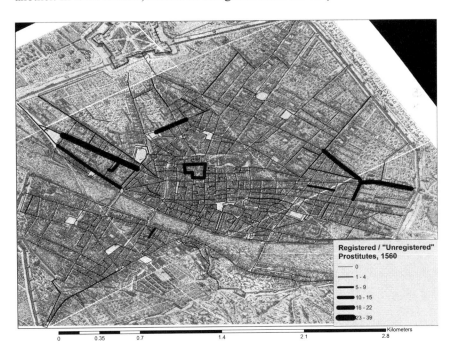

Figure 6.2 Concentration of registered and unregistered prostitutes (1560).

First, plotting where prostitutes lived might seem the most straightforward inquiry of all, since registered prostitutes were identified as such in the *Decima ricerca* and so appear as part of an occupational category in the DECIMA data base. Yet the exercise reveals one of the contradictions of the Florentine regulatory regime. It arises from the classic absolutist move of adopting strict laws and then offering the opportunity to purchase an exemption from them. In this case, while all prostitutes equally required a license, not all licences were equal. From November 1559 the Onestà distinguished between what were later designated the major and minor taxes (*tassa maggiore e minore*). The *tassa minore* was the standard license fee for public prostitutes, while the *tassa maggiore* was a higher fee that allowed a prostitute to practice outside the restricted zone and without wearing the yellow ribbon. This was part of the effort to raise funds for the convent of S. Elisabetta, also known as the Convertite, just inside the city walls from the Porta Romana, where prostitutes aiming to leave or retire from the profession could find a home. A law of 1553 ordering that all prostitutes' estates be seized for the benefit of the Convertite proved too hard to enforce since many prostitutes had spouses, children, and other beneficiaries. From 1559 a new law replaced stick with carrot: those signing on for the *tassa maggiore* that freed them from the spatial and sensory regulations also agreed to assign one quarter of their estates to the Convertite in their wills.[20] One year later, in 1560, fully 79 of Florence's 234 officially recognized prostitutes were paying the *tassa maggiore*. While still in the Onestà's registers, they did not have to declare their profession to *Decima* surveyors, and most indeed did not. As a result, the 1562 census of households and *bocche* delivered to Cosimo I counts only 134 self-declared prostitutes. Since we do have a list of those paying the *tassa maggiore* from 1560, we are able to overcome this limitation, find and plot their residences, and so come up with a more complete map of prostitutes' locations than DECIMA alone would generate. Figure 6.2 gives a better sense of where all prostitutes lived and where the largest groups were concentrated, a spatial reality that Florentines would have recognized from their own day-to-day movements around the city. The *tassa maggiore* directly undermined efforts to draw firm spatial boundaries around the zones of prostitution and created the situation that Colin Rose, Fabrizio Nevola, and David Rosenthal have described in their chapters here whereby prostitutes lived side by side with carpenters and bankers on Via dei Pilastri and in the neighbourhood of S. Ambrogio. While some prostitutes rented, Figure 6.3 shows that others owned their own homes and that these were concentrated in the three general areas of Via dei Pilastri/Via Pentolini, Via Palazzuolo/Borgo Ognissanti, and Via Guelfa/Via Tedeschi, all north of the Arno. Some were inside and some outside the approved zones. Authorities tried in 1568 and again in the 1590s to force those paying the *tasse maggiore* to at least continue to live in the approved areas, but it appears that this had no effect.[21]

Second, when we move to track actual prosecutions by the Onestà we can see that concerns around sound in particular dominate the records, while those having to do with general violations of the rules are less important.[22] From May 1560 through September 1562, the months when the *Decima* survey was under way, the

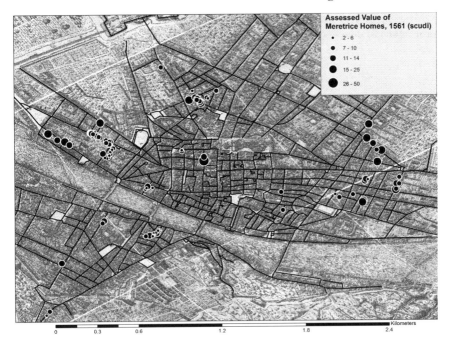

Figure 6.3 Assessed value of properties owned by prostitutes, 1561.

magistracy prosecuted 144 women and 63 men for a range of offenses. We need to remember that the bulk of these 207 prosecutions arose from public complaints rather than from direct arrests. Any Florentine could either make a verbal denunciation or write a complaint on a piece of paper and deposit it in a drum outside the Onestà's office across from the church of Orsanmichele in the city centre. The Onestà did indeed have two officers (*donzelle*) who walked through the city checking for licenses, seeing whether prostitutes were wearing their yellow ribbons, and confirming that they did not wear forbidden fabrics. It also lobbied to ensure that other Florentine police did not muscle in to make arrests and claim a fee. Yet, as Tessa Storey found in Rome, officers of the prostitution magistracy were often mocked and disregarded and were not particularly zealous in pursuing arrests. They feared entering red-light districts to openly confront women who had friends, relatives, and clients at hand to protect them. Like the Onestà magistrates who employed them, they often saw their job as one of coming to a mutually profitable accommodation with prostitutes rather than as serving as determined enforcers of regulations. As a result, the 207 prosecution records refer to perhaps fewer violations of Onestà regulations that we would imagine these officers pursuing, such as working without a license (6), violating sumptuary laws (5), failing to wear the yellow ribbon that marked a public prostitute (4), or failing to come to the annual St Mary Magdalen day sermon in the Cathedral (*metropolitana*) where a preacher would aim to persuade prostitutes to leave the profession (0). There were even relatively few prosecutions of women working outside the designated zones (10), and most of these were for those who were working too close to a convent. One borderline offense was operating without the special license required to work at night; 27 women were prosecuted for this. While most may have been arrested by the Onestà officers doing their rounds, some were likely turned in by neighbours fed up with the noise and distraction, while others were denounced by those prostitutes who had bought their *bollettino* and resented others' free-riding.

Yet all of these together amount to only a quarter of all prosecutions during the years in question. What Florentines found objectionable and denounced most often came down to three things that had more to do with disturbing neighbourhood life than with violating moral boundaries. The greatest number (55) had to do with insults, public mockery, and disturbing the peace. This included both direct verbal quarrels (*parole offese*) between individuals and the broader categories of *baccano* and *fatto la baia/baie*, the charivari-esque joking, mocking, hooting, or making fun of others that had people yelling and making a racket on the street. This was followed by a broad group of physical assaults (46), a category that men dominated. Charges and fines increased if offenders had used fists or clubs and particularly if they had drawn blood. In some cases it was groups of men that were being prosecuted for assault in what would have sounded like a battle on the streets; in others it was attacks on a prostitute by a client, neighbour, or relative. These two categories of insult and assault together were fundamentally noisy public disturbances, and they accounted for half of all prosecutions by the Onestà in the years when the *Decima* was being drawn up. The remaining specific offense was that of acting as pimp or procuress, and in most cases this amounted to running an unlicensed brothel. In some case, innkeepers and widows were charged with having lured honest and married women into the trade, sometimes keeping them locked up in an inn or home for months. In other cases, parents were charged with pimping their daughters or even their daughters-in-law. For the Onestà, this was a licensing offense; for neighbours, it was a racket best handled by making a secret denunciation or formal complaint. If we look ahead to prosecutions of the 1590s, we find that concerns about noise still dominated the Onestà's activities, suggesting that the sounds and public disorder around prostitution were more bothersome to neighbours than the question of whether prostitutes were wearing yellow ribbons or paying license fees.[23]

Third, the DECIMA mapping tool allows us to get a clearer understanding of the economic and occupational character of the neighbourhoods where prostitutes lived and worked and where complaints about the noise they generated were most common. As Figures 6.2 and 6.4 show, most of these were in what we might call Florence's inner suburbs, that ring between the second set of walls, built in the 1170s, and the third circuit, built 1284–1333. Here city blocks were larger, streets were wider, straighter, and longer, and traffic moved more quickly. And here people were poorer. This was where textile workers, day labourers, and rural migrants dominated, and Figure 6.5 gives the property evaluations that confirm its cheaper real estate. As Figure 6.1 shows, almost all the streets licensed for prostitution were outside the line of the former second wall, above all the busiest streets

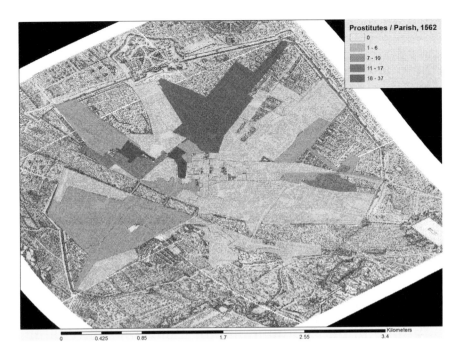

Figure 6.4 Registered prostitutes by parish, 1561.

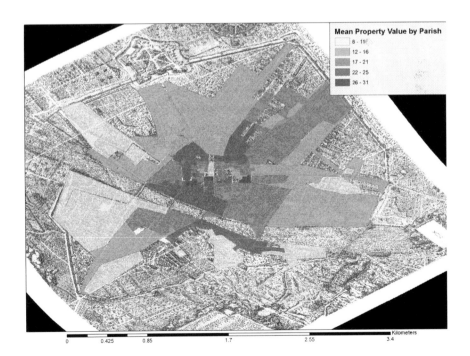

Figure 6.5 Mean property value by parish (in scudi), 1561.

for the sex trade like Via dei Pilastri and Via Palazzuolo. Via dei Pilastri and Via Pentolino actually followed the very line of that demolished wall. The central brothel was the only approved space for the sex trade located within the old Roman city ringed by the first wall, and indeed there were hardly any approved spaces between the first and second walls. This meant that prostitution was largely outside the ritual centre defined and crossed by the processions that Niall Atkinson has described. It was even outside the core area that the harsh legislation of the 1280s and 1290s had protected from moral pollution. While the two sets of walls protecting that core had been torn down, the new laws still preserved the core's distinct character. Its identity was written in densities and land values that may not immediately appear on a map or census but that come into focus when these two are brought together.

Florentines did not seek to hide prostitutes away in nooks, crannies, or alleys but moved them to the broader thoroughfares of these inner suburbs, where the city looked, felt, and moved differently. Housing stock was smaller and cheaper, more inhabitants rented than owned, population densities were lower, and there were none of the significant public buildings that Florentines took pride in and that visitors singled out for praise. Those prostitutes who owned their own houses tended to live here, though, as Figure 6.6 shows, prostitutes owned properties in

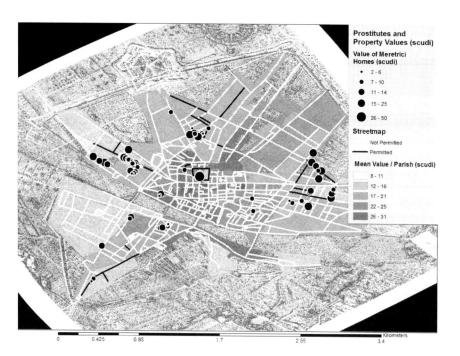

Figure 6.6 Prostitutes and property values, 1561.

all parts of the city, even the richest neighbourhoods, and did not concentrate in the very poorest areas. The transience that marked the inner suburbs was reinforced by the large number of prostitutes who took on names that identified them with towns and cities outside Florence: Tonina Bolognese, Maria da Palazzuola, Grazia da Siena, Agnola da Lucca. These weren't terribly exotic places, and very possibly the names were just professional tags like the more dramatic ones (like La Spiritata, La Persia, and La Smerelda) that other Florentine prostitutes adopted, particularly in the central brothel. Whether real or invented, these names tell something about the social and psychological spaces of prostitution and the people who moved through them. Most of the places by which sex workers identified themselves were within a hundred kilometres of Florence. This was the distance travelled by many young rural women who had been assaulted and who moved to nearby cities to escape their tainted reputations and either build a new life or enter the sex trade. It was also about the distance that many young labouring men – the target group for civic-regulated prostitution – travelled from around Tuscany to find work in the city. It is possible that the young working men who were looking for sex were drawn more by the familiar than by the exotic, and that young transient men and women from other towns in ducal Tuscany were both drawn to the same poor inner suburbs of the capital and continued living in proximity there. This associated the zones of prostitution with transience and linked them to worlds beyond the city walls.

As we saw earlier, the Onestà named some of the city's major streets in the inner suburbs only indirectly in its 1547 regulations. Via dei Pilastri was described by its shops and institutions but not by its name. Via Guelfa was given only as a street (unnamed) leading from the residence of the Barnabite monks to the Fortress of his Excellency the Duke. Niall Atkinson, Nicholas Eckstein, Fabrizio Nevola, and David Rosenthal write in this volume of how Florence's labouring class and poor marked their neighbourhoods with their feet and work, and navigated more by landmarks and uses than by streets and addresses. A widow's hostel, a convent, and the house of a famous courtesan spoke to a way of experiencing the city that was distinct from the 'routes of governmentality' that Cosimo I's *Decima* bureaucrats were tracing, though on a certain level it was the same space. The fact that both ways of describing streets enter into the Onestà's regulations underscores the mixed – and often contradictory – purposes that characterize early modern governance. The Onestà occupied both worlds, as indeed most Florentines did, and this was what led to many of Cosimo I's frustrations with it. The magistrates who set the boundaries also walked the streets, and some of them may have known Betta Strozzina very well.

The *Decima* gives us a window into the mental world of governmentality, and its panoptic view of city and state gives us tools to count and locate. DECIMA allows us to gather, visualize, and complicate that information. Using the two together in order to plot where prostitutes lived and worked, what prosecutions they faced most often, and what economic conditions marked their neighbourhoods allows us to see the kinds of spatial and sensory boundaries that Florentines raised, lived in, and manipulated. By highlighting the mixed and contradictory character of early modern civic regulations, it underscores just how little of urban life was truly or effectively regulated. In this way, the figures we generate are an opening and not an end to the inquiry – they raise further questions that are best approached through narrative sources that keep us closer to the city as a lived space and that help us bend the straight lines as Florentines themselves did. This is where spatial humanities moves a step beyond digital mapping. Taking a tool like DECIMA with us into the archives, we can take its cartographic and statistical abstraction and co-relate it to more long-standing relational ways of understanding space and place that emerge from other documents. This can give us a deeper view of the city that is textured and statistical, local and panoptic, living and abstract – and always partial.

Notes

1 Archivio di Stato di Firenze, *Onestà*, 1, c.37r.
2 M.S. Mazzi, *Prostitute e lenoni nella Firenze del Quattrocento*, Milan: il Saggiatore, 1991, 194–199. See also: J.K. Brackett, 'The Florentine Onestà and the Control of Prostitution, 1403–1680', *Sixteenth Century Journal* 24, 1993, 273–300; R. Trexler, 'Florentine Prostitution in the Fifteenth Century: Patrons and Clients', *Dependence in Context in Renaissance Florence*, Binghamton, NY: MRTS, 1994, 373–414.
3 N. Terpstra and C. Rose, 'DECIMA: The Digitally-Encoded Census Information and Mapping Archive, and the Project for a Geo-Spatial and Sensory Map of Renaissance Florence', *The Journal for Early Modern Cultural Studies* 13, 2013, 156–60.
4 For an expanded treatment of the material in this section, see N. Terpstra, 'Sex and the Sacred: Negotiating Spatial and Sensory Boundaries in Renaissance Florence', *Radical History Review* 121, 2015, 71–90.
5 The Florentine *braccia* measured 0.5836 metres. W.N.A. Boerefijn, 'The foundation, planning, and building of new towns in the 13th and 14th centuries in Europe: An architectural historical research into urban forms and its creation', PhD thesis, University of Amsterdam, 2010, 451.
6 These moves towards regulation by civic magistracies must of course be examined in the context of the Ciompi revolt. J. Najemy, *History of Florence*, Oxford, UK: Blackwell, 2006, 161–88.
7 M. Rocke, *Forbidden Friendships: Homosexuality and Male Culture in Renaissance Florence*, Oxford, UK: Oxford University Press, 1996. See also: Mazzi, *Prostitute e lenoni*, 144ff.
8 New legislation appeared in 1454, 1473, 1476, 1478, 1483, 1484, 1485, and 1488. Mazzi, *Prostitute e lenoni*, 168–81.
9 Regulations of 16 June 1527: ASF, *Onestà*, 1, 24v.
10 These reforms appear in the first volume of records of the *Pratica Segreta*, dating from 1545. On 14 April 1549, Cosimo appointed the Pisan Jacopo Polverini to investigate the finances and administration of the Onestà, and by 11 May he set out his wishes to the *Pratica Segreta*. ASF, *Pratica Segreta*, 1, #12, #14. For the 1561 table with full and reduced fines: ASF, *Camera Fiscale*, 2113, f591.
11 For the regulations on clothing of 1527, 1544, 1547, 1548, 1555, 1558: ASF, *Onestà*, ms. 1, ff. 24v, 32v-33r, 36r, 36v-37r, 38r. For the consolidated and revised regulations of 1577: ASF, *Onestà*, ms. 3.
12 ASF, *Onestà*, 3, f. 5r. In 1560 there were four recognized brothels: the central one in *Mercato Vecchio* and three others in Piazza Pradella, Via Romita, and Via dell'Ariento. ASF, *Acquisti e Doni*, ms. 291, 'Varieta – Onesta' Cl IX #27, np.

13 On the 100 *braccia* rule see the letter of 6 May 1561 to Duke Cosimo I: ASF, *Acquisti e Doni*, ms. 291, 'Onestà e Meretrici', np. Some rules stipulate monasteries as well as convents, but later regulation and prosecution emphasized only convents.
14 These prices come from the contemporary account books of the Casa della Pietà, a shelter for abandoned girls that was located on the edge of a red-light district in the textile district of Borgo Ognissanti. ASF, *Corporazioni religiose soppresse dal governo francese*, #112 (*Conservatorio di Domenicane denominato La Pietà di Firenze*), 2, ff. 102r, 129r.
15 Eighteen new regulations or decrees overhauled the Onestà's procedures from 1544 to 1560, and three warnings issued in the later 1560s showed that Cosimo I was alert to the magistrates' efforts to avoid or undermine the new regulations. ASF, *Onestà*, ms. 1, ff. 27r-43r. On regulations against courtesans: ASF, *Onestà*, ms. 3, ff.13v-14v; 17v. On fines paid for various offenses, see ASF, *Onestà*, 4.
16 Terpstra, 'Sex and the Sacred'.
17 ASF, *Onestà*, 3, 13v (1577 statutes), 38r-v (proclamations of January 1549 [sf], June 1572, September 1629); 43r-49v (May 1628, July 1628, October 1638, June 1639, December 1639). J.M. Hunt, 'Carriages, Violence, and Masculinity in Early Modern Rome', *I Tatti Studies in the Italian Renaissance* 17/1 2014, 175–96, partic. 177–78. For more on carriages and courtesans: T. Storey, *Carnal Commerce in Counter-Reformation Rome*, Cambridge, UK: Cambridge University Press, 2008, 165–66.
18 S. D'Amico, 'Shameful Mother: Poverty and Prostitution in Seventeenth Century Milan', *Journal of Family History* 39, 2005, 109–20.
19 As this concern abated by the 1630s, it was replaced by another that showed the continuing pull of the kind of moral preoccupations that had persuaded magistrates to avert sodomy with a brothel in 1403 or to prohibit prostitutes from posing as honest housewives in 1527. A significant number of prostitutes were married women, and generations of legislators and magistrates had chosen to ignore the fact that their professional activity constituted adultery. Grand Duke Ferdinand II moved against this in 1633 with a series of new regulations prohibiting the sale of licenses to married women and ordering that they be removed from the Onestà registry and then tried for adultery if later caught engaging in prostitution. ASF, *Miscellanea Medicea*, 26/20, ff. 10r-11r, 14r-15v; ASF, *Onestà*, 3, 39v-41r.
20 The *tassa maggiore* began as an additional 7 *lire* on top of the 15-*lire* license fee for four months, with lire 5.1.8 going to the Convertite and *lire* 1.18.4 going to the Onestà. ASF, *Acquisti e Doni*, ms. 291, 'Varietà – Onestà', np.
21 ASF, *Miscellanea Medicea*, 26/17, f. 2r-v.
22 The work is made complicated by discontinuous record keeping. Within the ASF's small Onestà deposit, there are three volumes tracking prosecutions: two (1441–1523), four (1593–1627), and six (1629–1647). The nineteenth-century historian Carlo Carnesecchi took notes from various sources on prosecutions from 1535 through 1624, but these were highly selective. The official records from 1560 to 1593 are found in the *Camera Fiscale* series that records prosecutions for all Florentine magistracies. The five volumes used here for the period of the *Decima* survey extend from 25 May 1560 to 18 September 1562: ASF, *Camera Fiscale*, 2110 (ff. 507–67), 2111 (ff. 669–92), 2112 (ff. 605–29), 2113 (ff. 589–604), 2114 (ff. 717–51).
23 Terpstra, 'Sex and the Sacred', 79–80.

Bibliography

Manuscript sources

Archivio di Stato di Firenze (ASF), *Acquisti e Doni*, 291.
——— *Camera Fiscale*, 2110, 2111, 2112, 2113, 2114.

―――― *Corporazioni religiose soppresse dal governo francese*, 112 (*Conservatorio di Domenicane denominato La Pietà di Firenze*), 2.
―――― *Miscellanea Medicea*, 26/17, 26/20.
―――― *Onestà*, 1, 3, 4, 6.
―――― *Pratica Segreta*, 1.

Print sources

Boerefijn, W.N.A., 'The foundation, planning, and building of new towns in the 13th and 14th centuries in Europe: An architectural historical research into urban forms and its creation', PhD thesis, University of Amsterdam, 2010.

Brackett, J.K., 'The Florentine Onestà and the Control of Prostitution, 1403–1680', *Sixteenth Century Journal* 24, 1993, 273–300.

D'Amico, S., 'Shameful Mother: Poverty and Prostitution in Seventeenth Century Milan', *Journal of Family History* 39, 2005, 109–20.

Hunt, J.M., 'Carriages, Violence, and Masculinity in Early Modern Rome', *I Tatti Studies in the Italian Renaissance* 17, 2014, 175–96.

Mazzi, M.S., *Prostitute e lenoni nella Firenze del Quattrocento*, Milan, Italy: Il Saggiatore, 1991.

Najemy, J., *History of Florence*, Oxford, UK: Blackwell, 2006.

Rocke, M., *Forbidden Friendships: Homosexuality and Male Culture in Renaissance Florence*, Oxford, UK: Oxford University Press, 1996.

Storey, T., *Carnal Commerce in Counter-Reformation Rome*, Cambridge, UK: Cambridge University Press, 2008.

Terpstra, N., 'Sex and the Sacred: Negotiating Spatial and Sensory Boundaries in Renaissance Florence', *Radical History Review* 121, 2015, 71–90.

―――― and Rose, C., 'DECIMA: The Digitally-Encoded Census Information and Mapping Archive, and the Project for a Geo-Spatial and Sensory Map of Renaissance Florence', *The Journal for Early Modern Cultural Studies* 13, 2013, 156–60.

Trexler, R., 'Florentine Prostitution in the Fifteenth Century: Patrons and Clients', *Dependence in Context in Renaissance Florence*, Binghamton, NY: MRTS, 1994.

7 Plague and the city

Methodological considerations in mapping disease in early modern Florence

John Henderson and Colin Rose

> *The places where the sickness was at its most severe were the extremities of the city, those which are inhabited by poor people....*
> —Rondinelli, Relazione del contagio stato in Firenze[1]

Early modern Europeans saw close associations among plague, poverty and the poorer areas of their cities. Historians have placed reactions to the plague within the wider context of developing policies towards the poor but have done less to study the relationship between disease and the physical environment. This chapter aims to bring these two together by exploring what methodologies might help examine the relationship among plague, the poor, and the physical environment in order to provide a more fine-tuned analysis of the impact of this disease on urban mortality. This type of examination can best be done at the local level, and we shall take the case of the impact of plague on Florence in 1630–31. This forms part of a forthcoming study by John Henderson that examines the impact of the epidemic on the city and on the developing policies of Grand Duke Ferdinando II de' Medici. The main themes include analysis of the relationship between public health and medical theory and the way in which this led to the implementation of a detailed survey of the city; the geographical spread of plague through Florence over the course of a year; the role of the *lazaretto* through the eyes of staff who worked in these isolation hospitals; the reactions and survival strategies of those at the lower end of society; and the relationship between the built environment and mortality.[2]

This chapter discusses methodological issues, leaving detailed results for the wider monograph. In the first section, John Henderson sets the context in plague studies generally and in his own long-standing research project as it developed from its beginnings in 1989 at the Centre for Metropolitan History at the University of London.[3] He then outlines the main measures taken by public health authorities during the epidemic, with a focus on the mortality crisis within the parish of San Lorenzo in 1630–31. In the second section, Colin Rose describes how he used DECIMA in order to map the spread of the plague through San Lorenzo, explaining some of the problems he encountered and the methodologies he developed while working with Henderson's extensive database.

Plague and historians

The seventeenth century saw the end of the second pandemic of plague in much of Europe, which began with the so-called Black Death of 1347–52 and continued to afflict the population on a regular basis for some three hundred years. Subsequently it returned briefly twice more, in Marseille in 1720 and in Messina in 1743, before finally almost completely disappearing from Europe. The reasons for its disappearance have been debated for many years, and no really satisfactory explanation has been provided, although one of the most widely held ideas is a belief in the efficaciousness of public health measures and in particular the isolation and quarantine of plague victims and their contacts. This was done at the level of the house and household, with the sick being shut up in their homes or taken off to isolation hospitals called *lazaretti*. This relationship between levels of mortality and the social, economic, and topographical character of the city reflects the interests of today's demographic historians and also the concerns of contemporaries, such as Francesco Rondinelli, cited at the beginning of this essay. The imposition of cordons sanitaire between states has been hailed as particularly effective.[4] In the case of early modern Italy, some indication of the effect of the quarantining of states emerges from a comparison of the geographical distribution of plague in the outbreak of 1629–33 and that of 1655–56. The first was confined to the north of the peninsula, while the second was limited to the south, except for Liguria.[5]

The study of plague in early modern Europe has, like plague itself, never quite disappeared, and interest has been rekindled within the past few years. This more recent revival of interest in plague has led to a series of new studies of Venice, Rome, Naples, Geneva, London, Barcelona, and Seville.[6] These studies look at medical theory and plague tracts, government policies and plague hospitals, the impact on art, and reactions of the resident population.[7] Much effort and many pages have also been expended on debates about whether 'historical plague' in the premodern period was in fact the same as bubonic plague in the postlaboratory era. DNA analysis of the dental pulp of those who died from historical plague epidemics has definitely shown the existence of *Yersinia Pestis* in medieval and early modern plague pits, although there do remain doubts about the applicability of these results across the whole period.[8]

One aspect that has tended to remain a minor theme until recently is the demographic impact of plague and its relationship to the urban environment. There are some exceptions. Robert Burr Litchfield's *Florence Ducal Capital, 1530–1630* provides a very useful general survey of the impact of the plague of 1630–31 on Florence.[9] The innovative studies of Guido Alfani include an essay in which Samuel Cohn provides a detailed demographic analysis of the impact of plague on Normentola in northern Italy and a monograph, *Calamities and the Economy in Renaissance Italy*, that gives a more extensive study of the impact of the plague ion the northern part of the peninsula within the wider context of war, famine, and the economy.[10]

The current research project on the 1630–31 plague in Florence first emerged in 1989 as an effort to undertake a comparative demographic analysis of plague in relation to the socioeconomic and topographical character of two of the largest urban centres in seventeenth-century Europe: London and Florence. It was envisaged as collaborative, with a joint methodology to be applied to both early modern cities. Within each city, areas were selected to provide a range of social and environmental conditions, from the more affluent to the very poor. Evidence for the incidence of plague and other deaths was studied in relation to surveys that revealed the character of the local communities. In the case of London, the main source examined was the Hearth Tax. Studying those parishes where complete tax records and parish registers survived allowed ambitious comparative socioeconomic analyses. This collaboration has generated numerous results, including Justin Champion's groundbreaking study of plague and its relationship to the built environment in early modern London, Graham Twigg's series of subsequent studies,[11] and a comprehensive project recently initiated at the London School of Economics to map changing mortality patterns in early modern London at the parish level.[12]

Plague in early modern Florence

The plague epidemic at the centre of this research project is that of 1629–33. It entered Italy in November 1629 during the Italian phase of the Thirty Years' War. Arriving on the tailcoats of both the French and the Imperial armies, it gradually travelled south until it arrived in Tuscany in summer 1630. It wreaked havoc on the way. For example, the two largest cities in the north, Milan and Venice, lost 46 and 33 per cent of their respective populations of 130,000 and 141,000. Smaller cities, such as Verona, were hit even more severely, with mortality rates reaching 57 per cent. By the time it reached central Italy in the spring of 1630, the epidemic had apparently lost some of its virulence, for Bologna suffered a slightly lower mortality rate of 24 per cent over the following months.[13]

This pattern continued as plague progressed further south. Florence itself only lost 12 per cent of its population of 75,000 between the late summer and the winter of 1630–31, although epidemic mortality did rise again briefly in 1633.[14] The seasonality of the epidemic in Florence can be seen in Graph 7.1; the highest

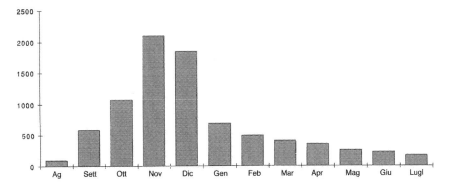

Graph 7.1 Plague deaths in Florence, 1630–31.

mortality was in the autumn and early winter of 1630, and then it gradually tailed off over the following seven months until the disease disappeared altogether by late July 1631.[15]

As the epidemic took hold, authorities debated about the nature of the disease. While some of the medical advisers to the Health Board suggested that it was merely a 'pestilential fever', in the end there was a general agreement that plague had indeed entered the city, and all the normal crisis measures were put into practice.[16] Debates about the cause of the disease were not uncommon in early modern European states at the beginning of epidemics, partly in order to avoid the panic and the inevitable commercial isolation of a state if plague was declared. In Florence, moreover, plague was not identified immediately since many assumed that it was a new occurrence of *patecchie* or typhus, which had broken out three times over the previous decade. Furthermore, the city had not actually experienced plague for about a century, although northern Italy had suffered from exceptionally virulent attacks in the 1570s.[17]

Once the Health Board had recognized the presence of plague, a series of routine measures were instituted to combat the 'invisible enemy'.[18] These included digging special plague pits outside the city, setting up isolation hospitals outside the walls, establishing a Health Board to run the whole operation, and appointing voluntary and paid officials to implement all these measures. Voluntary employees included members of the confraternity of the Misericordia, who transported sick and dead bodies and anybody who had come into contact with the sick. Physicians and surgeons were employed to inspect and identify plague cases and gravediggers to bury the dead; police were appointed to investigate and arrest those who broke plague regulations, as were judges to try offenders.[19]

One feature of Florentine plague measures that differentiated the city's strategy from those of other cities was the close involvement of the court.[20] The twenty-two-year-old Grand Duke Ferdinand II had recently come to power and was bent on proving himself to be a Christian and beneficent ruler. Consequently, he decided to remain in the city during the epidemic and took an active interest in the day-to-day administration of the emergency. He also contributed to the major costs of the measures, which included feeding the thirty-five thousand citizens who remained shut up in their houses for forty days when quarantine was imposed on all residents. He provided an example to his courtiers and employed them to undertake surveys of the poor and needy to decide to whom food and alms should be provided.[21]

Among these surveys was one at the beginning of the epidemic to address unsanitary conditions that were regarded as creating the conditions that caused plague.[22] 'Gentlemen of the Court' were appointed to identify which streets and households had leaking cesspits and defective water supplies that required mending, as well as which individuals slept in unsanitary conditions, either without a mattress or with a straw palliasse that was filthy and falling apart and needed replacing. Their survey contains the following accounts of the living conditions in a medieval tower at the Canto alla Paglia that had four separate apartments, each with problems of its own:[23]

> On the first floor of the said tower: to the widow Monna Lisabetta a new straw mattress; climbing another staircase: to Monna Lisabetta, wife of Bartolommeo Porta, another mattress; to Monna Francesca on the said floor: mend a cesspit.
> On the top floor: a mattress to Andrea the tailor; and instruct the landlord of the said [apartments], who is the above-mentioned Moscellaro, to have carried away all the rubbish in the said house because it causes a great stink.
> The house which is built next door to the son of the widow the stretcher-bearer: a new straw mattress and empty the well; the landlord of it is called il Grazzini.

This short extract from the Gentlemen's survey enables us to determine both how contemporaries characterized 'the poor' and how they thought their living conditions determined that poverty. First, this group of a half-dozen people was living in rented accommodation in cramped rooms in or next to a medieval tower. They were obviously living in squalid conditions with a landlord who was normally too mean to have the rubbish cleared away. In this and the house next door there were also problems with either the supply of clean water or the system to deal with human waste. We know that two of these women were widows, presumably living in straitened circumstances. They were too poor to buy decent mattresses, and it must be remembered that mattresses were mentioned here because they were seen as harbouring the poison of plague. Finally, two of the men would also have been regarded as potentially suspect within the context of plague – Andrea the tailor because he dealt with cloth and the stretcher-bearer because he came into contact with the sick.

The surveyors believed that these unsanitary conditions created and increased the corrupt vapours that were seen as fomenting plague. As the grand-ducal librarian Francesco Rondinelli put it, 'filth is the mother of corruption'.[24] The exercise continued throughout the month, and towards the end of August the members of the commission noted an alarming growth of 'misery, necessity and sickness' among the poor.[25] They saw a direct relationship between the built environment and disease, with the former creating the conditions that led to and exacerbated the spread of an epidemic.

The importance of outlining the Florentine authorities' varied reactions to plague is to emphasize that each of these separate activities generated records, a surprising number of which have survived.[26] Henderson's forthcoming monograph uses these to explore in detail the demographic aspect of the project.[27] Like Justin Champion's study of London, it analyzes an area of the city as a case study. In Florence this was the parish of San Lorenzo, the largest in the city, located in the northwestern quadrant with boundaries virtually co-terminus with the quarter of San Giovanni. In this period it contained about 14 per cent of the city's population.[28]

130 *John Henderson and Colin Rose*

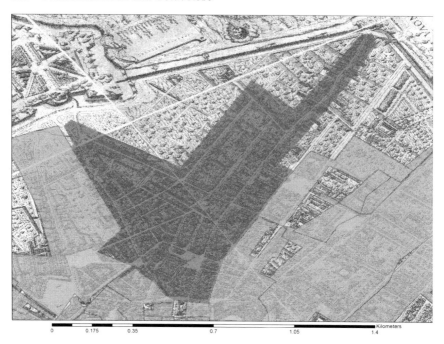

Figure 7.1 Buonsignori map of Florence showing the quarter of San Giovanni/parish of San Lorenzo.

San Lorenzo was chosen because of the survival of a rich cross section of records for both mortality and census-type information, which provide data on the socioeconomic and topographical character of the parish. Though best known for its close association with the Medici family, which had built their palace in San Lorenzo,[29] the parish had a very mixed social character. It contained a substantial concentration of artisan families, especially those working in the textile industries. It had streets dominated by patrician palaces, such as Via Ginori close to the centre, and others with a substantial number of large religious, monastic, and hospital buildings, such as Via S. Gallo, the arterial road leading to the northern city gate. Topographically, it was an area of contrasts, with substantial high-density housing mixed in with palaces and substantial ecclesiastical building complexes.

The initial aim in studying San Lorenzo was to examine the changing pattern of mortality and morbidity in the parish in relation to its social and physical character. A detailed database was compiled with the aim of mapping the results by linking them to a detailed reconstruction of housing types and density. This database is at the centre of the collaboration with the DECIMA project, as Colin Rose explains later in this chapter.

The broader comparative research study of which this forms a part has revealed significant differences between Florence and London. In England the vast majority of those who died from plague were buried in their parish. In major Italian cities, plague victims were buried either in extramural plague pits or in cemeteries at the isolation hospitals or *lazaretti*. This meant, in theory at least, that Italian city parish registers would not have included those who had died of plague, although there were exceptions in the case of some of the more affluent victims.

Fortunately, in Florence a series of registers has survived that indicates the impact of the epidemic of 1630–31 on the city. The most complete consists of lists of households visited by the representatives of the public health authorities during the autumn of 1630, when the epidemic was at its height. These record individuals taken to the isolation hospitals between autumn 1630 and the official end of the plague, in late July 1631. Inevitably, there are differences in the completeness of each source, the periods covered, and the level of detail provided.[30] The most problematic in terms of consistent detail provided about individuals were the records of burials attributed to plague.[31] The two most complete registers provide complementary information and together cover most of the period when plague was in the city. The first register covers a period of six weeks during the autumn of 1630, when mortality was at its height.[32] This is a record of those sent to the *lazaretto* of San Miniato, with a record of those who were buried, the houses that were locked, and the names of some of those who remained inside and who were provided with food by the city authorities. Two entries provide some idea of what happened when somebody was suspected of having plague:[33]

> Francesco di Domenico Castrucci, aged 15 months, lives in [Via] Campaccio next to Maestro Giovanni, surgeon, and opposite the Nuns of S. Appollonia; sent the said day [15 October 1630] through the report of Morandini. House seized.
>
> On 24 October 1630: Caterina di Francesco Porta, lives in Via di S. Zanobi next to Porta di S. Barbano, and her male child, are sent this day through the report of Morandini.
>
> In the house there remains only one person, locked up, and it has been ordered to lock the main door on the street.

In both instances the names of the main suspect are provided: in the first case it is Francesco, an infant of fifteen months, and in the second it is Caterina di Francesco Porta and her male child. All were sent to the *lazaretto* of San Miniato. Each had been identified as sick by one of the surgeons appointed by the Sanità in the quarter of S. Giovanni. Fairly specific details were provided about where they lived; for example, the infant Francesco lived in a house identified by the street (Via Campaccio) as well as in relation to a neighbour, the surgeon Giovanni, and by location behind the convent of S. Apollonia. These details enabled the brothers of the confraternity of the Misericordia to find the sick person they were to transport to San Miniato.

The second register recorded all the houses that had been locked because one or more of the occupants had been diagnosed with plague and taken off to the *lazaretto*; some had died there. This register covered the western part of the quarter of San Giovanni. There is a two-week overlap between these two registers, but the second one covers a much longer period, to the middle of September of the following year, six weeks beyond the official end of the plague epidemic. However, it provides much less specific information about those implicated. While the person who was taken to the *lazaretto* was identified, the co-residents who remained shut up in the house as members of the infected or suspected household were simply identified with a number:[34]

> 25 November 1630: Via Romita at the Madonna, Dorotea di Bartolomeo cook for having gone to S. Miniato; five remaining.
> 27 November 1630: Via San Zanobi next to the Porta di Barbano for the death of Madonna Laura; ten remaining.

There is sufficient detail to trace the spread of the plague from street and sometimes even sections of the street. In the case of Madonna Laura, the house was close to the one in Via San Zanobi where Caterina di Francesco Porta had been identified in the previous register as sick and subsequently carried to S. Miniato.

The next stage of the study was to place the morbidity data within a wider socioeconomic context to help us understand the factors underlying the spread of plague. In addition to the methodology employed for the analysis of the Great Plague in London, a particularly detailed series of records helped characterize the parish. Unlike in London, where hearth tax records survive from before and after the plague, in Florence a complete census of the city has survived only from a point two years after the epidemic had ceased (1632). This census assessed how many people had died from plague.[35] It also provides detailed information of the resident population, with names of heads of household by street and trade, together with the numbers of male and females within each household below and above the age of fifteen years. This enables one to provide a general characterization of the socioeconomic character of the parish of San Lorenzo after the plague. Litchfield's study, written after research for the present project was completed, provides a wider context for the present study, for he examined the impact of plague on the whole city for November 1630. Identifying the quarter of S. Giovanni as among the areas of the city worst affected, he provided a general characterization of the socioeconomic background of plague victims and the probable impact of the epidemic on the city's population as reflected in the 1632 census.[36]

One of the significant findings of the initial analysis is that the inhabitants of S. Lorenzo suffered more severely from the epidemic than did residents of the city overall.[37] During autumn 1630 a disproportionately high number of those admitted to the *lazaretti* (28 per cent) came from the parish, which contained about 14 per cent of the population of the city. This may very well be linked to the fact that the plague epidemic arrived from the north along the road to Bologna and first entered the city through the northern Porta San Gallo, from where it spread throughout the quarter of S. Giovanni. Slightly later the western part of the city also came to be infected, plague having been introduced through the Porta al

Prato. Although plague did break out in the other two quarters of the city, it was less severe in those areas.[38]

Just as some parts of the city had higher infection rates, so some parts of the parish of S. Lorenzo were more affected than others. The central question that arises at this point is: how far did the socioeconomic and topographical character of each street contribute to its fate? The results of this analysis cannot be more than hinted at here, but again it is useful to outline the methodology that will, as in the case of the study of the plague in London, help us to arrive at some tentative conclusions. Having determined the morbidity rates from plague for each street in the parish of S. Lorenzo, we next constructed a picture of the topographical and socioeconomic character of each street. The physical character was best reconstructed through a comparison of Stefano Buonsignori's 1584 map of Florence with the first really detailed and accurate map of the city in 1832, associated with the cadastral survey of that year.[39] With these two maps it was possible to obtain approximate measurements of the streets and buildings and then to put them together with data from the 1632 census, linking, for example, the number of houses listed in the fiscal document with those represented on both the 1584 and 1832 maps. The 1632 census also provides a wealth of information about the resident population, which, even if it has to be interpreted with caution, can help to characterize each household resident in the parish of S. Lorenzo. The results of the analysis of three streets with different profiles – Via de'Ginori, Via S. Zanobi, and Via Romita – will be presented briefly before we turn to Colin Rose's discussion of the methodology associated with mapping the plague epidemic.

The three streets chosen for analysis each presented different characteristics and had different rates of morbidity. The first, Via de'Ginori, was situated in the city centre and had a frontage of some 434 metres, the total of the frontage of the houses on both sides. It was one of the grandest streets in the parish and contained a series of large patrician palaces. According to the 1632 census, the street possessed a high proportion of heads of household with surnames and larger than average numbers of servants. Overall the street suffered very little from the epidemic; only seven cases of plague were reported, or 0.7 per cent of the total number of 1,046 in the whole parish over the course of the year 1630–31. Indeed, contemporaries noted that few patricians died over this year, and most deaths recorded in their houses tended to be those of servants.[40] Lower patrician mortality can presumably be attributed the fact that the owners had either fled to their villas in the countryside or remained shut up in their city palaces and thus had less contact with the outside world than the poorer sort who had to travel round the city to buy food or work.

While low morbidity rates may have been expected in these palatial, stone-built constructions, few studies of plague have attempted to go beyond the straightforward dichotomy between the rich and the poor. With a closer comparison between the factors mentioned earlier, a more nuanced picture emerges. Via S. Zanobi, in the north of the parish, was identified by the Health Board as having been particularly badly affected, and indeed its morbidity rate was 15 per cent of the parish total with 161 cases. Via S. Zanobi had a considerably longer street frontage than Via de' Ginori (810 versus 434 metres), but it had much greater housing density. The 1632 census recorded that Via de' Ginori contained 52 houses, whereas Via S. Zanobi had only 180. Occupational profile also differed: Via S. Zanobi was far from being patrician and had long been closely associated with textile production. In the 1562 and 1632 censuses, the majority of the heads of household were registered as employed to perform the more menial tasks of the wool and silk industries.[41]

The third street examined, Via Romita (today the top section of Via S. Antonino), is to the west of Via de' Ginori. Like Via S. Zanobi, it was long associated largely with the textile trade. Only sixty-six cases of suspected plague were reported (6.31 per cent of the parish total). Yet, because it was the shortest of the three examples, with a street frontage of only 183 metres, there were an average of two cases for each of its thirty-three houses, higher than in Via S. Zanobi with 1.12 cases for its 180 houses. One of the reasons for the difference was undoubtedly the density of the housing stock: Via Romita was the more crowded street; houses occupied narrow plots and contained, even after the plague, 7.6 people on average, while conditions in Via S. Zanobi were relatively more spacious, for houses contained on average 6.8 persons.

These correlations between the incidence of plague and the socioeconomic character of the streets represent only the first results of the analysis. Just as not all poorer areas within the city were equally affected, so not all the poorer streets had equivalent levels of morbidity even when contiguous. This question as to why this might have been the case will be explored in detail for the whole parish when an analysis of the socioeconomic profile of each street combined with its topographical character will provide a much more nuanced picture of the incidence of plague and its physical context.

Even during the initial stages of this comparative research project, it became increasingly clear how important it was to go beyond the graphic presentation of the data and represent it visually on a contemporary map. The aim then was to find a programme that could automatically link the database of plague mortality to the data from the census. In this way, we hoped, it would be possible to demonstrate clearly the chronological spread of plague and also to show clearly the relationship between patterns of mortality and morbidity and the socioeconomic and topographical profile of different streets within the parish. This was where the DECIMA project came in.

Mapping an epidemic's passage: change over time in the DECIMA HGIS

The plague of 1630–31 presented an excellent opportunity to test DECIMA's capacity for temporal mapping. This is possibly the most important aspect of HGIS for social historians, who are above all interested in process over event and in the effects of change on communities rather than individuals. The ability to analyze change over time is a major advance in historical cartography, which not only allows historians to demonstrate visually their research but also prompts new questions about the relationship between time and space. John Henderson's data set on the impact of the 1630–31 plague is a rich trove of temporal data.[42] Using the weekly totals of plague cases on a street-by-street basis and coupling these with analysis of street-level population density, DECIMA analyzes the impact of the plague with an eye to its movement from street to street. Mapping this data *over time* demonstrates that the plague of 1630–31 was fickle: some streets were hit extremely hard, while others were left relatively unscathed. This section describes the process of mapping an epidemic as a data set representing temporal change, the challenges encountered along the way, and the new forms of analysis and research questions that emerged.

The plague database covering the limited time frame of one year has provided the opportunity to develop DECIMA's capacity to map change over time. The complete data set required only minor modifications to become a time-enabled vector layer, with mensal plague morbidity attached to the street map of the parish of San Lorenzo, resulting in two layers in the DECIMA platform. One is a static data set that tracks the plague's weekly morbidity on a per-street basis and morbidity per capita, per metre of street frontage, and per household. This layer was comparatively simple to create and immediately lent a new dimension to the plague data, analyzing these significant variables in a single frame. The geographic dispersal of plague mortality at a given moment was made clear and led to the need for a layer that would demonstrate changes in mortality over time.

The second layer is the more dynamic of the two and organizes plague morbidity by monthly, rather than weekly, totals for simplicity's sake. It was created using a 'one-to-many join' operated through ArcMap's 'Make Query Table' tool. By arranging the plague data with time, rather than location, as the organizing principle, the HGIS researcher can use ArcMap not simply to show data at a given moment in time but also to demonstrate, visually, how those data change over time. This is a major advance in historical cartography. While projects such as *Mapping the Republic of Letters*, at Stanford University, the *Animated Atlas of African History*, from Brown University, and *The Atlas of Early Printing*, by the University of Iowa Libraries, all employ time lines and time-sliders to demonstrate, respectively, the progress of various 'Grand Tours', the development of colonial states in Africa, and the spread of print houses across Europe, DECIMA presents something distinctly different.[43] These projects maintain geography as their major spatial focus: time is used to show change over place, as travellers passed through Sicily, as colonial states were built and overthrown across the African continent, and as the printing press was developed in Strasbourg and rapidly picked up throughout Christendom. *Through, across, around*: geographical terms, shaping geographical thinking with the help of time. DECIMA's analysis of the 1630–31 plague reverses this and uses geography as an aid to temporal thinking: we show how streets and households suffered *during* the plague, how many sick people were taken away *throughout* its passage, and *when* the pestilence struck particular places and areas. John Henderson's data allow this, as they can use both geography and time to shape analysis.

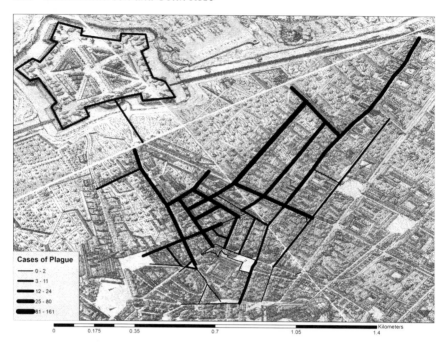

Figure 7.2 Total plague morbidity in San Lorenzo parish, 1630–31.

To my knowledge, DECIMA is the only HGIS project that employs street-level social data, organized by time, to map change over time for a social historical project.[44] That this type of approach is attracting interest can be seen from the ongoing research project of Neil Cummins, Morgan Kelly, and Cormac Ó Gráda on plague in early modern London, which has recently produced an animated map of the spread of plague by parish across the city during the epidemic (http://neilcummins.com/PlagueinLondon.html).[45]

In the analysis of the Florence data, space does not move, but time does, and as it moves so does the plague. The map shows how the plague struck harder in particular months and seemed almost to disappear from the parish of San Lorenzo at others, how it flared up in different times in different places, and how it seemed not just to follow the major transit routes but spread erratically through the neighbourhood from autumn 1630 to early summer 1631.

The preparation for this temporal analysis was not straightforward. The data themselves have some spatial limitations. Temporal mapping significantly changes the way social historians should think about time and its relation to space: to understand change, we should prioritize the first and use the second as the supporting material.

Old parish, new map: limitations of the San Lorenzo plague data

John Henderson's database of plague mortality tracks the 1630–31 epidemic across forty-five streets in the parish of San Lorenzo. The DECIMA street map, as it stood when Henderson first discussed his data, matched up to only twenty-four of those, a problem that diminished the scope and power of his database. The street map, built as it was from modern OpenStreetMap data, did not account for many of the small streets and *canti* (corners) in the parish, much less the Gomitolo del Oro or (between Borgo la Noce and Via S. Antonino) the vaguely named 'da S. Maria del Fiore'.[46] By continually refining the DECIMA street map, dividing modern streets into the pre modern segments, and working with visualizations of the parish provided by Nicholas Eckstein, I was able to identify another thirteen streets in San Lorenzo, bringing the total number of streets that I was able to match between the plague database and the street map to forty-three, a significant improvement that allows for a much more comprehensive analysis of the plague's impact over the course of 1630 and 1631

The richer the data set appended to DECIMA through projects like the plague data, the greater its analytical powers become and the more widely useful it is to a broad range of social, economic, and demographic historians, among other researchers. The focus of the plague morbidity GIS is the number of plague victims. The database includes a great many more data, such as total plague morbidity in relation to the socioeconomic structure of each street after the plague as recorded in the 1632 census; topographical information, including housing density and structure; and the results of the environmental survey in August 1630. This is all analyzed easily in the static layer of the plague map but is more difficult to conceive of on a temporal basis. Knowing the monthly population numbers and the resulting impact of plague morbidity proportional to those population figures would allow for more advanced temporal mapping. The DECIMA continues to improve on these challenges, as an organic and growing Historical GIS project, which by its nature tends never to be truly 'finished'.

Temporalizing spatial data: from street by street to month by month

The data in the plague database presented an immediate cartographic challenge. In Henderson's Excel© spreadsheet, mortality data were organized by street on the y-axis and by weeks on the x-axis (i.e. moving right and left through the database demonstrated temporal data, and moving up or down demonstrated spatial data). ArcMap, for all its analytical capabilities, will do only *exactly what its operator tells it*. Among other things, the program has been told that time exists on a y-axis, and in order to operate time in its cartography, this must indeed be the case in all data.[47] The data needed to be transformed from their form of presentation in Table 7.1 into a database organized by time, as in Table 7.2.

The organizational differences should be immediately apparent: the original data contain one row for each street, and across the columns of that row are inserted the temporal data, organized by weeks (a,b,c,d) in months (1–12). The y-axis (rows) is a geographic description of place: the street name, where the x-axis (columns) tracks temporal data. In the modified database, time exists on the y-axis: all thirteen rows of the second table are data for Via Sant'Orsola, one of the parish's harder-hit streets during the early stages of the plague.

138 *John Henderson and Colin Rose*

Table 7.1 Selection of John Henderson's original database

Via Week	10c	10d	11a	11b	11c	11d	12a	12b
Borgo la Noce		4	5	2	7	2	1	1
Borgo S. Lorenzo					2	1	1	5
Canto al Monteloro		1		2	2	1		
Canto alla Paglia						1		
Canto alle Macine	4			6	1	5	1	2
Canto del Giglio		2						
Canto di Bernadetto					1			
Canto di Puccino					1			
Da S. Maria del Fiore						1		

Table 7.2 Reorganized data prepared for temporal mapping

Street	Date	Cases
Via Sant'Orsola	1630/10/31	2
Via Sant'Orsola	1630/11/31	2
Via Sant'Orsola	1630/12/31	0
Via Sant'Orsola	1631/01/31	0
Via Sant'Orsola	1631/02/28	1
Via Sant'Orsola	1631/03/31	0
Via Sant'Orsola	1631/04/30	0
Via Sant'Orsola	1631/05/31	0
Via Sant'Orsola	1631/06/30	0
Via Sant'Orsola	1631/07/31	0
Via Sant'Orsola	1631/08/31	6
Via Sant'Orsola	1631/09/30	5
Via Sant'Orsola	1631/10/31	16

Moving down the y-axis, from 31 October 1630 to 31 October 1631, monthly totals of plague deaths are appended primarily to the date (the variable that changes) and secondarily to the street (which remains static on the y-axis, until one street has cycled through the full year; only then does the next street appear, with its thirteen rows, after which the name of the next street appears). In order for time to act as an analytical variable in GIS, it needs to be the operating y-axis, with geography (streets) secondary to time (months). This transformation took some consideration, but the end result is 408 entries that detail the progress of the plague over twelve months (plus a 'total' number, here faked by the date 31 October 1631) on forty-three streets.

Another of ArcMap's idiosyncratic programming characteristics is that geography must remain on the y-axis to be legible in the map as a 'shape'. This is a result of the nature of vector data. The street map of early modern Florence that is the basis of the plague analysis counts each street as a *line segment*, part of a *polyline feature*. Each street occupies a row in the layer's *attribute table*, which tracks the street shapes running down the y-axis and appends data, such as the name of the road, its length, and its current road type, in fields along the x-axis. The attribute table for the street map looks like this:

Table 7.3 Selection from attribute table of the DECIMA layer *San Lorenzo Streets*, extracted from OpenStreetMap vector data

OBJECTID	FME_TYPE	HIGHWAY	NAME	Shape_Length
1	fme_line	tertiary	Via Larga	0.007257
2	fme_line	residential	Via S. Gallo	0.008052
3	fme_line	residential	Via dell'Amore	0.001091
4	fme_line	residential	Via Panicale	0.00212
5	fme_line	pedestrian	Borgo la Noce	0.001265
6	fme_line	residential	Via Mozza	0.004172
7	fme_line	service	Via Romita	0.001167
8	fme_line	residential	Via dell'Ariento	0.002246
9	fme_line	pedestrian	Canto alla Paglia	0.001612
10	fme_line	residential	Via Sant'Orsola	0.000983

Each row in Table 7.3 represents a *shape* read by ArcMap and converted to a *line* that is the cartographic representation of a *street* in Florence. This is the only way that ArcMap will read shapes, as rows descending the Y-axis, with their attributes appended on the X-axis. The same is true for the polygon shapes that represent the city's various administrative and social divisions and for the point shapes that represent the individual household entries in the *Decima ricerche*, geolocated onto the DECIMA HGIS. Having reorganized the database of plague morbidity, simplifying it as I went, to make time the operating principle of the resulting GIS layer, I was then faced with the challenge of exactly how to append the new plague data, in which each street appeared in thirteen consecutive rows, to the DECIMA street map, which gave each street only one.

Appending temporal street attributes to a single street shape

The process of transforming the plague mortality data into a time-oriented data table was necessary preparation work in order to tag the temporal data to the street map of the city. The operation necessary to do so is referred to in database management circles as a 'one-to-many join', that is, the attaching of one piece of data (in this case, the individual street in San Lorenzo) to many pieces of data (in this case, the twelve months plus total of plague morbidity data for each of those streets). Performing this operation allowed for the creation of a time-based and enabled layer that would animate the impact of the plague as it travelled through time. In this layer, geography does not change, but this animation does allow us both to visualize the plague as a temporal phenomenon and also to analyze it as a process that was affected by the passage of time.

Creating the one-to-many join is relatively simple, but it requires a basic understanding of SQL querying (the expressions used to ask questions of a database). GIS software can be very finicky to use, and it is necessary to provide very exact instructions. The first join used for this project created the static map of plague data discussed earlier; this was a simple function of ArcMap's 'Join' command, which joined up as many street names as possible between the street map and the mortality data on a basic word-match: wherever the street map matched the plague database, the mortality data were appended to the street's attribute table. This can be done regardless of how the GIS is organized, as feature classes in a geodatabase or as shapefiles in a folder or series of folders. Once the two elements are layered in the GIS, the join is possible regardless of their location.

The one-to-many join requires that both elements be loaded in advance into the same *geodatabase* as a *feature class*, which must contain the *shape* of your desired layer, and as a *table*, which must contain the data for every iteration of the desired join. The first step in creating the time-dynamic plague map, then, was to load the street map and the plague table into a DECIMA geodatabase, where I had been previously working with the more flexible but less analytically robust shapefile formats. Once built, the geodatabase proved powerful enough that I migrated the entire DECIMA data set into it. Geodatabases are practical and effective ways to organize spatial-temporal data on a single machine or a local server, but they are difficult to employ in a WebGIS such as the DECIMA online portal. They provide significantly greater analytical capacities than shapefiles, such as the ability to create the one-to-many join necessary for temporally dynamic mapping.

With the DECIMA geodatabase operating, the next step was to create the one-to-many join. Using the ArcGIS toolbox, under 'Data Management Tools' and then under 'Table and Layer Views', I used the tool 'Make Query Table' to create this type of join. This tool allows one to query a feature of the geodatabase according to the characteristics of another database. To create the plague map, I input the time-organized mortality table and the street map feature class, selected all the fields from the plague data for output and only the 'shape' of the street map. The resulting table, which can be transformed quickly into a feature class layer, appends the shape of the street map to each instance of the street in the mortality table. It is organized by time and allows for the creation of a street map of the parish of San Lorenzo that can show both static representations of plague mortality in a given month and dynamic animations of the plague's impact over the course of a year. This chapter contains snapshots of that map; the dynamic version is accessible via the DECIMA Web portal.

Conclusion

The 1630 plague struck at a time when the ability of governments to record and archive information was rapidly growing, far outpacing the ability of governments to actually affect the course of a natural disaster of such magnitude. With a significant bureaucratic and courtly apparatus, Grand Duke Ferdinand II resolved to face the plague head on. Before it arrived, he organized a citywide inspection program designed to ward off the conditions that, in Florentine thought, bred sickness; it is not coincidental that these very conditions were those of poverty and urban decay. When, despite all these efforts, plague struck the city, Ferdinand remained while other nobles fled, and he continued to direct a program that sought to limit the plague's destructiveness. In reality, perhaps the most tangible result was the creation of large sets of records about who became ill, where they lived, and how the city managed the mounting numbers of plague victims.

Because of the relationship, noted both by modern historians and by their early modern subjects, between the conditions of one's physical environment and the onset of the plague, the records of morbidity drawn from various areas of the city must be placed in the context of those areas' economic and demographic characteristics. DECIMA helps to visualize the results of that analysis in ways that are lost in spreadsheets and their explication. Spatializing the spread of plague over time, as Henderson and Rose have done, shows how the plague struck Florence dynamically, moving from one street to another and then back. It also shows how particular streets close to the walls and accessible to gates were much more susceptible to illness than others. The housing densities, average property values, and occupational structures of these streets can be mapped against their experience of the plague to test the link between poverty and plague.

Mapping change over time carries its own challenges, with some of them again being specific to early modernist concerns. The methods used to record an epidemic may change between one epidemic and the next; indeed, they may evolve over the course of one plague. Ensuring the compatibility of data sets from different periods is essential. Here, with a limited time frame and a limited documentary basis, we were able to successfully map the recorded experience of the 1630–31 plague over its entire passage. Mapping change over time significantly increases the utility of HGIS and other platforms to social historians, as the plague map of Florence demonstrates nicely.

Notes

1. F. Rondinelli, *Relazione del Contagio*, Florence, 1634, 36.
2. J. Henderson, *Death in Florence*, New Haven, CT: Yale University Press, forthcoming; I am grateful to Yale University Press for allowing me to publish the material in this article which forms part of the forthcoming monograph.
3. I am very grateful to Derek Keene for his invaluable advice on the mapping of this epidemic.
4. A.D. Cliff, M.R. Smallman-Raynor, and P.M. Stevens, 'Controlling the geographical spread of infectious disease: Plague in Italy, 1347–1851, *Acta Medico-Historica Adriatica* 7, 2009, 197–236.
5. L. Del Panta, *Le epidemie nella storia demografica italiana (secoli XIV–XIX)*, Turin: Loescher, 1980, 161–69.
6. J.L. Stevens Crawshaw, *Plague Hospitals: Public Health for the City in Early Modern Venice*, Farnham, UK: Ashgate, 2012; I. Fosi (ed.), *La Peste a Roma (1656–1657), Roma Moderna e contemporanea* XIV, 2006; I. Fusco, *Peste, demografia e fiscalità*

nel Regno di Napoli del XVII secolo, Milan: Franco Angeli, 2007; A.L. Moote and D.C. Moote, *The Great Plague. The Story of London's Most Deadly Year*, Baltimore, MD: Johns Hopkins University Press, 2006; J.S. Amerlang (trans. and ed.), *A Journal of the Plague Year: The Diary of a Barcelona Tanner Miquel Parets 1651*, Oxford, UK: Oxford University Press, 1991; K. Wilson Bowers, *Plague Public Health in Early Modern Seville*, Rochester, NY: Rochester University Press, 2013.

7 S.K. Cohn, *Cultures of Plague: Medical Thinking at the end of the Renaissance*, Oxford, UK: Oxford University Press, 2010; G.A. Bailey, P.M. Jones, F. Mormando, and T.W. Worcester, *Hope and Healing: Painting in Italy in a Time of Plague, 1500–1800*, Chicago, IL: University of Chicago Press, 2004.

8 K.I. Bos, P. Stevens, K. Nieselt, H.N. Poinar, S.N. DeWitte, and J. Krause, 'A Draft Genome of Yersinia Pestis from the Victims of the Black Death', *Nature*, 478, October 2011, 506–10. For a recent discussion of the topic from both scientists and historians see: M. Green (ed.), 'Pandemic Disease in the Medieval World: Rethinking the Black Death', *The Medieval Globe* 1, 2014.

9 R.B. Litchfield, *Florence Ducal Capital, 1530–1630*, New York, NY: ACLS Humanities E-Book, 2008. Online. Available <http://quod.lib.umich.edu/cgi/t/text/text-idx?c=acls;cc=acls;view=toc;idno=heb90034.0001.001> (accessed 7 August 2015).

10 G. Alfani, *Calamities and the Economy in Renaissance Italy: The Grand Tour of the Horsemen of the Apocalypse*, London, UK: Palgrave, 2013; G. Alfani and S.K. Cohn, 'Nonantola 1630: Anatomia di una pestilenza e meccanismi del contagio: Con riflessioni a partire dalle epidemie milanesi della prima età moderna', *Popolazione e Storia* 2, 2007, 99–138.

11 J.A.I. Champion, *London's Dreaded Visitation. The Social Geography of the Great Plague in 1665*, Historical Geography Research Series, No. 31, London, 1995; J. Champion (ed.), *Epidemic Disease in London*, Centre for Metropolitan History Working Papers Series, No. 1, London, UK: Centre of Metropolitan History, 1992; G. Twigg, *Bubonic Plague: A Much Misunderstood Disease*, Ascot, UK: Derwent Press, 2013.

12 N. Cummins, M. Kelly, and C.Ó. Gráda, 'Living Standards and Plague in London, 1560–1665', *Economic History Review*, 2015, 1–32.

13 Del Panta, *Le epidemie nella storia demografica italiana*, 160: table 24.

14 J. Henderson, '"La schifezza, madre di corruzione": Peste e società a Firenze nella prima epoca moderna', *Medicina e Storia* 2, 2001, 23–56.

15 The figures for this graph derives from a letter sent to Francesco Rondinelli, a copy of which is contained in the library of the late Carlo Cipolla. I am very grateful for permission to use the data here.

16 Rondinelli, *Relazione del Contagio*, 26–27.

17 See, for example, Preto, *Peste e società a Venezia*; Cohn, *Cultures of Plague*.

18 On these measures in Florence in 1630–31 see: D. Lombardi, '1629–31: Crisi e peste a Firenze', *Archivio storico italiano* CXXXVII, 1979, 3–50; D. Sardi Bucci, 'La peste del 1630 a Firenze', *Ricerche storiche* X, 1980, 49–92; M.B. Ciofi, 'La peste del 1630 a Firenze con particolare riferimento ai provvedimenti igienico-sanitari e sociali', *Archivio storico italiano* CXLII, 1984, 47–75.

19 See Calvi, *Histories of a Plague Year*.

20 Cf. M.L. Leonard, 'Plague epidemics and public health in Mantua, 1463–1577', PhD thesis, University of Glasgow, 2014.

21 Contemporaries wrote a series of encomia about him, praising him for his role during the plague: Rondinelli, *Relazione del Contagio*, 66–67; M. Guiducci, 'Panegirico', in Rondinelli, *Relazione del Contagio*, 109–39.

22 Discussed in Henderson, *Death in Florence*, ch. 7; and see also: N.A. Eckstein, 'Florence on foot: An eye-level mapping of the early modern city in time of plague', *Renaissance Studies*, 2015.

23 Archivio di Stato di Firenze (ASF), Compagnie Religiose Soppresse da Leopoldo (CRS), 1418.II, nos. 210–12. See N. Eckstein article in this volume.

24 F. Rondinelli, *Relazione del contagio*, 24.
25 ASF, *CRS*, 1418.II, 28.8.1630.
26 J. Henderson, '"La schifezza, madre di corruzione"'; J. Henderson, 'Epidemie, Miasmi e il corpo dei poveri a Firenze nella Prima Età Moderna', *Storia Urbana* 112, February 2007, 17–37; 'More Feared Than Death Itself'? Isolation Hospitals and Plague in Seventeenth-century Florence', in: C. Bonfield, T. Huguet-Termes, and J. Reinarz (eds), *Hospitals and Communities, 1100–1960*, London, UK, and Bern, Switzerland: Peter Lang, 2013, 21–44.
27 Henderson, *Death in Florence*.
28 P. Pieraccini, 'Note di demografia fiorentina: La parrocchia di S.Lorenzo dal 1652 al 1751', *Archivio storico italiano* VII, 1925, 44–45, has 16 per cent over the whole period.
29 D. Kent, *Cosimo de' Medici and the Florentine Renaissance: The Patron's Oeuvre*, New Haven, CT, and London, UK: Yale University Press, 2000.
30 Litchfield, *Florence Ducal Capital*, 344–50.
31 AFM, 259: 'Morti in tempo di contagio dal 1630 al 1633'. Litchfield and, before him, Deanna Sardi Bucci, 'La peste di 1630 a Firenze', have plotted these data for the whole of the city (though the former concentrated on the November data), providing a useful context for the present study.
32 ASF, *Sanità*, 463.
33 Ibid., ff. 1r, 31v.
34 ASF, *Sanità*, 467, ff. 14r, 16r.
35 Cf. Champion, *London's Dreaded Visitation*. For the 1632 Florentine census see: BNCF, Palatino EB XV.2 See also the surviving sections of the census of the city taken in January 1631: *Sanità*, 465: 'Sesto di S. Spirito; Carte Strozziane Serie I.XIX: Sesto di S. Croce.
36 Litchfield, *Florence Ducal Capital*, 344–50, esp. 350: Table 7.1.
37 Henderson, '"La schifezza, madre di corruzione"'.
38 Litchfield, *Florence Ducal Capital*, 347–48.
39 See G. Fanelli, *Firenze nel periodo della restaurazione (1814–1864): Una mappa delle trasformazioni edilizie*, Roma, Edizioni Kappa, 1989.
40 Litchfield, *Florence Ducal Capital*, 346.
41 Ibid.
42 N. Eckstein, in this volume, uses geospatial data on the efforts of the Florentine *Magistrato della Sanità* to prevent a recurrence; here, Henderson tracks the plague itself, relying on the records of the sick and the dead to show its impact on a neighbourhood in Florence.
43 P. Findlen et al., 'Case Study: Travelers on the Grand Tour', *Mapping the Republic of Letters*. Online. Available <http://republicofletters.stanford.edu/casestudies/grandtour.html> (accessed 21 June 2015); N. Jacobs and R. Peñate, *Animated Atlas of African History*. Online. Available <www.brown.edu/Research/AAAH/index.htm> (accessed 21 June 2015); G. Prickman et al., *The Atlas of Early Printing*. Online. Available <http://atlas.lib.uiowa.edu/> (accessed 21 June 2015).
44 The *Republic of Letters* project is social historical, especially given its creator's interest in materiality and the relationships between things and the societies that produced them. Cf. P. Findlen (ed.), *Early Modern Things: Objects and Their Histories, 1500–1800*, London, UK: Routledge, 2013.
45 N. Cummins et al., 'Living Standards and Plague in London, 1560–1665', 1–32.
46 OpenStreetMap. Online. Available <www.openstreetmap.org/> (accessed 21 June 2015).
47 I am grateful to Marcel Fortin, Head of the Map and Data Library, Robarts Library, University of Toronto, for his patience in helping me develop the techniques required for this aspect of DECIMA and the entire project. The platform would be much thinner were it not for him. Cf. J. Bonnell and M. Fortin (eds), *Historical GIS Research in Canada*, Calgary, Canada: University of Calgary Press, 2013.

Bibliography

Manuscript sources

Archivio di Stato di Firenze (ASF), *Compagnie Religiose Sopresse da Leopoldo (CRS)*, 1418.
—— *CRS*, 1418.
—— *Sanità*, 463.
—— *Sanità*, 467.
Archivio della Fraternita della Misericordia della Firenze (AFM), 259.

Print sources

Albini, G., *Guerra, fame, peste: Crisi di mortalità e sistema sanitario nella Lombardia tardomedievale*, Bologna, Italy: Cappelli, 1982.
Alfani, G., *Calamities and the Economy in Renaissance Italy: The Grand Tour of the Horsemen of the Apocalypse*, London, UK: Palgrave, 2013.
—— and Cohn, S.K., 'Nonantola 1630: Anatomia di una pestilenza e meccanismi del contagion: Con riflessioni a partire dalle epidemie milanesi della prima età moderna', *Popolazione e Storia* 2, 2007, 99–128.
Amerlang, J.S. (trans. and ed.), *A Journal of the Plague Year: The Diary of Barcelona Tanner Miquel Parets 1651*, Oxford, UK: Oxford University Press, 1991.
Bailey, G.A., Jones, P.M., Mormando, F., and Worcester, T.W., *Hope and Healing: Painting in Italy in a Time of Plague, 1500–1800*, Chicago, IL: University of Chicago Press, 2004.
Biraben, N., *Les hommes et la peste en France*, 2 vols, Paris, France: Le Mouton, 1975–76.
Bonnell, J., and Fortin, M. (eds), *Historical GIS Research in Canada*, Calgary, Canada: University of Calgary Press, 2013.
Bos, K.I., Stevens, P., Nieselt, K., Poinar, H.N., DeWitte, S.N., and Krause, J., 'A Draft Genome of Yersinia Pestis from the Victims of the Black Death', *Nature* 478, 2011, 506–10.
Calvi, G., *Histories of a Plague Year: The Social and Imaginary in Baroque Florence*, Berkeley and Los Angeles, CA: University of California Press, 1989.
Carmichael, A.G., *Plague and the Poor in Renaissance Florence*, Cambridge, UK: Cambridge University Press, 1986.
Ceserani, G., et al., 'Case Study: Travelers on the Grand Tour', in G. Ceserani, *Mapping the Republic of Letters*, 2008. Online. Available <http://republicofletters.stanford.edu/casestudies/grandtour.html> (accessed 21 June 2015).
Champion, J.A.I. (ed.), *Epidemic Disease in London*, London, UK: Centre for Metropolitan History Working Papers Series, No. 1, 1992.
——, *London's Dreaded Visitation: The Social Geography of the Great Plague in 1665*, Historical Geography Research Series No. 31, London, UK: University of Edinburgh, 1995.
Ciofi, M.B., 'La peste del 1630 a Firenze con particolare riferimento ai provvedimenti igienico-sanitari e sociali', *Archivio storico italiano* CXLII, 1984, 115–38.
Cipolla, C.M., *Cristofano and the Plague: A Study in the History of Public Health in the Age of Galileo*, London, UK: Collins, 1973.
—— *Public Health and the Medical Profession in the Renaissance*, Cambridge, UK: Cambridge University Press, 1976.
—— *Fighting the Plague in Seventeenth-Century Tuscany*, Madison, WI: University of Wisconsin Press, 1981.

Cliff, A.D., Smallman-Raynor, M.R., and Stevens, M.R., 'Controlling the Geographical Spread of Infectious Disease: Plague in Italy, 1347–1851', *Acta Medico-Historica Adriatica* 7, 2009.
Cohn, S.K., Jr., *The Black Death Transformed. Disease and Culture in Early Renaissance Europe*, London, UK: E. Arnold, 2002.
—— *Cultures of Plague: Medical Thinking at the End of the Renaissance*, Oxford, UK: Oxford University Press, 2010.
Cummins, N., Kelly, M., and Ó Gráda, C., 'Living Standards and Plague in London, 1560–1665', *Economic History Review*, 2015.
Del Panta, L., *Le epidemie nella storia demografica italiana (secoli XIV–XIX)*, Turin, Italy: Loescher, 1980.
Findlen, P. (ed.), *Early Modern Things: Objects and Their Histories, 1500–1800*, London, UK: Routledge, 2013.
Fosi, I. (ed.), *La Peste a Roma (1656–1657), Roma Moderna e contemporanea* XIV, 2006.
Fusco, I., *Peste, demografia e fiscalità nel Regno di Napoli del XVII secolo*, Milan, Italy: Franco Angeli, 2007.
—— 'La peste nel Regno di Napoli, 1656–68: Diffusione e mortalitá', *Popolazione e Storia* 1, 2009.
Green, M. (ed.), 'Pandemic Disease in the Medieval World: Rethinking the Black Death', *The Medieval Globe* 1, 2014.
Guiducci, M., 'Panegirico', in F. Rondinelli (ed.), *Relazione del contagio stato in Firenze l'anno 1630 e 1633*, Florence, Italy: Landini, 1634, 97–124.
Henderson, J., 'Plague in Renaissance Florence: Medical Theory and Government Response', *Maladies et société (xii–xviiie siècles)*, in N. Bulst and N. Delort, (eds), Paris, France: Editions du CNRS, 1989, 165–86.
—— '"La schifezza, madre di corruzione": Peste e società a Firenze nella prima epoca moderna', *Medicina e Storia* 2, 2001, 23–56.
—— 'Historians and Plagues in Pre-Industrial Italy over the Longue Durée', *History and Philosophy of the Life Sciences*, 2004, 481–99.
—— 'Epidemie, miasmi e il corpo dei poveri a Firenze nella Prima Età Moderna', *Storia Urbana* 112, February 2007, 17–36.
—— 'More Feared Than Death Itself? Isolation Hospitals and Plague in Seventeenth-Century Florence', in C. Bonfield, T. Huguet-Termes, and J. Reinarz (eds), *Hospitals and Communities, 1100–1960*, London, UK: Peter Lang, 2013, 21–44.
—— *Death in Florence*, London, UK, and New Haven, CT: Yale University Press, [forthcoming].
Jacobs, N., and Peñate, R., *Animated Atlas of African History*, 2008. Online. Available <www.brown.edu/Research/AAAH/index.htm> (accessed 21 June 2015).
Kent, D., *Cosimo de' Medici and the Florentine Renaissance: The Patron's Oeuvre*, New Haven, CT, and London, UK: Yale University Press, 2000.
Leonard, M.L., 'Plague epidemics and public health in Mantua, 1463–1577', PhD thesis, University of Glasgow, 2014.
Litchfield, R. B., *Florence Ducal Capital, 1530–1630*, New York, NY: ACLS Humanities E-Book, *c.*2008. Online. Available <http://quod.lib.umich.edu/cgi/t/text/text-idx?c=acls;cc=acls;view=toc;idno=heb90034.0001.001> (accessed 07 August 2015).
Little, L.K., 'Plague Historians in Lab Coats', *Past and Present* 213, 2011.
Lombardi, D., '1629–31: Crisi e peste a Firenze', *Archivio storico italiano* CXXXVII, 1979.

Moote, A.L., and Moote, D.C., *The Great Plague. The Story of London's Most Deadly Year*, Baltimore, MD: Johns Hopkins University Press, 2006.

Palmer, R., 'The control of plague in Venice and N. Italy, 1348–1600', PhD thesis, University of Kent at Canterbury, 1978.

Pastore, A., *Crimine e giustizia in tempo di peste nell'Europa moderna*, Roma-Bari: Laterza, 1991.

Pieraccini, P., 'Note di demografia fiorentina: La parrocchia di S.Lorenzo dal 1652 al 1751', *Archivio storico italiano* VII, 1925, 39–76.

Preto, P., *Peste e società a Venezia*, Vicenza, Italy: Neri Pozza, 1978.

Prickman, G., *The Atlas of Early Printing*. Online. Available <http://atlas.lib.uiowa.edu/> (accessed 21 June 2015).

Rodenwaldt, E., *Pest in Venedig 1575–1577: Ein Beitrag zur Frage der Infektkette bei den Pestepidemien West-Europas*, Heidelberg, Germany: Springer, 1952.

Rondinelli, F., *Relazione del contagio stato in Firenze l'anno 1630 e 1633*, Florence, Italy: Landini, 1634.

Sardi Bucci, D., 'La peste del 1630 a Firenze', *Ricerche storiche* X, 1980.

Schofield, R.S., 'An Anatomy of an Epidemic', in P. Slack (ed.), *The Plague Reconsidered*, Matlock, UK: Local Population Studies, 1977, 95–126.

Scott, S., and Duncan, C., *Biology of Plagues. Evidence from Historical Populations*, Cambridge, UK: Cambridge University Press, 2001.

Slack, P. 'The Local Incidence of Epidemic Disease: The Case of Bristol, 1540–1650', in P. Slack (ed.), *The Plague Reconsidered*, Local Population Studies, 1977, 49–62.

——— (ed.), *The Plague Reconsidered*, Matlock, UK: Local Population Studies, 1977.

——— *The Impact of Plague in Tudor and Stuart England*, London, UK: Routledge, 1985.

Societia Italiana di Demografia Storica, *Popolazione, Società e Ambiente: Temi di Demografia Storica Italiana (secc. XVII-XIX)*, Bologna, Italy: Clueb, 1990.

Sonnino, E., and Traina, R., 'La peste del 1656–57 a Roma: Organizzazione sanitaria e mortalità', in *La demografia storica delle città italiane*, Bologna, Italy: Clueb, 1982, 433–52.

Stevens Crawshaw, J.L., *Plague Hospitals: Public Health for the City in Early Modern Venice*, Farnham, UK: Ashgate, 2012.

Twigg, G., *Bubonic Plague: A Much Misunderstood Disease*, Ascot, UK: Derwent Press, 2013.

Wilson Bowers, K., *Plague Public Health in Early Modern Seville*, Rochester, NY: Rochester University Press, 2013.

Part 3

Mapping motion, emotion, and sense

Using digital mapping to rethink categories and communication

8 Seeing sound
Mapping the Florentine soundscape

Niall Atkinson

Canto VIII of Dante's *Purgatorio* opens with a reflection on the way time was an effect of sound that brought a specific territory into being: 'It was now the hour that turns back the longing of seafaring folk and melts their heart the day they have bidden sweet friends farewell, and that pierces the new pilgrim with love if he hears from afar a bell that seems to mourn the dying day.'[1]

The evening bell, a sound that divided night from day, was one of the most universal sounds that echoed across early modern Europe.[2] For the traveller, the evening bell turned a strange place into a familiar territory of salutary promise and mitigated the longing for a distant home.[3] For Dante, bells could also transport those territories across space and extend the symbolic protective power of one's native city, a phenomenon with particular resonance for a writer in exile. The sound of the evening bell travelled widely in the Christian imagination, relaying from tower to tower across the landscape, accompanying both the peasant in the fields and the traveller on the road.[4] It ranged beyond the urban milieu in which it originated and carried its comforting message to those who found themselves in transit on the margins.

A city's soundscape was as much an expression of its identity as it was a medium through which social relations were forged and negotiated by both ritual and transgressive practices. And since the sound of an evening bell determined the limits of a city's legal control of a territory and its symbolic presence within the psychological geography of its inhabitants, mapping such networks of sound can shed a great deal of light upon the mutual effects produced by buildings and bodies on each other. This chapter focuses on Florence between the fourteenth and sixteenth centuries, taking Dante's cue about the relationship among the sound of a bell, the evocation of a social topography, and the maintenance of a collective memory embedded with the architectural matrix of the city.

To express such relationships, this essay explores certain techniques of visualization as a way of gaining a deeper and more intimate understanding of how Florentines experienced the civic relationships and networks in which they lived. These visualizations are based on and have been inspired by the DECIMA project's mapping of census data onto Stefano Buonsignori's sixteenth-century representation of the city. The DECIMA map evokes other mapping projects from both the fifteenth and nineteenth centuries that aim to measure and preserve. Yet

150 *Niall Atkinson*

it also opens ways of complicating such precise surveys, particularly as we bring in sense, sound, and ritual and see how lenses of politics, community, and the imaginary refracted all straight lines. As we map senses of the parish, sequences of bells, and paths of processions, we see how many different and dynamic topographies converged in the minds of Renaissance Florentines.

Multiple chorographies

Among the demographic data included in the entries for each household in Florence is the parish (*popolo*) in which the individuals in those households lived. Sometimes these were self-declared, but, as Colin Rose points out, sometimes it was the census takers themselves who placed a household in a particular parish. That may seem to be a minor point, but it does suggest that parishes were not

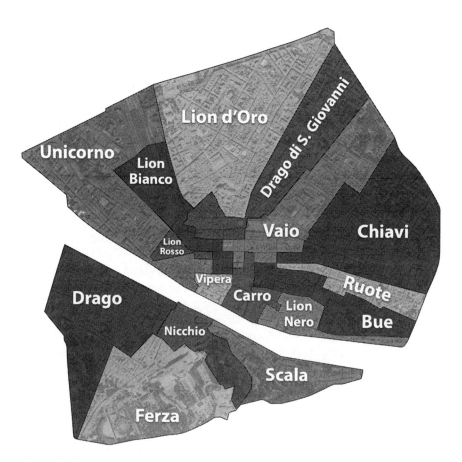

Figure 8.1 Map of the sixteen *gonfaloni* of Florence created after the political reforms of 1343 that reorganized the city within the new circuit of walls and replaced the old *sestieri*. Drawing by author.

formal in their organization and were defined by a general consensus rather than being imposed from without. This makes them rather different from the legislated borders of Florentine political wards (*gonfaloni*), which had precise demarcations and were an expression of the republican city.

Gonfaloni were no longer in use in 1561, so the only subdivision of the quarters (*quartieri*) that structure the *Decima* tax census of that year – Santo Spirito, Santa Maria Novella, San Giovanni, Santa Croce – is the parishes. However, the visualization of the parishes that emerges in 1561 does not conform to these divisions and points instead to a kind of social space that lies beyond conventional ideas about topographical borders and the territories they define. At the centre of this study, therefore, lies the parish. Where it is, who it defined, when it emerged, how it was demarcated – all these are questions whose answers are hardly self-evident, stable, or precise. In fact, parishes could be characterized as mental geographies that were brought into being by the sound of bells, not as a series of discrete acoustic territories but as a much more dynamic and interrelated phenomenon that tests the limits of our imagination to visualize them, in motion, in real historical time.

Digital mapping technologies give modern research the power to greatly enlarge the scale and scope, as well as the diversity, of historical research into Renaissance and early modern Florence. They allow us to test and confirm certain assumptions, while also providing the means of engaging in renewed ways with questions, assumptions, and experiments in charting the relationships between urban spaces and the production of knowledge, the inscription of social identity, the maintenance of collective memory, and the critical apparatuses necessary for such intellectual inquiry. These questions and experiments date back to the Renaissance itself and certainly could be traced even further back in time. Current technologies are not so much novelties as they are extensions and reiterations of an evolving dialogue about the nature of social space.

We can place the DECIMA project into historical context using two examples, from the fifteenth and nineteenth centuries. The first concerns techniques of translating spatial data reliably into a geographic representation, and the second deals with mapping social data onto a historical topographical rendering. By transforming the qualitative data of the 1561 census – names, addresses, occupations, rents – into the set of quantitative numerical coordinates and then using these coordinates to create a socio-spatial map of Florence, the DECIMA project realizes at a much larger scale a project of Leon Battista Alberti. In 1450, Alberti stood on the Capitoline hill in Rome, surveying the city around him. Using the most advanced surveying tools available, he plotted the relative positions of Rome's walls and a selection of its monuments and preserved them as precise numerical coordinates in tabular form (see Figure 8.2). The result was that anyone could reproduce an accurate map of Rome in the mid-fifteenth century by constructing a simple compass (Figure 8.3).[5]

The other example comes from the nineteenth century, in the form of a map made by Guido Carocci, the Royal Inspector of Fine Art and Antiquities in Florence and director of the National Museum of San Marco.[6]

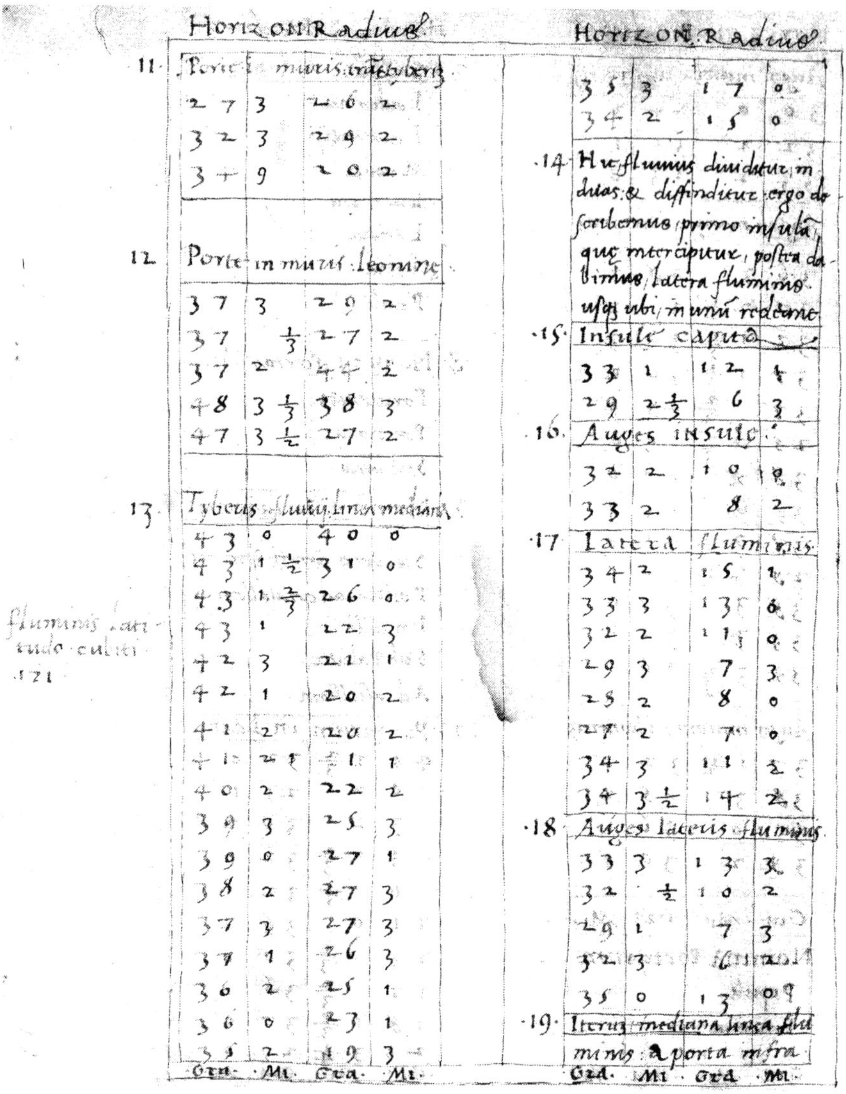

Figure 8.2 Leon Battista Alberti, *Descriptio Urbis Romae, c.*1450. These tables are taken from Alberti's treatise on mapping Rome. From his position on the Capitoline hill he tabulated the coordinates of the Aurelian walls, its gates, the river, and a selection of the city's monuments and then organized them into a database in which each site is expressed by two numerical quantities. The 'horizon' corresponds to the site's position relative to the Capitoline within a circle divided into 48 degrees. The 'radius' determines the distance of the site along a 'spoke' anchored at the centre of the map and divided into fifty-five equal sections (see Figure 8.3). (Photo courtesy of the Newberry Library, Chicago, Call # Case MS 102 27v).

Seeing sound 153

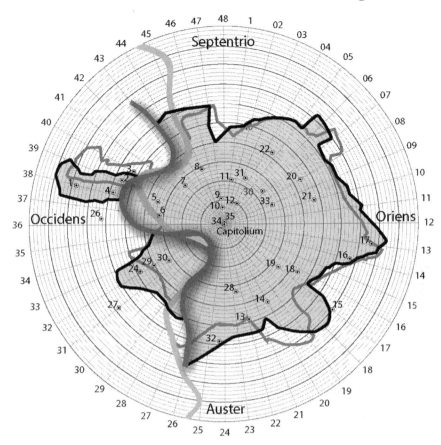

Figure 8.3 Plotting Alberti's coordinates onto a circular projection results in an endlessly reproducible and highly accurate map of Rome. It allows the user to trace the circuit of the Aurelian walls and the Leonine walls around the Vatican, the Tiber, and its island and to determine the relative positions of ancient and modern monuments around the city. Alberti's walls (black) and the course of the river (dark grey) can be compared with a map based on current cartographic coordinates (light grey). Drawing by author after Carpo and Furlan.

Carocci mapped the area of the Mercato Vecchio, today's Piazza della Repubblica, when it was slated for major redevelopment during Florence's brief tenure as the capital of Italy in the 1860s (Figure 8.4). The Mercato Vecchio was the antique forum and economic heart of the city for centuries. It was one of the earliest legally defined 'public' spaces in Florence, a zone of prostitution, the Jewish ghetto, and one of the most diverse social spaces of the city. Although it contained no monumental structures, it was the site of some of the city's oldest parish churches, with names recalling the area's local family power structures. It was also a slum. Unable to stave off the massive demolitions that were planned for the area, Carocci made an archaeological survey and saved many fragments of palaces, churches, loggias, works of art, and bells from wholesale destruction. In his topographical plan, Carocci overlaid contemporary building lines onto those of the fifteenth century and populated the map with demographic data taken from the city's 1427 *Catasto* tax census. Each citizen in the city and Florentine dominion had to declare all forms of wealth, credits, and obligations both familial and financial, and the *Catasto* is an archive representing different but related sets of demographic data more than a century before the 1561 *Decima* census. The way in which Carocci mapped these data onto both a historical and a contemporary map of the city makes it a methodological forerunner to the DECIMA project. DECIMA's digital organization of the data within an interactive GIS platform represents a much more versatile system that can facilitate a range of diverging projects. In my own case, what began as a simple mapping of the parishes in 1561 developed into a far more complicated series of questions that concern the way that Florentines constructed their communal identities in space through motion and sound.

Seeing sound

Consider the description of Florence's town hall, the Palazzo dei Priori (the modern Palazzo Vecchio), by the fifteenth-century textile merchant Goro Dati.

Sitting almost in the middle of the city (*quasi nel mezzo della città*) in a great square paved in brick, it was 'made entirely of stone of marvellous strength and beauty'.[7] Dati was fully aware of the rhetoric of power on display. He revelled in the building's symmetry, in the poetic response that the tower made to the base on which it sat, and in the 60-*braccia* (34.8m) height of both sections, decorated with matching projecting arches supporting fortified rooflines of corbelled brackets and crenellations.

Dati's description does not end with what he sees but continues with what he hears. 'And up in this tower are the bells of the commune, that is, the great bell that weighs 22,000 pounds, and that of the council, and the bell of the clock, which you can hear throughout the entire city sounding the hours of the day and the night.'[8] From the vertical visual poetry of the building, Dati moves to the horizontal acoustic axis created by the building's bells, which extended its authority out across the entire city. Marking time, the execution of justice, and the evening prayer, accompanying civic rituals, and announcing official news, the civic bells of the Palazzo dei Priori enveloped all Florentines within a common acoustic zone that expressed their unity. For Dati, the aural power of the state completed the building's spectacular beauty. The acoustic expression of the regime's authority was crucial for Dati because, in a city whose densely packed structures allowed little room for long, clear sightlines, the power to render that authority present through sound was a crucial element in the representational apparatus of the state.

Dati's account demonstrates how space was a function of sound for Renaissance Florentines. Lasting topographies were built on entirely ephemeral acoustic foundations. Consequently, visualizing the territories formed by sound provides important insights into the ways in which the built environment was infused with social, political, and religious meanings through temporally bounded acoustic

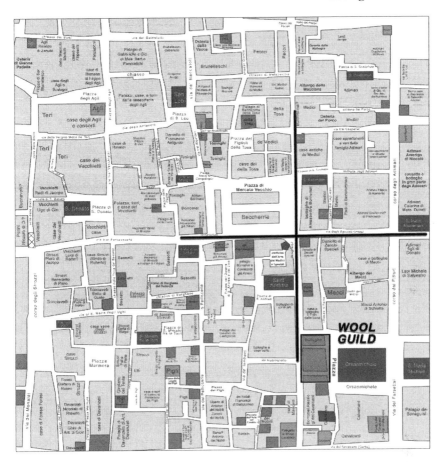

Figure 8.4 Map of the area around the Mercato Vecchio of Florence showing fifteenth-century building lines and including spatialized demographic data from the 1427 *Catasto*. Giovanni Villani's ideal axes are shown intersecting at the southwest corner of the market, and the relative position of the Wool Guild's headquarters to this ideal central point is highlighted in the lower left of the map. Drawing by author after Guido Carocci.

overlays. Such topographies were necessarily fluid and never static; they emerged and receded with the sounds that defined them. Yet this fluidity fully emerges only through the visualization of documentary sources, as information embedded in texts becomes evident in translation between media.

Translating the all-encompassing sound of civic authority expressed by Dati's description of the city's most important bell tower down to the level of the parish introduces some immediate complications. The political divisions of the city were subsumed into the sound of the commune's bells. In contrast, the regular repeated pealings of parish churches represented an alternate topography of micro-territories extending out in all directions to envelop their communities and define them from a world beyond. But this acoustic subdivision would generate overlapping boundaries of sonic dissonance. What would the borders of these micro-regimes look like, and how could they be represented and understood? Such borders would have been necessarily indistinct. Would Florentine legal restrictions on the height of towers and the size of bells have kept them functioning within a certain sonic and spatial order as good acoustic neighbours?

Using the spatialized data of DECIMA, Colin Rose and I created a map of parish geography (Figure 8.6). Rose has described how we systematically catalogued each individual household and generated the map's boundaries from those coordinates.[9] The map yielded some surprising initial results. Parish churches rarely sat in the middle of the community of souls over which they presided. More often than not, they sat at the extreme edges of their domain. This is true both for the smaller, older parishes in the crowded centre and for the larger parishes that extended to the periphery of the Renaissance city. The DECIMA-driven map shows how parish boundaries were set not by laws and linear planes

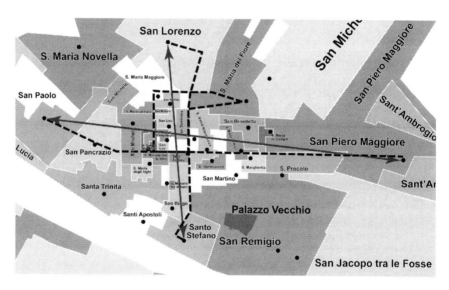

Figure 8.5 Map showing the extent of the Rogation Day processions that ultimately led to the churches of San Lorenzo, San Paolo, San Piero Maggiore, and Santo Stefano, the four churches that make up the sacred axes of the city's holy geometry, according to Goro Dati. This illustrates how these sacred coordinates were contained with the placement of the churches and then actualized by ritual movement through the city. Along the way, the songs sung to titular saints of parish churches and the sequential ringing of bells as the procession passed plotted out this sacred geometry, linking its spatial coordinates to the Florentine imagination. In this rendering, the cross made by linking the churches with 'straight' (*via diritta*) lines actually finds its centre in the Mercato Vecchio, but at its northern edge. Note how San Jacopo tra le Fosse also lies completely outside the zone defined by those who identified it as their parish church.

but by the mobility of parishioners within their communities, their attachment to the patronage structures of these communities, and the marriage and business alliances that were evolving over time. If we were to dive into the data of other *Catasti* and censuses, we could generate a more comparative analysis that would visualize this morphological change and might help to explain how some parish churches, such as Santa Maria Maggiore, San Tommaso, and San Jacopo tra le Fosse, were stranded entirely outside their parish's supposed geographical boundaries.[10] We might also understand how others, like the cathedral chapter and San Miniato fra le Torri, extended over noncontiguous territories separated by several blocks.[11] Despite the fact that some parishes may have been dissolved, redistricted, or rezoned over time, George Dameron points out that Florentine parishes, by and large, stubbornly retained local control and patronage well into the fourteenth century.[12] DECIMA shows that creating a systematic and authoritative map of Florentine parishes is likely impossible. More important, it may actually miss the point.

To demonstrate this, I would like to consider two examples of the ways in which Florentines forged and maintained communal bonds by sonically inscribing them into the spaces of their city. It is only in seeing these sounds by mapping out the topography of specific soundscapes, acoustic gestures, and aural rhythms that we can begin to understand how sound was a critical medium that brought both space and community into being and provided the means for its multiple articulations.

Let me begin with the architectural dimensions of the political struggles of late medieval Italian communes in central and northern Italy to establish the rule of law and a more equitable – at least in its rhetorical expressions – patriarchal state. The most paradigmatic image of this struggle was the visual profile of these cities rendered as a circuit of walls containing a dense topography of towers. Most were the mute, defensive towers of family clans that lived in fortified enclaves. Yet the civic towers of newly emerging regimes were rising higher, literally and figuratively in the case of Florence. Their height and prominence transformed them into acoustic transmitters, a phenomenon still visible in the bell tower of the Bargello (the Palace of the Podestà), where Florence installed the apparatus of civic justice.

It is through these civic towers that the city built a mass communication system with which it addressed its citizens, making the soundscape part of the same political motivations and spatial logic of urban planning policies that often appropriated or overlay private properties in order to create public institutions.

Along with the Palazzo dei Priori, the Bargello's civic bell tower was part of a triad of enunciative forms that organized the city through images, texts, and sounds. Flags, laws, and bells together constituted a multipronged urbanism and were always on display during the collective celebrations and calls to arms that preserved and celebrated the republic. This urban strategy was also, more subtly but perhaps more enduringly, built into the very fabric of the city by the daily acoustic regime constructed by the Florentine government in order to regulate economic, political, spiritual, and civic life every day, from daybreak to sunset.

Figure 8.6 The full map generated by DECIMA suggests that the larger outer parishes were extended from the churches, most of which lie close to the older circuit of walls. Rather than defining rigid boundaries, the irregular outlines of the parishes actually seem to represent persistent overlap across streets and within building lots. As a result, this map can be only approximate. Note how Sant'Ambrogio extends deep into territory associated with San Piero Maggiore and is divided in two by that parish, which also surrounds it. The church of Sant'Ambrogio, meanwhile, is located at the hinge of its two territories. This suggests strong divisions within this area in terms of allegiance to particular parish identities that are spatially antagonistic.

Pure white areas represent zones for which no parish data are given. In the outer areas of the city this result from open areas that are represented in the Buonsignori map by gardens and uninhabited spaces. In the centre the white square just to the north of the parish of San Andrea (see Figure 8.5) is the Mercato Vecchio. The area around the church of San Martino is white because there are no data in the *Decima* for that area.

The churches named and numbered with Arabic numerals represent the 'official' sequence of parish bells as they were rung by the Ciompi to organize their revolt on July 20, 1378, as extracted through torture. The churches labelled with Roman numerals represent the sequence of bells heard and then identified by a witness who stood in the Piazza della Signoria by the Palazzo Vecchio during the event. Although he names different churches, his map follows the general spatio-acoustic sequence, where Camadoli would correspond to the two proximate churches of the Carmine and San Frediano. San Piero Gattolino is correctly identified and San Giorgio replaces San Niccolò. Across the river, Sant'Ambrogio replaces San Piero Maggiore perhaps because of the strong association that parish had with the Ciompi identity and laborers. On the basis of the actual irregular spatial division of the two parishes, as suggested earlier, the witness was more or less accurate in his identification of the bell ringing in this area. Noting Via San Gallo is important because the street had numerous religious institutions, though no parish churches, and any number of bells in proximity but it seems to correspond to the bell of San Lorenzo. One anomaly seems to be the lack of any reference at all to the bell of Santo Stefano, whose parish the listener was actually standing in. This might be explained by the fact that the 'official' sequence of bells was not the one actually heard.

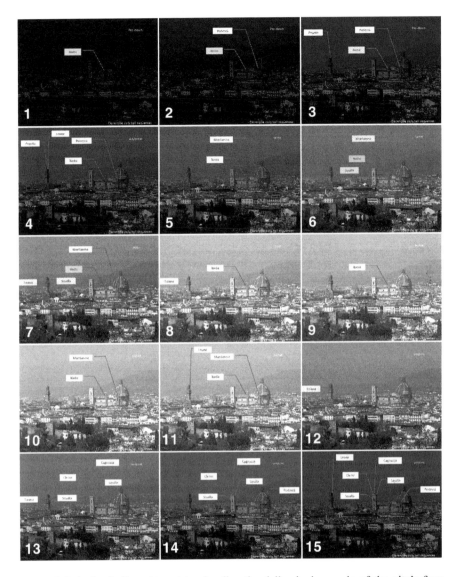

Figure 8.7 Author's first attempt to visualize the daily ringing cycle of the city's four principal bell towers as it was described in the city's statutes. Each image identifies the bells that rang at certain times of the day from the city's four principal bell towers from dawn until nightfall. Although the series gives an idea of the temporal arc of the daily soundscape, it does not effectively visualize how the system was based on a call-and-response dialog between towers. Such a phenomenon became visible only in a 'live' visualization loop created in Google Earth by Peter Leonard and then further developed in an ArcGIS environment that traced the Rogation processions.

This daily schedule is articulated in the city's statutes. Working out the daily sonic schedule is complicated, yet when that information is translated into a series of images of the Florentine skyline with the daily acoustic schedule fixed along a sequential chain, deeper resonances begin to emerge (Figure 8.7).

From this very rudimentary visualization one can easily discern that the republican communal government inserted its sonic markers into the spaces between the regular sounding of religious time by the Benedictine monks at the ancient Abbey of the Badia (formally known as S. Maria di Firenze) and the canons at the cathedral of S. Maria del Fiore. In other words, rather than breaking down the traditional sacred soundscape that gave meaning to the Florentine day, the government harnessed the unifying capacity of bells to orchestrate a rhythmic harmony between church and state.

When this daily regime is more systematically embedded within a digital visualization schema, the more complex nature of bell ringing comes to light, demonstrating how the soundscape was not merely a system of sequential sounds marking time. When we translate the sequence into a time-based animation in Google Earth, what becomes immediately clear is that towers were not only speaking at particular moments in the day but also listening. They were acoustic transmitters but also acoustic relay hubs. The ringing of bells did not simply mark a point in time. It was integrated into a larger system of call and response in which sound became meaningful only in its rhythmic relationship to other sounds. As a result, what we can elaborate as the psychological experience the city's particular temporal rhythms was a product of sound and did not exist independent of its aural iteration [13]

Goro Dati understood and admired the unifying function of the city's civic bells. These sounds created a cohesive Florentine space that dissolved the particularizing, localizing spaces of family, religion, politics, and taxes. That was Dati's dream. It was the dream of a city emerging victorious from a protracted war with Milan and in search of political stability because behind the aural harmony lay the constant threat of sonic disorder and, therefore, political disorder. Hardly more than a generation earlier, Florentines had stood in the same square and listened carefully to the bells of the commune to gauge complicated political shifts in the volatile summer of 1378. The witness Benedetto Acciauoli later wrote of hearing not the sound of authority but a scuffle breaking out in the piazza at Terce, the third canonical hour of prayer in the morning, and then a sudden call to arms.[14] It was just at that moment that he heard a succession of bells begin to ring in alarm around the city: from Camaldoli, then San Piero Gattolino, San Giorgio, several churches in Via San Gallo, Sant' Ambrogio, and 'in many other places' (Figure 8.6).[15]

The immediate translation Acciauoli made from what he heard into a spatial topography was, in effect, a parish map.[16] Parish bells communicated not only with their parishioners or with the cathedral but also with one another in that summer of 1378. In doing so they built unstable, temporally bound, sacred, but socially transgressive acoustic topographies that were put in motion directly under the radar, so to speak, of the more global reach of civic bells; authorities took this seriously enough to torture those involved in order to learn of the sequence of bells with which the Ciompi called supporters to arms. This sonic motion of local

Seeing sound 161

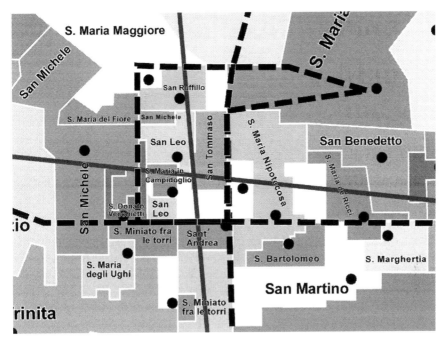

Figure 8.8 Detail of the parish map created by Atkinson and Rose from the demographic data found in the 1561 *Decima* with the location of parish churches represented by black circles. This image shows the small and irregularly shaped parishes in the centre of the city. Many of the parish churches are located at the edge of the territories they represent. The church of San Leo is located just outside its own jurisdiction in the parish of Santa Maria in Campidoglio. The church of San Tommaso is located across the city's main north-south thoroughfare from the parish itself. The church of San Miniato fra le Torri lies between the two noncontiguous territories to the north and east of the church. The parish of San Michele is divided into two sections by a satellite zone of the parish belonging to the cathedral, Santa Maria del Fiore, whose main territory lies on the other side of the city centre.

The dashed lines represent the routes (after Toker) of the Rogation processions that originated at the cathedral in the upper right and traced the cross-axes of the city on their routes to different parish churches. This map shows how often these processions would pass directly by parish churches in the centre of the city and suggests all the possible acoustic exchanges between bells and voices that could occur along each itinerary. This allows one to 'see' how the parish was an ephemeral, serial, and sonic phenomenon brought into being through motion.

bells relaying messages and communicating across and beyond the bounds of parishes means that a very different set of maps would be required to represent not the fixed space of parish borders but the sonic dynamism that came into being when those bells sounded.

At first glance, the Ciompi revolt's inversion of the city's acoustic regime appeared to be an anomaly. However, the instructions for late medieval religious processions in Florence, found in the *Mores et consuetudines ecclesiae florentinae*,

162 *Niall Atkinson*

which was compiled in the first third of the thirteenth century, clearly show how the acoustic mechanism of revolt was also very deeply embedded in traditional parochial soundscapes.[17] This helps to explain the severity of the crimes for which the Ciompi were punished. They were ostensibly sent into exile for the crime of ringing church bells out of order, but the real transgression was the way they succeeded in throwing into complete disarray a political and religious harmony that insisted on an aural hierarchy from centre to periphery.[18] Parish churches were not simply pale echoes of the voice of the commune or only passive players in the liturgical ringing sequence of the cathedral. They had a critical and active role to play in the construction of aurally based communities.

Idealizing geometry

In his fourteenth-century chronicle of Florence, Giovanni Villani takes the reader on an imaginary walk around and through the city. He names, measures, and describes the entire circuit of newly built walls designed to encompass a rapidly expanding urban demography.[19] The journey starts in the east, on the north bank of the Arno River, systematically tracing the edges of a large polyhedron, noting each turn to orient the reader in space and thereby evoke a very clear visual image.

Having taken account of the city's bounds, he enters through one of its gates and measures and names the principal axes of the city, imposing a geometric unity on the city.

From the Porta alla Croce to the Porta del Prato d'Ognissanti, along the straight street through which the palio is run; 3,350 *braccia*.

From the Porta di San Gallo to the Porta Romana there are 5,000 *braccia*.

From Porta alla Croce to Mercato Vecchio, 2,200 *braccia*, and almost the same from there to the Porta a Prato.

From San Gallo to the Mercato Vecchio, 2,200 *braccia*.

From Porta Romana to Mercato Vecchio, 2,800 *braccia*.

Villani's map is wrong from a strictly modern cartographic point of view. It recalls David Friedman's claim that when Florentines described their city in words they transformed it into an ideal and harmonious geometry that 'glossed over specific topographical details, giving a generalized account of regular and recognizable shapes'.[20] Villani's ideal axes set in motion the flow of goods and people through the city and sanctify that motion by imagining that a cross defines the city's geometry. He names it as such and locates the headquarters of the powerful merchant guild of wool manufacturers precisely at this crossing.[21] This same cross was the armature of a deeper sacred topography that was still firmly embedded in the Florentine psyche a century later and evoked by Goro Dati in his description of the city. Recounting the rebuilding of Florence after its destruction in the fifth century by Attila, Dati notes that the builders had a coherent and unified plan that echoed the sacred axes of Christian Rome.[22] Florence's own S. Pietro lay just inside the Romanesque walls of the city, and following a straight line ('*via diritta*') across the city one encountered the church S. Paolo, just *outside* those walls (*fuori della città*), like Rome's S. Paolo Fuori le Mura.[23] Dati bisects the line connecting these churches to form a cross – he is explicit about this – with another 'straight' street running from the church of S. Lorenzo, at the northern edge of the twelfth-century walls, to Santo Stefano a Ponte, just north of the Ponte Vecchio. Dati notes that these two lines cross in the very centre of the city at Florence's own capitol and Roman Forum (i.e. the Mercato Vecchio).[24] Thus, Saints Peter, Paul, Lawrence, and Stephen, four early Christian martyrs, all buried in Rome and all inscribed into an ideal geometry of Florentine space (Figure 8.5). Where does the idea for this kind of sacred topography come from?

An early Florentine tradition linked the city's Christian topography in a similarly weak but significant way to Rome.[25] As Franklin Toker notes, processions of the canons of Florence deliberately ignored the rising importance of mendicant churches and the diagonal roads that inflected the Roman orthogonal grid by continuing to process along the ideal cosmic cruciform geographic orientation of the city's Roman core.[26] It was the act of processing along the axial grid, rather than the churches' actual spatial location, that overlaid the sign of the cross onto the city during the annual spring Rogation processions. These processions were intentionally anachronistic in the way they continued to demarcate the older topography of the city precisely at the moment when Florence was expanding its territory with new sets of walls and secularizing its political institutions. The processional cross was built over three successive days, linking four increasingly marginalized churches – dedicated to the same four early Christian martyrs in Rome, Peter, Paul, Lawrence, and Stephen – into the axes that both Villani and Dati celebrated as the central element of Florence's urban geometry.[27] In doing so, the Rogation processions not only valorized the threatened primacy of the cathedral chapter but also etched an older Christian topography into the city's living collective memory (Figure 8.8).

Acoustic itineraries

But what about sound? In mapping out the directions for these liturgical processions, the integrated coordination of movement, itineraries, voices, and bells comes to the fore. The sounds of the liturgical calendar rang out from the cathedral bell tower and flowed along the sacred axes of the city as a series of acoustic exchanges between parishes and the populace. The Rogation processions began with all the cathedral bells ringing to call the clergy and city to assemble. After the sounding of Terce, the singing began and hardly stopped for the entire ritual. Litanies or prayers were sung in every church visited and sermons were said, but the most significant element of the ritual, the one that links sound to space in the most fundamental way, is one that goes barely noticed in the text. As the procession went forth and returned, participants sang Antiphons, verses, and 'responses appropriate to the saints that are titular of the churches by which we pass or to which we are headed'.[28] Churches along Florentine processional routes were ordered to ring their bells as those processions passed by, setting up the most profound acoustic relay by which parishes took part in a collective dialogue with one another, the cathedral clergy, and the general populace of the city. The procession ended with the singing of the mass in the cathedral and all the parish churches simultaneously, coordinated by the ringing bells of the cathedral bell tower.

A similar dynamic occurred during a procession on the feast of Saint Agatha (5 February) meant to ward off the threat of fires in the city. All the cathedral bells rang at Terce in a special triple sequence to gather the clergy and the people. The procession was marked by the singing of the four gospels at specific points along the periphery of the second set of city walls and the river, with the participation of parish priests along the way. More important, the participants sang directly to the saints whose relics they passed along the way as they processed behind an image of Saint Agatha that led them through the streets.

Parishes came into being through an exchange of voices and bells synched to a collective bodily motion. A traditional parish map of fixed linear boundaries misses the point of how parishes were understood as a psychosocial geography and the different ways they were organized by such processions, Parish churches and bells functioned not as static transmitters speaking to a fixed community around them. Instead, they integrated fluid, localized communities into a larger network of diffuse territories that emerged and receded through the acoustic exchange of voices and bells. They were not exclusive sonic zones but were deliberately merged through an acoustic choreography where bells on the edge of their own territory were expected to communicate with a mobile populace moving from one parish through another. And even if these processions were small, listeners throughout the city would have been able to follow and mentally map the journey because Florentines could orient themselves and the sound of bells in space in very meaningful ways. It does not matter if the resulting maps – of processions and revolt – do not conform precisely to a literal geographic reality. Such a literal spatial map may have meant less to sixteenth-century parishioners who experienced their local community in motion, on the ground, and in an active dialogue of call and response along urban itineraries that continually reminded inhabitants of who and where they were, which saints lived there, and how they were connected by an ephemeral network of territories defined by vectors of moving sounds.

It is these dynamic territories, which were at the intersection of real space and the mental imagination of Florentines, that digital mapping technologies like DECIMA can begin to decode and represent in meaningful ways. Their promise of mapping movement and the general sequence of acoustic exchanges that Florentines could map in their own minds with remarkable precision can lead to more profound knowledge about the dynamics inherent in ritual movements, especially in the way they were connected to deeper psychological forms by which Florentines understood the city.

This is why the sonic relay that initiated the Ciompi revolt was not simply a disruption of the sonic order. The succession of church bells rippling through the city also confirmed how Florentines experienced real and imagined space. When parish bells rang during the 1378 revolt, they were accompanied by processions of the faithful, moving between parishes, led by an image, inscribing alternative itineraries onto the city's topographic archive.[29] Just as processions of the cathedral canons were attempts to reverse their increasing political irrelevance in the mercantile city through a complex sonic choreography, so too the Ciompi put an acoustic strategy into play with parish bells whose sound was supposed to ring through the city.

The more senses and purposes we map, the more our maps multiply, and the more necessary it is to have some tool that can help choreograph them. The parish map based on the geocoded rendering of DECIMA generated a skewed topography that suggested that parishes were flexible and mobile. Their limits were not the fixed boundaries of political jurisdictions but were set by people as they moved from one dwelling to another and so were capable of travelling with these parishioners. By injecting that map with various dimensions of the city's soundscapes derived from documentary sources – the aural regime heard by Dati, the prescriptive information of the cathedral liturgical processions, and the sonic disruptions of the Ciompi revolt – we find that the parish emerges as a more complex social entity. It is not clear whether the Florentine parish was simultaneously a place where a building was located and the mental territory of a thinking, listening, and mobile soul. However, in the itinerant acoustics of church rituals, each parish came into being with the ring of a bell. It was a performative territory that belonged both to the church and to Florentines as they moved through the city, across space and over time. The same territory was a different parish at different times, while the sonic reach of a parish bell into neighbouring territories bound those communities together into an acoustic exchange. This defined them in very different ways from the great bells of the commune that acoustically drowned out those boundaries in pursuit of a much more unified and perhaps submissive collection of souls.

The importance and the challenge for mapping multiple soundscapes rests in being able to render these multiple identities as distinct but interpenetrating. They were ephemeral but no less powerful, real, and imagined topographies. DECIMA's digitized geography of the 1561 *Decima* census can facilitate a range of mapping projects that would be impossible without its data arranged along geographic coordinates. The social mapping that it presents can be used to generate more maps so that multiple dimension of Florentine ritual and social life can be overlaid onto the spaces that were so meaningful to the construction of their multiple identities.

Notes

1 D. Alighieri, *The Divine Comedy: Purgatory*, C. Singleton (ed.), Princeton, NJ: Princeton University Press, 1980, VIII, 1–6.
2 The fourteenth-century jurist Albericus de Rosate articulated this fact in this way: '*campanae deputatae ad segregandum diem, a nocte sicut communiter est in omnibus civitatibus.*' A. de Rosate, *Commentarii in Primam Digesti Veteris Partem*, Venice, 1585, ad D.2.12.8.
3 One of Dante's early commentators was more prosaic in his explanation, believing that the sound was simply the evening bell signaling the closing of the city gates, so that the quickened pace was not from a stimulated heart but from an anxious mind trying

to reach the town before nightfall: '*quando fit sero, si peregrini audiunt pulsare unam campanam, que vocatur in Ytalia squilla, quae significat finem diei, pungunt se, idest conantur velocius ire, propter applicare ad portam antequam claudatur*'. J. de Serravalle, *Translatio et comentum totius libri Dantis Aldigherii*, M. da Civezza and T. Domenichelli (eds), Prato, Italy: Giachetti, 1891; F. Novati, 'La 'Squilla Da Lontano' È Quella Dell'ave Maria?' in F. Novati (ed.), *Indagini E Postille Dantesche*, Bologna, Italy: Nicola Zanichelli, 1899, 143.

4   See the poem quoted by F. Novati, 'Squilla da lontano', 140.
5   L.B. Alberti, *Leon Battista Alberti's Delineation of the City of Rome (descriptio Vrbis Romæ)*, Tempe, AZ: Arizona Center for Medieval and Renaissance Studies, 2007, 77–79, 97–99.
6   A.M. Ghisalberti (ed.), *Dizionario biografico degli Italiani*, vol. 20, Rome, Italy: Istituto della Enciclopedia italiana, 1977.
7   G. Dati, 'Istoria di Firenze', in A. Lanza (ed.), *Firenze contro Milano: Gli intellettuali fiorentini nelle guerre con i Visconti (1390–1440)*, Rome, Italy: De Rubeis, 1991, 263.
8   Ibid. '*e in su esso sono le campane del Comune, cioè la campana grossa che pesa 22 migliaia di libber, che non ha pari al mondo, e quella del Consiglio e quella dell' Oriolo, la quale si sente per tutta la città sonare l'ore del dì e della note.*'
9   Note that there is an area in the centre where parish information is missing, likely because of the high incidence of workshop properties.
10 See Figure 8.5.
11 Ibid.
12 Mapping these spatial distortions over time is one goal of this study through the creation of a series of overlaid maps that trace the changing morphology of Florentine parishes over time. On the structure of Florentine parishes within the diocese see G.W. Dameron, *Florence and Its Church in the Age of Dante*, Philadelphia, PA: University of Pennsylvania Press, 2005, 28–42; D. Peterson, 'An Experiment in Diocesan Self-Government: The 'Universitas Cleri' in Early Quattrocento Florence', in M. Zangarini (ed.), *Preti nel medioevo*, Verona, Italy: Cierre, 1997, 195–220; G. Brucker, 'Urban Parishes and Their Clergy in Quattrocento Florence: A Preliminary Sondage', in A. Morrogh et al. (eds), *Renaissance Studies in Honor of Craig Hugh Smyth*, vol. 1, Florence, Italy: Giunti Barbèra, 1985, 17–28.
13 N. Atkinson, 'Sonic Armatures: Constructing an Acoustic Regime in Renaissance Florence', *The Senses and Society* 7, 2012, 45.
14 The term the author uses is 'serra', which can mean either siege, barricades, or a general state of military threat. See S. Battaglia and G.B. Squarotti, *Grande dizionario della lingua italiana*, vol. 18, Turin, Italy: Unione tipografico-editrice torinese, 1961, 745.
15 G. Scaramella, 'Lettera d'anonimo sul tumulto dei ciompi (23 July, 1378)', in Scaramella (ed.), *Il Tumulto dei Ciompi – cronache e memorie*, Bologna, Italy: Nicola Zanichelli, 1917, 141. Although the letter is dated three days after the events and, therefore, the writer would most likely have discussed the various churches whose bells were rung, there is no reason why he would not have been fully aware of the encircling movement of the alarm, which he foregrounds in his experience.
16 The fact that he also got the map 'wrong' – in comparison with the planned sequence of rings as they were extracted through torture on the eve of the revolt – is less significant than the general spatial 'correctness' of the sequence of sounds he plotted in his mind. In fact, we cannot be sure, on the basis of what we might know about the reliability of tortured confessions, which map corresponds more closely to the actual experience of Florentines that morning who were listening in real time. A. Acciaioli, 'Cronaca', in G. Scaramella (ed.), *Il Tumulto dei Ciompi*, 22.
17 The text of the thirteenth-century liturgical calendar is found in *Mores et consuetudines ecclesiae florentinae*, Florence, Italy: Petri Alegrinii, 1794. It is also transcribed in F.

Toker, *On Holy Ground: Liturgy, Architecture and Urbanism in the Cathedral and the Streets of Medieval Florence*, London, UK: Harvey Miller, 2009, 265–84, Cf. 119–47.
18 N. Rodolico, *La democrazia fiorentina nel suo tramonto (1378–1382)*, Rome, Italy: Multigrafica Editrice, 1970, 441–45, shows that the charge was against ringing parish bells independent of the bells of the commune. '*Ceperunt se coadunare in aliqua multitudine gentium armatarum et fecerunt pulsari campanas quampluriam ecclesiarum ad martellum divisim et per se a campanis populi et Communis Florentie. . . .*'
19 G. Villani, *Nuova cronica*, in G. Porta (ed.), Parma, Italy: Fondazione Pietro Bembo, 1990, bk. 10, ch. 257.
20 D. Friedman, *Florentine New Towns: Urban Design in the Late Middle Ages*, New York, NY: Architectural History Foundation, 1988, 201.
21 See Figure 8.3.
22 See Figure 8.5.
23 G. Dati was most likely referring to *San Paolino*, originally called *San Paolo*, which was founded either in 335 ce, according to a fifteenth-century inscription, or in 805 ce by Charlemagne (Villani) in front of the west gate of the city, near the present Via Palazzuolo. Paatz even suggests that the church was a conscious 'copy', at least in terms of placement, of Saint Paul's in Rome. See W. Paatz and E. Valentiner, *Die Kirchen von Florenz, ein kunstgeschichtliches Handbuch*, Frankfurt am Main, Germany: V. Klostermann, 1952, vol. 4, 591 and n.2.
24 G. Dati, 'Istoria di Firenze', 262–63.
25 Three versions of the city's Roman origins are found in O.V. Hartwig, *Quellen und Forschungen zur ältesten Geschichte der Stadt Florenz*, Marburg: Elwert, 1875–80, 37–65. The earliest version of the narrative is found in the thirteenth-century *Chronica de origine civitatis*, copied by the fourteenth-century chronicler D. Compagni, either of which versions Dati almost certainly read. Compagni's text has been translated in D. Bornstein (ed.), *Dino Compagni's Chronicle of Florence*, Philadelphia, PA: University of Pennsylvania Press, 1986.
26 F. Toker, *On Holy Ground: Liturgy, Architecture and Urbanism in the Cathedral and the Streets of Medieval Florence*, London, UK: Harvey Miller, 2009, 131–36.
27 See Figure 8.5.
28 Ibid., 121.
29 Contemporaries also noted that the Ciompi marched behind the image of an archangel holding a sword and the arms of the Florentine *popolo*. It was this flag that Trexler saw as the foundation of their corporate identity, to which I would add the sounds they made through the ringing of bells. For a contemporary reference to the Ciompi flag see M. di Coppo Stefani, *Cronica Fiorentina*, Rerum Italicarum Scriptores, L.A. Muratori (ed.), vol. 30, Città di Castello: S. Lapi, 1903. For an analysis of the dynamics of flags in 1378, see R. Trexler, 'Follow the Flag: The Ciompi Revolt Seen from the Streets', in *The Workers of Renaissance Florence: Power and Dependence in Renaissance Florence*, Binghamton, NY: Medieval and Renaissance Texts and Studies, 1993, 30–60.

Bibliography

Print sources

Acciaioli, A., 'Cronaca', in G. Scaramella (ed.), *Il Tumulto dei Ciompi – cronache e memorie*, Bologna, Italy: Nicola Zanichelli, 1917, 13–34.

Alberti, L.B., Carpo, M., Furlan, F., Boriaud, J-Y., and Hicks, P., *Leon Battista Alberti's Delineation of the City of Rome (descriptio Vrbis Romæ)*, Tempe, AZ: Arizona Center for Medieval and Renaissance Studies, 2007.

Alighieri, D., *The Divine Comedy: Purgatory,* C. Singleton (ed.), Princeton, NJ: Princeton University Press, 1980.
Atkinson, N., 'Sonic Armatures: Constructing an Acoustic Regime in Renaissance Florence', *The Senses and Society* 7, 2012, 57–84.
Bornstein, D. (ed.), *Dino Compagni's Chronicle of Florence,* Philadelphia, PA: University of Pennsylvania Press, 1986.
Friedman, D., *Florentine New Towns: Urban Design in the Late Middle Ages,* New York, NY: Architectural History Foundation, 1988.
Dati, G., 'Istoria di Firenze', in A. Lanza (ed.), *Firenze contro Milano: Gli intellettuali fiorentini nelle guerre con i Visconti (1390–1440),* Rome, Italy: De Rubeis, 1991, 209–98.
Ghisalberti, A.M. (ed.), *Dizionario biografico degli Italiani,* vol. 20, Rome, Italy: Istituto della Enciclopedia italiana, 1977.
Hartwig, O.V., *Quellen und Forschungen zur ältesten Geschichte der Stadt Florenz,* Marburg, Germany: Elwert, 1875–80.
Novati, F., 'La "Squilla Da Lontano" È Quella Dell'ave Maria?', in F. Novati (ed.), *Indagini E Postille Dantesche,* Bologna, Italy: Nicola Zanichelli, 1899, 137–50.
Paatz, W., and Valentiner, E., *Die Kirchen von Florenz, ein kunstgeschichtliches Handbuch,* vol. 4, Frankfurt am Main, Germany: V. Klostermann, 1952.
Rodolico, N., *La democrazia fiorentina nel suo tramonto (1378–1382),* Rome, Italy: Multigrafica Editrice, 1970.
Rosate, A. de, *Commentarii in Primam Digesti Veteris Partem,* Venice, 1585.
Scaramella, G. (ed.), 'Lettera d'anonimo sul tumulto dei ciompi (23 July, 1378)', in G. Scaramella (ed.), *Il Tumulto dei Ciompi – cronache e memorie,* Bologna, Italy: Nicola Zanichelli, 1917, 139–48.
Serravalle, J. de, *Translatio et comentum totius libri Dantis Aldigherii,* M. da Civezza and T. Domenichelli (eds), Prato, Italy: Giachetti, 1891.
Stefani, M. di Coppo, *Cronica Fiorentina, Rerum Italicarum Scriptores,* L.A. Muratori (ed.), vol. 30, Città di Castello, Italy: S. Lapi, 1903.
Toker, F., *On Holy Ground: Liturgy, Architecture and Urbanism in the Cathedral and the Streets of Medieval Florence,* London, UK: Harvey Miller, 2009.
Trexler, R., 'Follow the Flag: The Ciompi Revolt Seen from the Streets', in *The Workers of Renaissance Florence: Power and Dependence in Renaissance,* Florence, Italy; Binghamton: Medieval and Renaissance Texts and Studies, 1993, 30–60.
Villani, G., *Nuova cronica,* G. Porta (ed.), Parma, Italy: Fondazione Pietro Bembo, 1990.

9 Mapping fear
Plague and perception in Florence and Tuscany

Nicholas A. Eckstein

Is it possible to map an emotion like fear?[1] I intend this question in a literal sense: can digital mapping technology such as that being used by the DECIMA team be exploited to represent people's fear of a happening, a series of events or situation in a specific time and place, or to track the spread of such fear from one location to another? Are such phenomena susceptible to representation on a plan such as the Buonsignori map? This essay presents some thoughts on these and related issues that have arisen from my current interest in the way Florentines responded to the threat of plague in the sixteenth and early seventeenth centuries. Fear of plague ran deep in this period, and we should not be surprised therefore that the population's anxiety levels spiked when rumours of disease began to spread. But it is also clear that people never really stopped worrying: fear of plague did not disappear in periods when there was no immediate threat, and when a serious illness appeared, one of the first things that people asked themselves and others was whether the new malady was 'true plague'.

What would it mean to 'map' this kind of fear, and by what means could one do it? Several issues and potential stumbling blocks immediately present themselves. First and foremost, we would have to decide exactly what it is that we are trying to measure. Much has been written in recent times about the practical and theoretical challenges that face historians who attempt to write the history of emotions, including the question of what emotions actually are.[2] In this instance it is necessary to think about what 'fear of plague' really meant for early modern Florentines and whether that emotion is a measurable quantity. By what means did it travel, and is it possible or feasible to track its progress on a map? Can one, indeed, plot fear in the way one would identify a physical landmark or track the advance and retreat of an army? What would such a map look like? While there are many similar questions that cannot be addressed in an essay of this length, there is one that must be posed. Assuming that it is indeed possible to produce such a map, what would be the point? What, if anything, would a map of fear demonstrate?

One advantage in the present context is the survival of an archive containing thousands of letters written by officials of Florence's permanent health magistracy, the Officers of Health, or Sanità.[3] This voluminous correspondence reveals that whenever plague threatened the city, the Sanità received frequent, often daily, written reports that told them what was happening in other cities. In formulating their own reports on such intelligence, the Sanità's officials unfailingly expressed themselves in a clear, matter-of-fact style. Explicit references to emotion are not particularly numerous, but the letters are written with such attention to detail that one is always aware of the atmosphere of tension and anxiety in which they were written. One example involves the plague that struck Florence in August 1630 and that returned in fits and starts until May 1633. Prior to its arrival, there had been months of tension as correspondents, first those in major cities in northern Italy, later those located in regional Tuscan towns, reported news of plague. By June the Sanità was receiving almost daily updates. One, written on 8 June 1630, refers to a 'great fear' (*grandissimo timore*) gripping the inhabitants of Bologna.[4] The terms in which the growth of such fear is described, as well as the process by which news was communicated, emerge clearly in the Sanità's correspondence. What is demonstrated by these letters, not just those for 1630 but those written during every similar crisis with which the Sanità had to deal, is that reports of disease spread principally by gossip, rumour, and word of mouth. In addition to forming part of the Sanità's systematic response to the risk of plague, the letters are an artefact of the often haphazard and inconsistent way that news of potential disaster travelled. They are replete with the language of hearsay, of reports both confirmed and unsubstantiated.[5] One such communication, by giving a taste of the rumours that were swirling in northern Italy in mid-1630, helps us to understand what must have been a perennial dilemma for the Sanità – that its officials were forced to react on the basis of information that may or may not have been accurate. Written on 8 June, the letter was penned in Florence by a health magistrate named Giovanfrancesco Guidi, who reported that the Sanità had received written word from officials in Bologna advising that:

> Modena has placed a ban on Bologna. No other specific warnings have come in, except that the same rumour [*voce*] has been spreading in that city. From the health officials of Genoa we had a letter dated the 31st of May just passed, in which they ask us if it is true that in Bologna and Ferrara there have been cases of contagion; in Venice we understand that they have banned Ferrara, albeit that in letters sent by the merchants we are given to understand that trade has been resumed with the said city of Ferrara. And in a letter from Clemente Falconieri, commissioner of health at the Pietramala pass, written on the fifth day of June . . . one hears that in Bologna two entire families have died, (albeit, it is said, as the result of ordinary, non-contagious maladies), and that therefore the Bolognesi are in great fear on account of the said mortality, and he [Falconieri] says that he's heard this without explaining from whom.[6]

Three days later the rumours had intensified, and Guidi wrote again: 'It appears that the suspicions of contagion in the city of Bologna are increasing all the time.'[7] He emphasized that the Sanità officials had been working assiduously, not simply receiving information but actively investigating and weighing what people were saying. Beyond listening to the:

> opinion circulating in this city [Florence] in the letters of merchants and others, in our office we have gone to the trouble of quizzing the Dominican fathers now returned from the chapter that has just been held in Bologna, and in particular from two of the fathers, one from Santa Maria Novella and the other from San Marco . . . and from them we have learned that in Bologna reports and rumours [*fama e voce*] were circulating that there were deaths from contagion there, and that the Cardinal Legate had not explicitly denied this to them, at the same time as he tried to assure everyone that the city was safe. And it has been reported to our chancellor by the prior of the canons regular of San Iacopo Soprarno that one of their fathers who has arrived here seriously infected had gone to Lucca to seek refuge in one of their convents. He said that he had asked this favour fearing that Florence had sent orders to its borders to block anyone coming from Bologna and that he therefore feared being banned himself, having heard that in Bologna many houses had been sealed. . . .[8]

Compared with the lifeless managerial jargon favoured by twenty-first-century bureaucrats, the prose of Sanità's official letters is terse, functional, and direct. Quoting and paraphrasing the oral testimony of first-hand witnesses, the letters testify vividly to a rising tide of reports and rumours of plague – so-called *fama*, *voci*, and *romori* – and the fear that it carried.[9] Whether one is referring to the people who passed on such rumours or to the impact of the latter on the emissaries reporting to the Sanità in Florence, there can no doubt as to the emotional state that they reflected and provoked: people were afraid.

As I have already indicated, large numbers of equally detailed letters survive in the Sanità's archive. So the thought immediately occurs: with so much available evidence, surely it should not be too technically difficult to use digital technology to plot the places where the plague's presence had been reported to reveal how Florentine population's fear of approaching disease mapped itself on to the Florentine *contado* and regions beyond. One can even imagine a time-lapse animation that would use information from the Sanità's reports to dramatize the plague's appearance in other cities and its progress from place to place, in exactly the same way that television documentaries such as the BBC's classic *The World at War* represented the advance of a military foe. The comparison is apt, given the Sanità officials' frequent recourse to martial language and the clear evidence that they confronted the threat of advancing plague as they would a military invasion. Especially in this sense one wishes almost instinctively for a map that might express the siege mentality of a fearful population bunkered within its walls. It is a seductive thought because it is so easily visualized: a calendar in one corner of the computer screen ticking over the days as the plague, represented as a black smudge, appears in Bologna and Ferrara and subsequently engulfs small centres close to Florence.

Unfortunately, a map such as this is just that bit too easy to imagine, because it is not immediately clear exactly what it would purport to measure or represent. In the first place the obvious point must be made that, based as such a map would be on reports received and solicited in Florence by the Sanità's officials, it could in no way be accepted as an accurate charting of the plague's actual movement. While the Sanità was the clearinghouse for a huge volume of news, nearly all of the reports were anecdotal. What the Sanità officials ostensibly 'knew' about the disease can in no way, therefore, be accepted as reliable: their correspondence is not a scientifically reliable record of the exact path taken by the plague prior to its arrival in Florence or of how rapidly it spread. As often as not, witnesses and officials were not even sure what disease they were describing. Beyond this, there are equally important questions about attitudes and public opinion. That anxiety about the perceived threat of plague was spreading seems beyond question, but the reports in the Sanità's correspondence do not tell us about what might loosely be called public opinion or the word on the street. On the contrary: the evidence contained in the Sanità's correspondence tells us only about the anxieties of several quite limited groups of people, who include eyewitnesses, citizens who passed on the reports of others at second or third hand, and still others who mediated what must on many occasions have been pure gossip. As for the actual letters of the Sanità, they represent the distillation of these various kinds of information by a group of educated, mostly aristocratic, officeholders who tailored their message for reception by other members of the ducal government of which they were members and for the Grand Duke himself. The letters of the Sanità are not remotely comparable to a twenty-first-century poll, which for all its flaws is conceived for a specific purpose and is based on a rigorously constructed survey of a carefully selected sample of the population. Mapping the reports of fear in the Sanità's correspondence looks more and more difficult and, on the surface at least, less and less useful.

This is not to say, however, that such evidence cannot inform a mapping exercise. To benefit from it requires that one identify its great strength, which is the insight that the Sanità can provide into the attitudes that informed upper-class perceptions of plague, the terms in which the officials mediated these perceptions, and their impact on the measures that the Sanità implemented for dealing with such crises. Not only do I believe that it is possible to map fear in a literal sense; I believe that doing so can enhance our understanding of what we are looking at when we make use of a visual resource such as the Buonsignori map. In what follows, I wish to discuss an approach that will not simply add to knowledge of the specific landmarks that are identified on such a map but that may also in a general sense enrich our understanding of how Florentines thought about certain kinds of places and how changing circumstances could modify contemporary spatial perception.

To explain what I mean requires some background and a few words about two separate though theoretically and methodologically complementary projects on urban space with which I am currently engaged. In both I have at different points made use of the software package in Google Earth to plot the locations of various features, and in both cases I have encountered problems and challenges that have subsequently proved instructive. My principal source for the first project is the Florentine *Catasto*, the tax census implemented for the first time in 1427 and conducted intermittently with various modifications until its final iteration in 1480. In the second project, I have exploited the written record of a walking survey of Florence conducted in August 1630 by an aristocratic confraternity on the orders of the Sanità. The purpose of this 'Visitation' (*Visita*), as it was called, was to inspect poor households throughout the entire city with the intention of identifying conditions that, according to contemporary medical thinking, could produce noxious miasmas that would in turn give rise to plague.[10] Danger signs and objects of suspicion included evil smells, refuse, soiled bedding and furniture, overflowing cesspits, leaking pipes, and the like. Once notified of the presence of such problems, the Sanità would ensure that they were rectified. My argument is that, like a host of other Florentine censuses and surveys, the *Catasto* and the Visitation reflect a way of thinking that Florentines had used for centuries to conceive and describe the urban places and spaces of their city and their relationship to the physical environment. Elsewhere I have described this mode of perception as a kind of culturally encoded global positioning system, whose coordinates were the familiar landmarks, spaces, and people encountered in the pursuit of their everyday lives.[11] In the *Catasto* one sees this at work in the method used to describe the locations of the urban properties that householders were required to declare to the officials who ran the tax system. A residential house, for instance, was identified not by a street number but in relation to the adjacent properties that surrounded it, which were called 'confines' (*confini*). One example of the literally tens of thousands found in the returns (*portate*) filed by householders is a residence in the middle of Florence inhabited by one Antonio Benzi in 1427, which he described as:

> 'A workshop or in other words a house with vaults underneath it.' As in every other such declaration, Antonio accompanied this description with a numbered list of the property's *confini*: '1. Via Porta Rossa; 2. The aforementioned house; 3. The alley [*chiasso*] of the Bostichi family; 4. Part [of the property belonging to] Niccolò di Miniato.'[12]

In 1630, the volunteer lay brothers who carried out the Visitation for the Sanità instinctively activated the same mental process as they walked from door to door to inspect the homes of the Florentine poor. Because they had to guide other officials and repairmen to these properties to fix the problems that they discovered, the 'Visitors', as they called themselves for the duration of the exercise, employed the geometrical logic of the *confini*, locating people and households in physical relation to familiar street corners, churches, or well-known landmarks. Proliferating throughout the report are linguistic coordinates expressed by prepositional phrases that begin with 'next to', 'opposite', 'behind', 'on the other side of', 'over', 'under', or 'between'.[13] Typical of this language is an entry in which the surveyors described the location of a leaky drain in need of attention as 'in the street of San Iacopo in Campo Corbolini, going towards Piazza Madonna on the left-hand side: . . . the house opposite the baker, next to the corner'.[14]

In even the most arid administrative document, Florentines mentally mapped their city by relating places to one another in sequences that often resemble itineraries.[15] Landmarks were identified not by placeless bureaucratic descriptors but by names that reflected a degree of local knowledge or that resonated with a connection to the local community. Not that this kind of engagement with urban space was new, let alone specifically Florentine. It can be seen at work in the ancient world and informs a well-known exchange in Terence's play *The Brothers*, in which a slave named Syrus attempts to send an old man, Demea, on a wild goose chase. Syrus is momentarily tripped up at one point by Demea's unexpected familiarity with the neighbourhood being discussed:

SYRUS: Do you know that arcade down by the market?
DEMEA: Of course I do.
SYRUS: Go uphill past it, straight along the road. When you get to the top, there's a slope downwards: hurl yourself down that. Next, there's a little shrine on this side, and there's an alleyway thereabouts.
DEMEA: Which one?
SYRUS: There where there's also a fig-tree.
DEMEA: I know it.
SYRUS: Go down that one.
DEMEA: But you can't get through that alleyway!
SYRUS: You're absolutely right! Really! Can you believe I'm a human being? I made a mistake: go back to the arcade; yes, you'll get there much more directly this way, and there isn't so far to walk. Do you know the house of wealthy old Cratinus?
DEMEA: I do.
SYRUS: When you've passed that, go left straight along that road; when you come to the temple of Diana, go to the right. Before you reach the gate, just by the pond, there's a bakery, and a workshop opposite: that's where he is.[16]

In the *Catasto* and the *Visita*, just as in Terence's play, Florentines conceived their city in terms of elemental relationships that were repeatedly renewed in the recurrent cycles of their everyday sociability. As Michel de Certeau has observed of our own world, such personal transactions, which are the building blocks of urban sociability, take place on the ground and are activated in horizontal movement, by walking.[17] Herein lies the challenge at the core of the present essay: it is difficult to represent, let alone to capture the essence of, these ephemeral relationships on the abstracted, schematic format of a two-dimensional plan, which by definition regards the city from above. My *Catasto* project, which uses the source in a way not previously attempted, provides an example of this problem. In their magisterial study *Les toscans et leurs familles: Une étude du 'Catasto' florentin de 1427*, David Herlihy and Christiane Klapisch-Zuber constructed an

Mapping fear 175

unprecedentedly large database of the 1427 *Catasto*'s many categories of demographic, financial, and economic information.[18] While much narrower and more selective, my survey differs from theirs in that it addresses the dynamic element of change. Whereas Herlihy and Klapisch-Zuber studied the entire city and the surrounding *contado* in a single year, I am focusing on *portate* from one section of central Florence in three surveys: 1427, 1458, and 1480. In building a database from the *portate*'s lists of urban properties, which include the *confini*, my objective is to provide the evidential foundation on which to base small narrative histories that plot the fifteenth-century evolution of selected streets, micro-neighbourhoods, individual piazzas, and street corners, all important nodes of community and sociability. However, a problem arises in trying to map these phenomena.

When I began this inquiry, I was worried that I might struggle to compile a critical mass of useable evidence. Would I invest a lot of time only to discover that too little of the right kind of data had survived, especially for nonelite citizens, whose *portate* frequently contain little detail? In the event, I discovered that my real problem lay at the other end of the spectrum. Even allowing for the interactivity of a digital map, which provides a variety of means to present detailed results, the plethora of narrative detail that I discovered on individual households turned visual presentation of the necessary data into a genuine practical obstacle. Figure 9.1 helps illustrate the point. It shows the intersection of Borgo Santi Apostoli and its eponymous piazza in

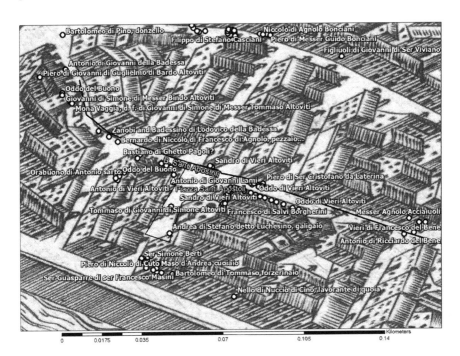

Figure 9.1 Florence: intersection of Borgo Santi Apostoli with Piazza Santi Apostoli and environs, displaying a sample of households declared in the 1427 and 1480 *Catasti*. (Sources: ASF, *Catasto*, 74; *Catasto*, 1008).

central Florence as they appear on the Buonsignori map. Overlaid on this map are the locations of households reported for this zone in the *Catasto* surveys of 1427 and 1480. Each white circle and its accompanying name represent the tax return of a single household. This map includes only a sample of the households for which *portate* survive in this zone, and it totally excludes the results from 1458. Even so, the map is visually crowded. And the problem is exacerbated if one attempts to show the evidence available for individual households, as Figure 9.2 demonstrates.

This image displays some notes to myself about the palace household of the patrician citizen Sandro di Vieri Altoviti, who made his declaration in 1427. The observations appear in a window based on the pop-up windows that one can display in Google Earth by hovering a computer mouse over one of the household icons and clicking. As the volume of data on Sandro's household makes clear (and much more is available), a conventional plan such as this is not adequate to the task of presenting a view of such large amounts of demographic data in a useful way. It needs to be said that it is of course possible to present data more selectively than this. Evidence for all but a single year can be hidden to obtain a clearer view (as has been done here with 1458). Alternatively, albeit with somewhat more difficulty, comparable data from different years can be sequenced for a small area. It is also possible to display a single datum, such as the location of artisanal workshops. In this way, for instance, it is possible to represent the

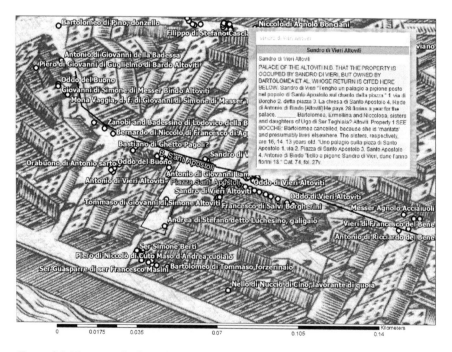

Figure 9.2 Notes on the household of Sandro di Vieri Altoviti, overlaid on data from Figure 9.1. (Sources: ASF, *Catasto*, 74; *Catasto*, 811; *Catasto*, 1008).

distribution of workshops in a single area or to trace changing patterns of ownership and/or the distribution of one or more occupations.[19]

Resolving logistical challenges such as these, however, avoids my central question, which is how one might represent in visual form the 'prepositional' relationships that are encoded in the *confini* and that are overtly expressed in the written record of the 1630 Visitation. These belong to what Henri Lefebvre has called 'spatial practice', the sphere where people enact individual and collective perceptions of urban space in their daily routines.[20] Such relationships are spatially embedded in and inextricably connected to the urban fabric, but they are not trigonometric formulae; their sociological texture, cultural amplitude, and subjectivity are hard to capture in the two-dimensional medium of a city plan. Nothing could be easier than to pinpoint on a map the 'house with a tower, the two of them joined together, for my habitation', which Lorenzo Carducci declared to the *Catasto* officials of 1458. Tied equally to the physical space of his family's residential enclave, though much less susceptible to visual presentation, is the little history contained in the lines that follow Lorenzo's list of *confini*, in which he explained that 'right beneath, under the said tower', there were formerly two workshops that the family used to rent out but that had been empty for years (indeed, since the first *Catasto*, in 1427) because the ground-floor space was to be incorporated in a plan to renovate and extend the principal Carducci domicile.[21] Lorenzo's account, far from the only one of its kind for this part of town, demands explanation with reference to important mid-fifteenth-century changes in the physical, occupational, and socioeconomic character of the ancient and wealthy neighbourhood huddling around the Borgo Santi Apostoli and Via delle Terme just to the north. Perhaps we must conclude in the end that historicizing phenomena such as these in a way that relates contemporary perceptions of the physical environment – including class-inflected attitudes as to who should be living where – is an operation best left to conventional narrative analysis.

Or, perhaps not. Awareness of the need to enrich understanding of how contemporary Florentines occupied, moved through, negotiated, and thought about the places and spaces of their city is a principal motivating factor behind the *Hidden Florence* project, conceived and authored by Fabrizio Nevola and David Rosenthal and described elsewhere in this volume. *Hidden Florence* is a mobile phone app that simulates the ground-level experience of a fictionalized early modern Florentine, named Giovanni, who takes modern visitors on a guided walking tour of *his* Florence. The app's ingenious conceit is its exploitation of GPS and mobile digital technology, which transform visitors from passive listeners into active participants by communicating an intimate sense of the relationship that bound citizens of a past era to the urban environment. Unlike conventional guidebooks, whose usual function is to embed sites and monuments in a positivistic meta-narrative of Western history, *Hidden Florence* imparts a generic sense of the overlapping and often competing associations by which Florentines were attached to their urban environment and the different contexts in which they engaged with it. Without doubt the user learns many canonical facts about the city's history, but it is this experiential, immersive dimension that makes *Hidden Florence* such a distinctive innovation. And it is this quality that one would very much like to incorporate into a map.

I have sought to evoke this kind of spatial experience in my recent article on the Visitation of 1630 (Figure 9.3).[22] One purpose of that argument is to suggest how the Florentine citizenry's 'prepositional' awareness of urban space can be historicized by demonstrating how at different moments it was influenced by specific factors – such as fear of plague. Contemporary medical thinking, which held that plague arose from damp, filth, decay, and detritus, understandably made people wary of the poky, badly ventilated spaces that were the lot of the Florentine poor. It was exactly this concern that motivated the determination in 1630 to 'purge' lower-class accommodation 'of every piece of garbage and dirt, bleaching and cleaning them so as to remove all hint of bad odour, filth being the mother of corruption, and this of plague'.[23] Every entry in the reports of the Visitation exudes the contemporary population's deeply embedded fear of such conditions. Because the reports are structured as lists and the entries of which these lists are composed retain the original order in which households were visited, reading them creates the sensation of walking with the Visitors and of seeing through their eyes. One entry at a time, this vicarious walking tour of the city discloses the ground-level vision of another 'hidden Florence' whose urban taxonomy has nothing to do with parishes, quarters, or *gonfaloni*, the civic and ecclesiastical divisions that historians

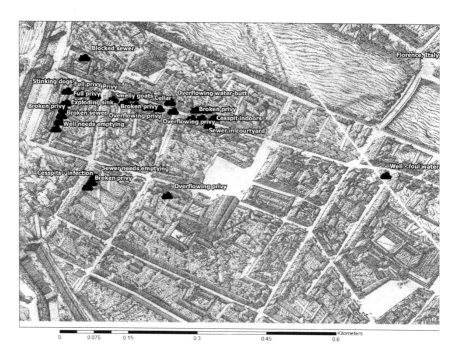

Figure 9.3 View of western Oltrarno, Florence, displaying selection of households reported in August 1630 'Visitation'. (Source: ASF, *CRSPL*, 1418, Arcangelo Michele, Filza 5, Fascio A, *Visite de'quartieri*).

usually discuss in reference to the city's medieval and Renaissance history.[24] Here the visitor discovers no hint of the rhythmic palatial exteriors and ordered vistas of the early Renaissance republic celebrated by the humanist chancellor Leonardo Bruni. In the lists of the Visitation one discovers a Florence turned inside out, its viscera on display in an alienating confusion of squalid, rubbish-choked courtyards and claustrophobic, airless rooms. Here desperate widows and emaciated children are as likely to sleep on the bare earth or a bench as on a clean mattress. All over the city, foul and stagnant water throws out poisonous odours from putrid cisterns, wells, blocked and broken drains,[25] collects in basements,[26] or courses along the street.[27] And at every turn the poisonous stench of human excrement erupts from the cesspits or black wells (*pozzi neri*) used by every household.[28]

Because the Sanità needed to know where to send the volunteers who would pre-empt the danger posed by these putative micro-emergencies, the Visitors made sure to identify the exact location of every overflowing cesspit, leaking drain, rotting mattress, or pile of rubbish. In doing so, they employed a narrative version of the principle exemplified in the *Catasto*'s *confini*, locating everything that they found in physical relation to neighbours, contiguous houses, or other recognisable landmarks. One typical set of directions singled out a cluster of small and obviously deprived households in Via Chiara, on the northwest side of what is now the Central Market: 'In the first house next to the baker, to the tenant on the ground floor, [supply] one mattress; half-way up the stairs, [supply] another; on the first floor on the mezzanine [supply] another.'[29] Thumbnail portraits of the local terrain like this would instantly have been comprehended by contemporary Florentines because they combined the kind of objective data that we expect to find in a modern directory with local knowledge – characteristic of Terence's earlier-cited play – that was a common possession of most if not all inhabitants at the time. In the present context it is necessary to state the obvious, namely that in the absence of this local knowledge, the twenty-first-century scholar is unable to follow the Visitors' directions with such facility. Reading the Visitation record, it is always clear what street the Visitors were in when they wrote their directions because they never failed to specify this fact. Often we can tell precisely where they must have been standing, especially when a prominent landmark or feature such as a street corner is involved. More frequently, however, it is impossible to identify the exact spot to which they refer. As historians of Renaissance Florence know well, while the city's street plan has changed relatively little over the centuries, the same cannot be said for the streetscape itself, let alone the interiors of even those buildings that have survived.[30] Without secure reference points like these, we often cannot be sure of just where the Visitors turned to enter a doorway, descend into a cellar, or walk into an internal courtyard.

A complete and faithful reconstruction of the Visitors' itineraries is not, therefore, a realistic objective. But having said this, and acknowledging the margin of error that I describe, I have found that plotting the locations described in the Visitation remains a useful research exercise because it reveals spatial clusters that reinforce our knowledge of how contemporaries thought about and approached plague (Figure 9.4).

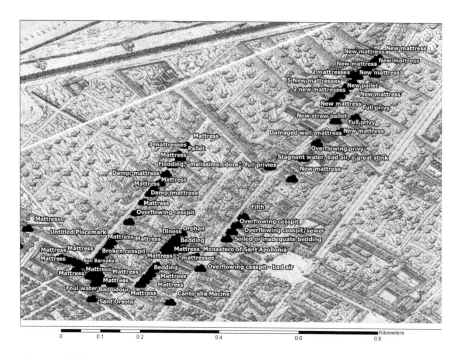

Figure 9.4 View of the area (*sestiere*) of San Giovanni, Florence, displaying selection of households reported in August 1630 'Visitation'. (Source: ASF, *CRSPL*, 1418, Arcangelo Michele, Filza 5, Fascio A, *Visite de' quartieri*).

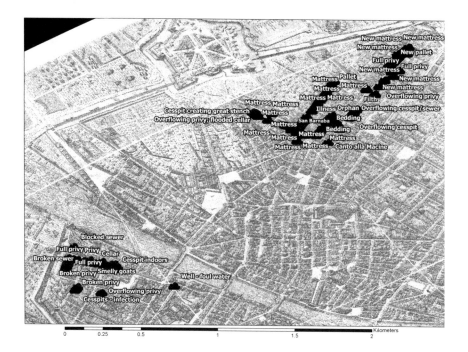

Figure 9.5 View of Florence displaying data from Figures 9.3 and 9.4.

Figures 9.3, 9.4, and 9.5, which represent just the beginning of such an exercise, make this point by showing two such clusters in different locations on the urban periphery of Florence. Figure 9.3 reveals that the Visitors responsible for surveying the western zone of Oltrarno, the area of Florence that lies on the south bank of the river Arno, found poor households in the vicinity of the San Frediano gate, where dirt and odours caused by broken cesspits and privies – and in some cases inappropriately housed animals – posed a risk to public health. Large numbers of poor people, including unskilled workers in the wool industry, had lived in this part of town for centuries, and the colloquial name for the area, Camaldoli, had become a byword for poverty and social unrest.[31] Equally predictable (Figure 9.4) is the similar picture that the Visitation uncovered northwest of the Medici palace in the area between Via San Gallo and the walls, which, as the Buonsignori map makes clear, was much less urbanized than it is today. Here as well, the Visitors discovered large numbers of poverty-stricken women and men living with the dangers of broken, dysfunctional, or flooded privies and soiled bedding. Given that the conditions thought to produce plague were so closely associated with poverty and poor housing and the fact that large numbers of poor people lived in marginal neighbourhoods like the two shown in Figures 9.3 and 9.4, one is hardly surprised that the Visitors discovered so many of the risk factors for which they were looking in this part of town.

In creating Figures 9.3 and 9.4, I used a small black cloud icon to indicate places where the Visitors discovered the various factors responsible for the noxious odours that contemporaries so deeply feared. Readers familiar with the Google Earth, where I originally entered this data, will know that the program allows users to zoom in to produce a highly detailed view; alternatively, user can zoom out to simulate a panoptic gaze. In Figures 9.3 and 9.4 I have reproduced this effect against the background of the Buonsignori map. In Figures 9.5, which places the viewer high above the city, the angle of vision causes the black icons to merge – they smear and appear to colonize street corners, thoroughfares, and small neighbourhoods. This effect, which began as unintended visual by-product of Google Earth's zoom tool, seems to me serendipitously metaphorical in the present context, and I believe that its retention can be justified as something more than a visual rhetorical flourish. As I have argued,[32] the written reports of the Visitation may be understood as a textual artefact preserving a spatialized mental projection of the citizenry's fear of plague on to the Florentine streetscape. As a visual shorthand for that collective emotion, the sinister black clusters are surprisingly apt, in both historical and representational terms. They express well the contemporary population's apprehension of pestilence as a malodorous vapour seeping from the filth and squalor of the city's poor and crowded neighbourhoods, corrupting the air, adhering to inanimate surfaces and skin, spreading itself from person to person.

Mapping fear in this way does more, however, than confirm something that we already know about Florentine spatial sensibility, namely that upper-class Florentines had always been negatively biased against the urban periphery.[33] Figures 9.3, 9.4, and 9.5 show the beginnings of a spatially and temporally contingent map that may illustrate how Florentines felt in certain circumstances and at specific moments about other features of the urban terrain. Earlier in this essay I remarked that one of the things one learns from extended reading of the Sanità's sixteenth-century correspondence is that Florentines did not stop worrying about the risk of infection when plague was not imminent. Like the twenty-first-century fear of catastrophic fire experienced by rural Australians, this emotion remained in the background until the inevitable crisis that forced it to the front of active attention.[34] A map composed along the lines of Figures 9.3, 9.4, and 9.5, therefore, has the potential to suggest how a perennial background anxiety about plague could inform the Florentine community's collective attitude towards the particular kinds of urban places from which infection could be expected to launch its next assault on the community, whenever that might be.

Because early modern Florence never had a working-class ghetto, the population's suspicion of places where poor people lived or regularly congregated did not relate exclusively to the city's edge. As the Visitation record demonstrates in more detail than almost any other surviving document, every part of Florence was peppered with enclaves of deficient housing filled with suffering poor. It seems reasonable to assume, therefore, that wealthier citizens worried more about health risks that were literally next door than they did about identical problems that manifested themselves out of sight on the urban periphery. In 1630, the Visitors reported that workers from the nearby Medici Chapels at San Lorenzo had transformed an alcove right behind the Medici place into a de facto *pissoir*, 'generating an mighty stink [*grandissimo puzzo*], as they also do under the portico, where the said workers also congregate'. It was therefore necessary 'to place these public conveniences [*luoghi comuni*] somewhere else, and to make sure that they are properly ventilated'.[35] Cramped, badly ventilated accommodation was jammed between major thoroughfares and behind palaces of the elite throughout the city centre, as in the case of several desperate households in the courtyard of the Donati tower and in the tower itself, where the Visitors discovered 'people dying of hunger'.[36] Citizens abreast of contemporary thinking about the causes of plague would therefore have known that whenever and wherever they walked in Florence, the deadly precursors of disease – dirt, decay, corrupting air – lurked just metres away and on all sides in the hovels that filled the city's laneways and back streets. They would also have been justified in worrying about what lay beneath their feet, given the networks of drains designed to carry away both water and ordure and that periodically heaved their sickening contents to the surface. Just off the Piazza Madonna, behind the cupola of San Lorenzo, the Visitors discovered a drain pumping effluent directly into the street, while in the middle of town was a 'ditch running under the houses of the corridor as far as the Ponte Vecchio, which receives [matter from] all the privies in the said houses. It needs to be deepened, because it channels and carries away all the filth, and the shopkeepers say that it is throwing out an evil odour'.[37]

As already observed, we do not have the data necessary to create a map that would show the precise location of every problem located by the Visitors in August 1630. The Visitation record, however, contains more than enough evidence to allow for a map that would highlight examples of the kinds of perceived danger spots that were under surveillance during the looming crisis of that year and that in my opinion would have constituted a permanent concern for members of the governing classes. In other words, I believe that by using the digital means available to the DECIMA team, it should be possible to overlay the Buonsignori with a range of place markers showing generic urban features onto which contemporary citizens projected a quite distinct variety of collective fear. Locating and highlighting the fetid little piazzas and courtyards, open drains, stagnant cisterns, and broken cesspits and the many crowded, desperate households that appear in the Visitation report may provide an additional lens that can refine our vision of such representations as the Buonsignori, as well as enriching the context in which one appreciates other features (such as the location of the early modern city's many female sex workers). To the places I have already mentioned should be added the city's gates, ingress through which was banned during emergencies to people who did not carry an official *bolletta* declaring them disease-free, as well as minor entrances such as the now vanished Porticciuola delle Farine, on the western edge of the city by the Arno. In a letter dated 7 June 1630 one cannot miss the smoking anger of the Sanità's magistrates at one Capitano Francesco Novellucci of Prato, who had sneaked into the city via this route, having earlier been denied access further north at the Porta al Prato.[38] Additionally, there is a class of ephemeral spaces created by the measures that the government took in its efforts to contain the spread of plague once it had been detected. These include the private houses that were boarded up and sealed – often with the inhabitants inside – when the presence of plague was suspected or proved, as well as entire streets that were temporarily quarantined until, it was hoped, the plague had exhausted itself.

In my own current work I am extending this exercise in spatial mapping beyond the city walls and into the dominion of the Grand Ducal State. In this wider context one discovers, extending over many decades, a recurrent determination on the part of the Sanità to implement nothing less than a Tuscan-wide combined intelligence and military operation that aimed to seal borders, if necessary by terrorizing (*dar terrore*) those seeking unauthorized entry to Florentine territory.[39] Unfailingly, this policy targeted the poor, as in 1555, when the Sanità urgently spread word throughout the *contado*, 'above all in the markets and the churches', that Tuscany's starving poor would be prevented from entering Florence to beg because 'being badly nourished and fed they are frequently contagious'.[40] Panning outwards to view the region reveals a spatial consciousness on the part of the Sanità's officials that does not differ in principle from that which governed the government's perception of the city itself. Arterial roads in the *contado* were a major concern, as these were the routes most likely to be used by would-be arrivals. On the other hand, they were relatively easier for the authorities to police. A much greater worry was Tuscany's frighteningly porous borders, where Florentine troops, no matter how brutally they sought to enforce their authority, could not possibly hope to monitor every right of way. Like the city's down-at-heel interstices, remote and relatively untrafficked terrain away from major routes were danger zones. It was via minor roads, passes, and trails, even water-courses, that 'wayfarers and foreigners' could pass unchecked, evading official guards 'by malice or fraud'.[41]

Investigating the phenomena described in this brief essay has the potential to extend beyond the example of a single crisis, teaching us more about how

Florentines of the governing classes engaged emotionally and otherwise with aspects of the physical and spatial environment that often escape attention because they are not deemed architecturally significant or aesthetically attractive or indeed because they lie outside the city. In addition, such study can also contribute to the history of emotion by allowing us to parse and historicize the affective dimension of such engagement. The emotion refracted through the lens of the Visitation report and the Sanità's correspondence was not merely a fear of mortal disease. Beneath the surface in these sources ran another and even more fundamental anxiety, which was the citizenry's dread of the civic disorder and social breakdown that accompanied the crisis of epidemic disease. Again and again, it is clear that when the city's governors took action to contain the poor in their homes, to quarantine streets and entire neighbourhoods, and to prevent unauthorized entry to the city, when they attempted to prevent the mass movement of poor citizens across subject territories or sent troops to the borders to deny entry to illegal arrivals they were spatially performing one of the citizenry's most intense emotions – the fear of losing control.

Notes

1   I wish to register my warm thanks to Colin Rose for translating the data contained in my 'kmz' files from Google Earth into the form that they take in the figures accompanying this essay. I owe you one, Colin.
2   B.H. Rosenwein, 'Worrying about Emotions in History', *The American Historical Review* 107, 2002; W.M. Reddy, *The Navigation of Feeling: A Framework for the History of Emotions*, Cambridge, UK, and New York, NY: Cambridge University Press, 2004.
3   *Ufficiali di Sanità* (*Sanità*). For an other approach to digital mapping of this plague, see the article by Henderson and Rose in this volume.
4   *Sanità*, 37, fol. 40r.
5   On the circulation of news in official circles and throughout the urban population see F. de Vivo, *Information and Communication in Venice: Rethinking Early Modern Politics*, Oxford, UK: Oxford University Press, 2007; on rumour and gossip, E. Horodowich, *Language and Statecraft in Early Modern Venice*, New York, NY: Cambridge University Press, 2008, especially ch. 4.
6   *Sanità*, 37: fol. 40r.
7   Ibid., fol. 43r.
8   Ibid. Sealing houses, often with sick families inside, was an expedient implemented by health authorities in this period with the intention of preventing plague from spreading. See C. Cipolla, *Cristofano and the Plague: A Study in the History of Public Health in the Age of Galileo*, London, UK: Collins, 1973, 33; G. Calvi, *Histories of a Plague Year: The Social and the Imaginary in Baroque Florence*, Berkeley and Los Angeles, CA, and Oxford, UK: University of California Press, 1989, passim.
9   *Sanità*, 37, fols 34r, 41r, 43r.
10 See N.A. Eckstein, 'Florence on Foot: An Eye-Level Mapping of the Early Modern City in Time of Plague', *Renaissance Studies* 30, 2016.
11 More detailed treatment of the themes relating to this project appear in Eckstein, 'Florence on Foot'.
12 Archivio di Stato di Firenze (ASF), *Catasto*, 1008, fol. 230r.
13 See N.A. Eckstein, 'Neighborhood as Microcosm', in Roger J. Crum and J.T. Paoletti (eds), *Renaissance Florence: A Social History*, New York, NY: Cambridge University Press, 2006, 228; Eckstein, 'Florence on Foot'. The written record of the Visitation survives in ASF, *Compagnie Religiose Soppresse da Pietro Leopoldo*, 1418, Filza 5, Fascio 8, hereafter cited simply as 'Visita', the name used by the surveyors themselves.

14 Visita, fol. 57r.
15 N.A. Eckstein, *Painted Glories: The Brancacci Chapel in Renaissance Florence*, New Haven, CT, and London, UK: Yale University Press, 2014, 52–53.
16 Terence, *Terence: The Comedies*, P. Brown (trans.), Oxford, UK: Oxford University Press, 2006, pp. 86–87.
17 M. de Certeau, *The Practice of Everyday Life*, Berkeley and Los Angeles, CA, and London, UK: University of California Press, 1988, ch. 7.
18 S. Herlihy and C. Klapisch-Zuber, *Les Toscans et leurs familles: Une étude du catasto Florentin de 1427*, Paris, France: FNSP Editions de l'école des hautes études en sciences sociales, 1978.
19 E.g. W. Jacobsen, *Die Maler von Florenz zu Beginn der Renaissance*, Munich, Germany: Deutscher Verlag, 2001, 702–9.
20 W. Lefebvre, *The Production of Space*, D. Nicholson-Smith (trans.), Oxford, UK, and Cambridge, MA: Blackwell, 1991, 38.
21 *Catasto*, 811, fol. 205r.
22 Eckstein, 'Florence on Foot'.
23 F. Rondinelli, *Relazione del contagio stato in Firenze l'anno 1630 e 1633*, Florence, Italy: J. Guiducci and S. Franchi, 1714, 22.
24 E.g. D.V. Kent and F.W. Kent, *Neighbours and Neighbourhood in Renaissance Florence: The District of the Red Lion in the Fifteenth Century*, Locust Valley, NY: J.J. Augustin, 1982; N.A. Eckstein, *The District of the Green Dragon: Neighbourhood Life and Social Change in Renaissance Florence*, Florence, Italy: Olschki, 1995.
25 *Visita*, fols 16r, 28r, 95r.
26 *Visita*, fols 5v, 25r.
27 *Visita*, fols 59v, 62r.
28 *Visita*, fol. 48v.
29 *Visita*, fol. 58v.
30 E.g. B. Preyer, 'The "chasa overso palagio" of Alberto di Zanobi: A Florentine Palace of about 1400 and Its Later Remodeling', *The Art Bulletin* 65, 1983, 387–401.
31 Eckstein, *The District of the Green Dragon*, 8.
32 Eckstein, 'Florence on Foot'.
33 Eckstein, *The District of the Green Dragon*, 6 ff.
34 See Reddy, *The Navigation of Feeling*, 111.
35 *Visita*, fol. 63r.
36 *Visita*, fol. 43r.
37 *Visita*, fols 62v, 52r. The reference is indeed to Vasari's famous corridor, which links the Palazzo Vecchio to the distant Palazzo Pitti, south of the Arno: 'Un fosso sotto le case del corridore sino al ponte Vechio che riceve tutti li destri di dette case, converia farlo affondare, perché corra, e porti via l'inmonditie e si ha relatione da' botegai che getta cativissimo odore.'
38 Entrance via the weirs on the Arno was prohibited in 1630; Rondinelli, *Relazione del contagio*, 22. For the incident on 7 June, see *Sanità*, 37, fol. 41r.
39 Ibid., fol. 42v.
40 Ibid., fol. 3v.
41 Ibid., fol. 6v.

Bibliography

Manuscript sources

Archivio di Stato di Firenze (ASF), *Catasto*, 811, 1008.
——— *Ufficiali di Sanità (Sanità)*, 37.
——— *Compagnie Religiose Soppresse da Pietro Leopoldo (Visita)*, 1418.

Print sources

Calvi, G., *Histories of a Plague Year: The Social and the Imaginary in Baroque Florence*, Berkeley and Los Angeles, CA, and Oxford, UK: University of California Press, 1989.

Cipolla, C., *Cristofano and the Plague: A Study in the History of Public Health in the Age of Galileo*, London, UK: Collins, 1973.

de Certeau, M., *The Practice of Everyday Life*, Berkeley and Los Angeles, CA, and London, UK: University of California Press, 1988.

de Vivo, F., *Information and Communication in Venice: Rethinking Early Modern Politics*, Oxford, UK: Oxford University Press, 2007.

Eckstein, N.A., *The District of the Green Dragon: Neighbourhood Life and Social Change in Renaissance Florence*, Florence, Italy: Olschki, 1995.

––––––– 'Neighborhood as Microcosm', in R.J. Crum and J.T. Paoletti (eds), *Renaissance Florence: A Social History*, New York, NY: Cambridge University Press, 2006, 19–54.

––––––– *Painted Glories: The Brancacci Chapel in Renaissance Florence*, New Haven, CT, and London, UK: Yale University Press, 2014.

––––––– 'Florence on Foot: An Eye-Level Mapping of the Early Modern City in Time of Plague', *Renaissance Studies* 30, 2016, 25.

Herlihy, S., and Klapisch-Zuber, C., *Les Toscans et leurs familles: Une étude du catasto Florentin de 1427*, Paris, France: FNSP Editions de l'école des hautes études en sciences sociales, 1978.

––––––– *Tuscans and Their Families: A Study of the Florentine Catasto of 1427*, New Haven, CT: Yale University Press, 1985.

Horodowich, E., *Language and Statecraft in Early Modern Venice*, New York, NY: Cambridge University Press, 2008.

Jacobsen, W., *Die Maler von Florenz zu Beginn der Renaissance*, Munich, Germany: Deutscher Verlag, 2001.

Kent, D.V., and Kent, F.W., *Neighbours and Neighbourhood in Renaissance Florence: The District of the Red Lion in the Fifteenth Century*, Locust Valley, NY: J.J. Augustin, 1982.

Lefebvre, H., *The Production of Space*, D. Nicholson-Smith (trans.), Oxford, UK, and Cambridge, MA: Blackwell, 1991.

Preyer, B., 'The "chasa overso palagio" of Alberto di Zanobi: A Florentine Palace of about 1400 and Its Later Remodeling', *The Art Bulletin* 65, 1983.

Reddy, W.M., *The Navigation of Feeling: A Framework for the History of Emotions*, Cambridge, UK, and New York, NY: Cambridge University Press, 2004.

Rondinelli, F., *Relazione del contagio stato in Firenze l'anno 1630 e 1633*, Florence, Italy: J. Guiducci and S. Franchi, 1714.

Rosenwein, B.H., 'Worrying about Emotions in History', *The American Historical Review* 107, 2002.

Terence, *Terence: The Comedies*, P. Brown (trans.), Oxford, UK: Oxford University Press, 2006.

10 Locating experience in the Renaissance city using mobile app technologies
The *Hidden Florence* project

Fabrizio Nevola and David Rosenthal

Introduction: the kinetic city

Hidden Florence is a smartphone app in which a 'contemporary' character, a late fifteenth-century wool worker dubbed Giovanni, invites the user to go with him on two walks around the city.[1] The first walk is focused on the parish of Sant' Ambrogio, the neighbourhood in which Giovanni lives; the second guides the user around the dense urban centre in which he works. Of all the seventeen stops on Giovanni's itinerary, Site 3 of the neighbourhood walk, Via dei Pilastri, may well be the least visually spectacular, yet it quickly takes us to the heart of the agenda that underpins the project – to explore how mobile technologies can offer historians a tool and a methodology for researching and conveying urban experience as a dynamic relationship between place and identity.

As users 'walk' into Via dei Pilastri, they discover a fairly typical *centro storico* 'canyon'. Two rows of apartments buildings, four storeys of shutter-blinkered windows, face each other across the narrow street. With earphones plugged in and one eye on the smartphone screen, they see their own geolocated avatar as it moves along a much earlier Via dei Pilastri, the one painstakingly drawn by Stefano Buonsignori in his 1584 map of Florence (Figures 10.1 and 10.2).

The Buonsignori map reveals that the streetscape of the past was also something of a canyon, a continuous wall of terraced dwellings, three storeys rather the present four, typical of the housing developed by religious institutions in the predominantly artisan districts of the urban outskirts. The app asks users, after 'walking' a few metres along Pilastri, to find a hole in the wall, probably used for selling wine. Once they have found it, users trigger the audio, and Giovanni starts to talk. He tells users that the house they are standing in front of is rented by the wine seller, an out-of-towner called Pierfrancesco, who lives there with his family of eight people. The house next door is owned, unusually, by an artisan, a shoemaker who rents it to a dyer called Cesare, a man who is notoriously unlucky at dice. Further up, at the streetcorner, there are a couple of shops, a bakery and a firewood store, the latter run by a literate man who has also acted as scribe for the local confraternity for ten years. Giovanni continues in this vein for a minute and then says: 'I know, I'm starting to sound like a *Catasto* official doing the rounds for a tax census. But it is a kind of a census every time you walk down the street, it's as if you're measuring the neighbourhood.'

Figure 10.1 Via dei Pilastri, detail from Stefano Buonsignori, *Nova pulcherrimae civitatis Florentiae topographia accuratissime delineate*, 1594 (Harvard Map Collection), as viewed on screen in the *Hidden Florence* app (© University of Exeter).

In Via dei Pilastri, the Giovanni character keys into a number of urban historical themes – neighbourhood and community, networks and literacy, streetcorners and shops as social junctions – and both the 'discover more' audio and the brief articles on the app's website delve into these issues further. But what the character also underscores is the significance of movement in this ecology

Locating experience 189

Figure 10.2 Hidden Florence app user on Via dei Pilastri.

of the street. In recent years, movement has become increasingly intrinsic to the analysis of everyday urban experience; indeed, recent sociology has coined the notion of a 'mobility turn' in the humanities, a phrase designed to echo the 'spatial turn' identified by the cultural geographer Denis Cosgrove more than a decade ago.[2] Historians of early modern Italy, adapting the ideas of influential thinkers such as Michel de Certeau, have started to incorporate everyday movement into an already vigorous scholarship addressing the spatialized politics of urban existence.[3] Movement, essentially walking, is seen as one practice through which city dwellers effectively produced urban spaces and social relations (and as 'an intensely social activity', as Filippo de Vivo points out, rather than the solitary and alienated practice sometimes imagined by the theorists of the twentieth-century city).[4] Walking, suggests Niall Atkinson, was one of the critical ways identity was shaped. In the often crowded streets of the early modern city, he argues, people were constantly engaged in relocating and re-establishing their sense both of self and of community externally, in a physical fabric alive with personal and familial, local and civic resonances.[5]

Hand-held devices enabled with GPS (global positioning systems) are clearly well placed to develop such lines of investigation, to apprehend and communicate the complex and, above all, kinetic relationship between city dwellers and the built environment. Giovanni tells users that simply walking down the street is like 'measuring the neighbourhood'. Everyday movement, we want to suggest, recalled, affirmed, and modified urban knowledge for the early modern city dweller – and it frames that knowledge as a dialogue between the actor in motion and the urban fabric. As Giovanni measures, or re-creates, the neighbourhood, he also in effect maps his own sense of identity, tracing out ideas of self, territory, and community as he puts one foot after the other. Meanwhile, twenty-first-century users are offered a sense – and an interpretation – of a non-elite Quattrocento man's engagement with the journeys, spaces, and objects that they, too, are experiencing. As they walk from site to site, they are invited to confront the similarities and disjunctures between past and present and to consider how getting there is as important as being there.

The sections that follow more fully unpack our approach in *Hidden Florence* and consider the potentialities and issues associated with locative media. The sections roughly mirror the way the app unfolds for users – from the remarkably detailed 1584 Buonsignori map, which allows a degree of navigability and immersion not possible with previous maps of the city, to the specific sites and objects that engage users with the material culture of public space, to the audio and the invented Giovanni character. Despite the chronological dislocation with the map, we chose to set the app historically around 1490. *Hidden Florence* was a research experiment, but it was also conceived as a pedagogical tool and a way to engage as wide a public as possible in what in effect is an alternative tour of the city. The Quattrocento and the early Medici tend to be the focus of the many history and art history courses run in Florence, and they also represent the 'Renaissance' as widely promoted to tourists. Giovanni, pitched as a textile worker, was designed as a vehicle not only to explore everyday urban experience but also to raise questions about perception and the politics of place in a period most visitors will already have encountered through the city's monumental sites and its most mythologized figures.

Buonsignori's map and locative media

Like the DECIMA project that constitutes the primary example for this collection, *Hidden Florence* adopts Stefano Buonsignori's map. As far as we know, it is the first geolocated app to adopt a premodern map, what we might loosely describe as a sixteenth-century streetview interface.[6] Towards the middle of the city centre walk, Giovanni brings the visitor to the Piazza della Signoria (City Centre, Site 4). In Buonsignori's map, the piazza is rendered as one of the largest open city-centre spaces, the surveyor's southwestern vantage point offering a clear view onto the square, which is dominated by the imposing mass of the Palazzo Vecchio.

As is well known, Buonsignori made his map for Grand Duke Francesco de' Medici during his tenure as court 'cosmographer'; nowhere is this more evident than in the depciton of the Piazza della Signoria, which is placed at the visual centre of the huge (123 × 138cm) map.[7] Significantly, the elaborate display of statuary assembled along the *aringhiera* and beyond to the Neptune fountain and Giambologna's equestrian monument of Cosimo I are prominently visible, emphasizing the reordered princely space that supplanted the civic centre following the Medici accession.[8] But Giovanni, speaking to us from the last decade of

Figure 10.3 Piazza della Signoria, detail from Stefano Buonsignori, *Nova pulcherrimae civitatis Florentiae topographia accuratissime delineate*, 1594 (Harvard Map Collection), with *Hidden Florence* avatar (© University of Exeter).

the the fifteenth century (almost a century before the map was made), has a different point to make – about rare citizen participation in *parlamenti* and popular politics in the piazza. He invites the viewer to look for the fourteenth-century marble sculpture of Justice, high up above the arcade of the Loggia dei Signori. A symbol of the city's pre-ducal republican institutions, the loggia is rendered invisible in Buonsignori's map, whose perspectival angle privileges sites of Medicean monarchical rule over monuments of civic government (Figure 10.3).

This is a powerful reminder of the fact that the cartographic gaze is not necessarily objective and that urban space as it is constituted on the printed page of the map represents the politics of sixteenth-century Medici patronage.[9] Buonsignori's was an innovative piece of map making, combining a more traditional axonometric ('bird's-eye view') approach with the more technically accurate ichnographic (figure ground) survey to create an unusual compound view of clear street networks and recognisable elevations.[10] Thus the key network of streets can be understood – and is indeed revealed to be quite similar to the modern layout in most areas – while landmarks also stand out as prominent. This combination lends itself especially well to the function of depicting a version of city in which particular monuments stand out in the city fabric – a representational form loaded with period-specific meaning.

In the DECIMA project, the precision of the sixteenth-century map has been updated and rendered GIS-compliant so that information from the census documents can be accurately plotted using location coordinates.[11] As Leah Faibisoff shows elsewhere in this volume, by understanding the movement of census officials along the city streets as they compiled their documents, it is possible to propose a plausible location for each household and shop they visited.[12] While DECIMA's use of the map is locked to a detailed GIS rendering, the approach we took with the app designers we worked with at Calvium was somewhat more approximative and experiential. In *Hidden Florence*, Buonsignori's map is adopted as a navigational tool – not something it was designed for – allowing modern-day users to walk through the city and experience the streets and piazzas as they are depicted in the Renaissance map. The GPS functions of the smartphone plot users' locations – using a simple avatar, a Renaissance-robed version of the Google streetview yellow man – and allow the authors to present information to them as they approach sites of significance for Giovanni, the guide-character.

Within the app, we wanted to show users their location on the historic Buonsignori map as well as on a modern street map of Florence.[13] That meant turning the historical map into a set of map tiles that could be selected and presented by the app as appropriate, while also providing three map zoom levels to give users both an overview of the neighbourhood and a detailed view of a few local streets. The superb detail of Buonsignori's printed map made this zoom function possible but also raised problems relating to how to limit the amount of memory needed to build the map into the app. Consequently, we created historic tile sets only for the areas of Florence visited through the app. Having selected the relevant sections of Buonsignori's map and stitched them together as a composite image in an image editor, we rotated, scaled, and skewed it until it lined up with a modern street map imported as a base layer (OpenStreetMap). When the match was good, we discarded this layer and exported the composite historic image. Finally, we geolocated that image by defining the latitude and longitude of its borders. The end result is a historic Google-like map that provides an amazingly accurate representation of what would have been around the visitor in Buonsignori's time.

The use of the historic map as a navigational tool both historicizes the experience of moving through the city and estranges users from their surroundings; by so doing it highlights ways in which the Florence of today is different from its Renaissance self. The historical elisions and inconsistencies that occur between the app's visual interface map (a rendering of the city in the 1580s) and the narrative underpinning the discussion of the site as it was in 1490 also offer a useful entry point to thinking about locative media and the creative practice that underlies the app design. Apps like *Hidden Florence* encode content (e.g. sound, film, text) onto fixed places, identified by their geospatial codes (e.g. GIS), and trigger that content by users' movement into proximity (e.g. using geo-fences or i-beacons).[14] Tagging information to place in a way that allows it to be unlocked by movement has been termed 'urban markup', a process enabling information to be encoded onto the fabric of the city in far more informal ways than epigraphs, inscriptions, or signage.[15] The implications for such technologies – which in quite simple ways visualize the long-established concept of the city as palimpsest – for urban and architectural history are significant.[16] On the one hand, the approach enables a more embodied, practised research process, which is discussed further in the following section. On the other hand, working with multiple sorts of information – the underlying base map, the historic Buonsignori map, the historical content voiced by the Giovanni character, the modern photographic cues delivered on screen, and the present-day urban fabric itself – the app can be understood as a locative media experiment that highlights the degree to which the city can be experienced as historically permeable, adaptive, and layered.[17]

Thus, when Giovanni steps into the Piazza della Signoria, he is at once in the 1490s, in the 1580s, and in the present day. While he describes fifteenth-century popular government practices of groups gathering in the piazza to voice, at least in theory, the opinion of the crowd, as users we to some extent experience his account informed by the crowds (of tourists) that fill the piazza with us, while at the same time we might historicize that view through the representation of it by Buonsignori, visible on screen. In spite of the fact that only a brief account is provided of the phenomenon (Giovanni speaks for no more than two minutes at any one site), users will understand the visual and social history of that particular space in quite a different way to how they might through more traditional text-based communication. Through the affordances of locative media, sensory experience – audio, visual, environmental – is placed at the heart of a new way of approaching and understanding historical 'data'.

If we return to the Via dei Pilastri example discussed at the outset, we might contrast Buonsignori's view with that which emerges from the 1561 *Decima* documents. The former offers a fairly generic view of a working-class residential district with simple housing scarcely differentiated along the street front, while the archival document offers a highly detailed record of largely rented housing in multiple ownership, of workers and their professions, mouths to be fed, and rent due, some of it to the nearby nuns of Sant'Ambrogio. In *Hidden Florence* a compound understanding is proposed, by which a user walking along the street is offered a sense of who might have lived behind these doors and what their stories were – Buonsignori's map combines with the modern city to unpack the dense archival evidence so that we can see and hear the streetscape of the neighbourhood.

Material culture of urban space

Rendering Buonsignori's map responsive to movement through the smartphone or tablet is really only the first step in the process by which *Hidden Florence* engages users. The second step is to return users to a more direct dialogue with the extant city fabric at selected sites, where material evidence provides the visual cue for the brief commentaries on everyday life provided by the Giovanni character. While much of the content and interpretation voiced by Giovanni might be described as sociocultural history, the *Hidden Florence* app seeks also to be a work of art and architectural history in that it engages users above all in exploring the extant material culture of the public spaces of the Renaissance

194 *Fabrizio Nevola and David Rosenthal*

city. In so doing, we argue, it also reshapes our undertanding of the embodied experience of urban space and the complex meanings inscribed on particular places in the past.

We might consider the site in the neighbourhood walk that follows Via dei Pilastri, the Monteloro tabernacle on the northern corner of the intersection of

Figure 10.4 Canto di Monteloro: intersection of Via dei Pilastri and Borgo Pinti, detail from Stefano Buonsignori, *Nova pulcherrimae civitatis Florentiae topographia accuratissime delineate*, 1594 (Harvard Map Collection), as viewed on screen in the *Hidden Florence* app (© University of Exeter).

Locating experience 195

Figure 10.5 Canto di Monteloro: intersection of Via dei Pilastri and Borgo Pinti.

Via dei Pilastri and Borgo Pinti (Sant' Ambrogio, Site 5). Florence, like most Italian cities, is peppered with street shrines, which mostly cluster around street corners (Figures 10.4 and 10.5).

As Edward Muir has pointed out, they are a visual reminder of how the sacred permeated everyday life in Italian cities, as people moved around doing their daily business.[18] While a number of the more significant Florentine tabernacles have undergone restoration in recent years, attention has tended to focus on the paintings that adorn these streetside shrines, with the prevalent concern of art historians to establish their attribution and, in many cases, to guarantee their preservation by relocating the often damaged frescoes to museums.[19] Much less attention tends to be afforded to their physical placement, its wider urban context, and the social histories of devotional practices that rotated around these objects and sites. Giovanni observes:

> I don't usually come up this way. . . .
> I know! I can hear you saying it's just a block from where I live, in Sant'Ambrogio. But the thing is, this is another district, someone else's turf.
> This *canto* or street corner tells the story. Look at the street shrine there, on the left. It's a pretty old painting – they say it's been there for generations. But the symbols in the frame – they were added just a few years ago. They show golden hills and a cross above them – *monti d'oro* – That's the name of these crossroads.

Look on the other side of the street and you'll see another stone marker – just like the one I showed you at Sant'Ambrogio. This is another *potenza* neighbourhood. It's the Monteloro *potenza* territory, and as the stone says they fear God, *timor domini*; you'll hear those words from every fraternity in town. In fact, there was a tavern here – the Candeli (the candles) – that was only just recently closed down because people got too rowdy . . . too close to Our Lady you see. It's also too close to the nunnery of Santa Maria Maddalena, just up the road there. That symbol with the hills? That's the convent's symbol. . . .

By choosing the Monteloro tabernacle, the app aims to draw the user's attention to an all-too-often ovelooked feature of the streetscape, the sort of site whose very ubiquity and association with popular devotional practice set it apart from the body of works traditionally invested with scholarly attention. Giovanni's commentary then inscribes the site with a variety of overlapping meanings that contextualize those practices in the light of everyday neighbourhood community life. In the second half of his account, he explains how the shrine is managed by the men of a local confraternity, who keep the site clean and dignify the Madonna with a crown and robes on special occasions, and even that its name derives from the coat of arms of '*monti d'oro*' (golden hills topped by a cross) of the nearby convent of Santa Maria Maddalena.[20] But Monteloro is also the name of one of the city's carnivalesque artisan brigades (*potenze* or 'powers') that carved out 'kingdoms' across Florence, a neighbour and sometimes rival to Giovanni's own brigade of the Red City (Sant'Ambrogio, Site 1). This is brought home by directing the viewer's gaze across the street to the Monteloro *potenza*'s territorial stone marker, a visible expression of a largely 'secular' tavern-based sociability – in this case the tavern that intermittently existed on the same street corner.[21]

Here, then, the app moves out of the map into the physical fabric of the city. The Giovanni commentary is brief and touches on many issues – religious enclosure, confraternal devotion, carnival brigades and drinking, the signage assembled at a street corner – but they come together because the information is 'performed' on site in a close interaction between the audio guide and the visual traces in front of the user. Thus the technology facilitates an embodied engagement with the meanings of the site, where our physical presence and our experience of movement to and through that site are integral to our understanding of it.[22] Sites such as street corners were nodes in networks of information, sociability, and devotion; they were places where key services such as taverns, apothecaries, and bakeries clustered and where neighbourhood groups and local lineages marked themselves physically and ritually and through artistic and architectural elements such as loggias and street shrines. Writing for locative media makes these places newly significant, framing a process of enquiry that can lead to fresh research questions and findings.

Microhistory and the making of 'Giovanni'

Engaging both researcher and user in a close reading of the relationship among actors, places, and objects raises, as pointed out earlier, issues of perception and identity – and this leads to a closer consideration of the Giovanni character. Our decision in *Hidden Florence* to focus on everyday social experience and a nonelite perspective is informed to a significant degree by microhistorical approaches. First developed in Italy in the 1970s, in reaction to what was perceived as the perspective-flattening (we might say axonometric) scientism of quantitative history and the *longue durée*, *microstoria* is perhaps less a methodology than an 'exploratory stance'.[23] Yet it has a number of persistent features. Most fundamental is the idea that a micro-analysis of specific scenarios and their actors can illuminate larger social and cultural processes, mentalities, conflicts, and appropriations. In keeping with this, microhistorians have given ample room to contingency and agency, in particular (though not exclusively) the agency of nondominant individuals or groups. In this respect, microhistory finds an affinity with the analysis of urban space and movement set out by de Certeau, who suggested that apparently simple activities such as walking constituted creative assertions of agency by ordinary city dwellers – a politics of everyday life.[24] Last, microhistory has been distinctly committed to 'thick' description and narrative devices as a means of critically reconstructing experience, in short, bringing the past to life.[25]

Locative media offer a powerful vehicle for developing microhistorical-type approaches, and the *Hidden Florence* app represents one model for putting this into practice. Clearly the character at the centre of the app, 'Giovanni', is not a recovered voice, a Ginzburgian miller contextualized and probed through narrative reconstruction. While there are parallels with microhistory's use of fictive techniques, he is entirely a fiction. We must also stress that we made no intention to invent an 'authentic' period voice like those attempted by Simon Schama in *Dead Certainties (Unwarranted Speculations)* or Robin Bisha with her invented voice of an eighteenth-century Russian noblewoman.[26] Giovanni, who addresses the present-day user directly, in nonperiod language, is unambigiously a device that playfully replaces the modern tourist guide with a pseudo-contemporary one. Nonetheless, he sits loosely within this strand of experimental history. The reasons for choosing this model were linked to our desire to locate the experience of ordinary, often overlooked, Florentines. Certainly, there are nonelite sources that could have been used. The most obvious example is the diary of the apothecary Luca Landucci (1450–1516). Giovanni in fact refers to Landucci when he stands at the Strozzi palace (city centre, site 9), which was close to the apothecary's shop, and some of the detail of his narrative there is drawn from the diary.[27] However, our aim was to explore the journeys of a late fifteenth-century artisan man organized around routines of home (neighbourhood) and work (city centre). No single source could have provided a voice that would have allowed the linked-up and cross-referenced perspective that any Florentine would have had on the city as a whole and that we wanted to represent – at least not one that would have allowed us to engage users with a range of specific sites through the functionality of an onsite mobile app.

Here, inventing a character allowed a further degree of experimentation. Giovanni is pitched as a *battilano* or wool beater, a labourer at the base of the textile industry's hierarchy and a figure for whom little unmediated source material exists. We wanted to imagine not simply the urban world of a male labourer but how a 'descendant' of the revolutionary Ciompi wool workers of 1378 might read his city. In the introductory audio, Giovanni starts by saying he is a Florentine, baptized like every other inhabitant of the city in the ancient baptistery. But he quickly points out that he is 'not a banker or great patron but a humble wool worker – Giovanni the magnificent wool beater'. His ironic use of the honorific customarily given to Lorenzo de' Medici establishes a wry and politically aware voice, and he

Figure 10.6 Red City *potenza* stone on the corner of the church of Sant'Ambrogio.

Locating experience 199

goes on to say that Lorenzo 'orders the republic more or less as he likes it, a friend to all of us, so long as all of us show our love for the house of the Medici'. It is a theme continued at Site 1 in the neighbourhood walk of Sant' Ambrogio, where Giovanni stands outside his parish church and invites users to examine the stones wrapped around the street corner there by the Red City *potenza* (Figures 10.6 and 10.7).

Figure 10.7 Red City *potenza* stone on the corner of the church of Sant'Ambrogio as viewed on the 'found it' screen in the *Hidden Florence* app (© University of Exeter).

He explains that noncitizens such as he are barred from holding office in the Florentine republic but that, on certain festive days, the *potenze* elect kings ('I was king once myself') and play a game that turns the world upside down, so that the rich briefly become the 'subjects' of the poor.[28]

Just how irreverent or reflective a 'typical' wool worker would have been is a matter of speculation, yet the voice we chose to give Giovanni is informed by a significant body of research. The brief revolution of 1378 was a bid by textile workers and other artisans excluded from guild government – the Ciompi labourers their most radical wing – to seize a place at the civic table. As Niall Atkinson explains in his chapter in this volume, outlying neighbourhoods, such as Giovanni's Sant' Ambrogio, where most textile workers lived, were the flashpoints of worker organization.[29] In the fifteenth century, that social geography became more emphatic as the palace building boom destroyed cheaper housing in the centre (one of the themes at the monolithic Strozzi palace).[30] Yet, while class tensions remained and there were sporadic instances of industrial agitation, there was far less class conflict. If this was the result of a more vigilant government apparatus, it also was the case that Florentine elites, armed with a humanistic ideology of the civic good, closed ranks around a more conciliatory approach, a combination of charity, the granting to workers of the right to associate in confraternities, and the cultivation of new patronal attitudes and vertical networks.[31] This patronage – or 'friendship', as Giovanni uses the term – is especially evident in the case of the increasingly authoritarian Medici. Lorenzo de' Medici openly sponsored the *potenze*, groups that speak at once to an acute awareness of the deep social rifts that all Florentines experienced in their daily lives and to the perceived need to mitigate hostility through a form of civic representation for the politically excluded.[32]

The point was to underscore how contemporaries might read their city in very different ways, how place evoked and shaped a politics of memory and identity, of subjectivity in short. This is brought into stark relief at 'iconic' civic sites such as the guild church of Orsanmichele (City Centre, Site 2) and, as discussed earlier, at the Piazza della Signoria, where Giovanni goes as far as to say that 'the game is rigged'. As Stephen Milner has argued, the piazza may have been a space theatrically produced by dominant groups, but it was also, borrowing from de Certeau, a 'practiced place', never able to shut down resistance to supposedly authoritative representational strategies.[33] In other words, reception, while sharing common features, partially depended on the receiver, the person standing in front of an object, and the notions about self and community carried by that person.

If these issues condition Giovanni's voice, as the earlier examples of Via dei Pilastri and the tabernacle at the Canto al Monteloro pointed up, there was a broad range of themes we wished to address. It is worth detailing one more site to give a fuller sense of how *Hidden Florence* exploits the 'invented character' model. The city-centre alley of Vicolo del Giglio, parallel to the main processional thoroughfare of Via dei Calzaiuoli, is one of two sites where Giovanni tells a complete story (Figure 10.8).[34]

Locating experience 201

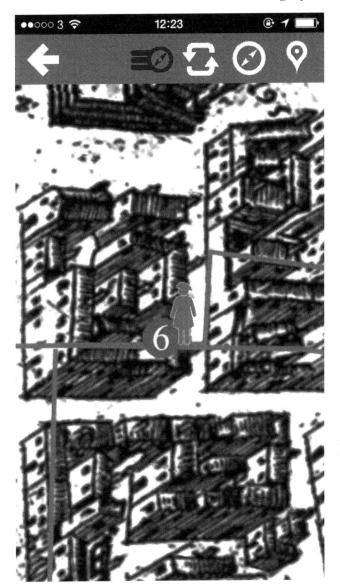

Figure 10.8 Vicolo del Giglio, detail from Stefano Buonsignori, *Nova pulcherrimae civitatis Florentiae topographia accuratissime delineate*, 1594 (Harvard Map Collection), as viewed on screen in the *Hidden Florence* app (© University of Exeter).

In this case there is a close affinity with the microhistorical mode, where a source 'story', often extrapolated from trial records, is critically reconstructed to shed light on broader issues. Here, while the effect is the same, the arrow points in the opposite direction: the story is a fiction, one into which a number of wider themes are condensed.

Giovanni invites users to enter the alleyway and to keep on walking to the end at the other side into the Corso.

> And while you do, I've got a great story to tell you. One evening about a month ago, I came down here with a few wool-beaters from the shop. All men from the neighbourhood, all brothers in our *potenza* of the Red City. We were heading to the Fico. It's the best-known tavern in Florence. A magnet for men of every rank. They come to satisfy their desires, for women... or men (some aren't bothered either way). Or they come to gamble. Or just to talk and drink that golden Trebbiano wine. Anyway, we get to the Fico, and who's there but a crowd of weavers from Santa Lucia all of them from the *potenza* of the Prato. Now the Prato is supposed to be the head of all the *potenze* in Florence, but we don't worry too much about that. Well, we all start drinking together, but then a couple of the Prato boys start to give our Michele a hard time. They said he's 'kept like a women' by some Giorgio or other. They even threaten to shop him for sodomy to the Officers of the Night. So our Michele throws a punch. Now I don't know if Michele is a sodomite, and to be honest I don't care (though he is getting a bit old for that kind of thing). But the sneering of these Prato weavers? None of us were going to put up with that. Before you know it we're dragged in to a fight and the tavernkeeper throws the whole lot of us out into the alley. We should have left it there, but our blood was boiling. We picked up some stones and started a proper street fight. Just like we do as *potenze*. It was almost like May Day. Except on May Day the cops usually stay out of our way. Not this time. When we spilled out the other end of the alley and into the Corso they came at us. We had a bit of luck though. The Prato men were out first and the *birri* were too busy arresting them to notice us slipping away towards the Mercato....

The aim of this story – as with Giovanni's narratives at several other city-centre sites – was to suggest how the urban core was a special arena of social interaction. By day, it was alive with the rhythms of work, commerce, shopping, and street performance; hundreds of wool beaters such as Giovanni headed daily to work in the *botteghe* of the wool merchants.[35] After dark, the city centre continued to exert a pull, mainly because of well-known taverns such as the Fico.[36] Bringing Giovanni to the Fico with cohorts from the Red City neighbourhood *potenza*, then having them run into members of the 'imperial' brigade from Santa Lucia sul Prato, on the opposite side of the city, was designed to suggest how city-centre taverns were hubs of sociability for men from across Florence.[37]

At the same time, Giovanni's story draws out aspects of Florence's sexual topography, as well as reflecting on gender identities and masculinity more widely. The city centre, particularly its taverns, also featured prominently in the pursuit of sex; it was a hub both for prostitution – the Fico was one of the *osteria* in what effectively was the red-light area between the Mercato Vecchio (the present Piazza della Repubblica) and the Baptistery – and for male sodomitical encounters.[38] While homosexuality was highly transgressive, as many as two-thirds of the male population under the age of forty in late fifteenth-century Florence had at some point been officially implicated as sodomites. Sex between men was widely understood as a life stage, linked to oppositional and hierarchical notions of gender. The 'norm' was for teenagers to take what was understood as a passive 'feminine' role, males in their twenties and thirties the active 'masculine' role.[39] Denunciations to the Officers of the Night, established in 1432 to prosecute the vice, regularly and derogatorily characterized the passive partner as being 'kept like a woman'.[40] Thus the taunt against a member of Giovanni's cohort labelled this man as emasculated and dishonourable. It would have been especially stinging since, as Giovanni implies, he was no longer a teenager. The ensuing street brawl represented a re-assertion of virility, and this is linked back to the more formal hypermasculine ritual of the *potenze*, in particular the stone fight, an emblematic form of combat between the city's artisan kingdoms, a means by which they claimed public, and civic, space.[41]

Conclusion: the city as experience

New technology delivered through an app allows the historian to revisit old questions in the study of the Renaissance city and to open up new ones; it enables both researcher and user to approach the evidence in such a way that knowledge is constructed in new ways that are deeply inflected by their being experienced onsite. Kevin Lynch was the first to show that the meanings of urban space and how it is assembled to fashion an image can be accessed only through experiential analysis.[42] As Diane Favro indicated at the turn of the milenium, urban and architectural historians have followed the work of the urban theorist in seeking to recover the experience of cities in the past, through the adoption of empirical and experimental methods.[43] Moreover, as was discussed at the outset, the spatial turn in early modern studies can also be said to have taken a 'mobility turn', the new attention to the everyday politics of movement through the cities of the past arguably informed by the recent revival of psychogeography as both a practice and a literary genre.[44] Locative media both enable the delivery of historical *dérive* and serve to focus the researcher's perspective on a fine-grained engagement with site-specific urban space, as opposed to the more distant analysis of patterns and typologies, to evoke the dichotomy set up by de Certeau in his formulation of practiced place.

Thus, it is worth considering that while the *Hidden Florence* project began life as an experiment in the application of new technology for public engagement purposes, it has emerged as a worthwhile research practice in its own right. The format proposed is one that is infinitely extensible: given the wealth of studies on Florence, it is easy to imagine multiple walks that would engage different aspects of the city's early modern history, all of them overlaid on Buonsignori's map. Our intended next step – which is inevitably contingent on further funding – is to develop an editing platform that would ease the creation and addition of new stories/walks to the existing app and possible new apps developed for other cities. Moreover, mobile technology offers considerable pedagogical opportunities.

Initial feedback shows some take-up by onsite courses, while trials with students suggest that writing for locative media involves students in compelling ways, by harnessing technologies with which they are familiar from their everyday lives but that rarely find their way into the humanities classroom.

In conclusion, if we recall de Certeau's famous observation from the top of New York's World Trade Centre, we might say that the use of GPS location coordinates in H-GIS projects (such as DECIMA) maintains a panoptic and hierarchical vision on the city, while their adoption in locative media projects (such as *Hidden Florence*) delivered onsite shapes an experience that aims to recover the practices of everyday life in the past. Here meaning, narrative, and intention emerge and make sense only through the embodied practice of movement and the kinaesthetic dialogue that is established between past and present and the standing material culture of the city.

Notes

1 Released in July 2014 to the AppStore and GooglePlay, *Hidden Florence* is a collaboration with the developers Calvium Ltd, funded by the Arts and Humanities Research Council (AHRC, UK) and published by the University of Exeter. For an accompanying website including all audio content, brief articles by the authors, and details of the project team see: www.hiddenflorence.org. Unless otherwise stated, all content in the app and website is by the authors. For reasons of space, footnotes focus on supporting the theoretical framing of the project rather than the extensive specialist scholarship that underpins the app's content.

2 T. Shortell and E. Brown, 'Introduction: Walking in the European City', in Shortell and Brown (eds), *Walking in the European City: Quotidian Mobility and Urban Ethnography*, Farnham, UK: Ashgate, 2014, 5; D. Cosgrove, 'Landscape and Landschaft', *German Historical Institute Bulletin* 35, 2004, 57–71. Highly influential here are M. de Certeau, 'Walking in the City', in de Certeau, *The Practice of Everyday Life*, Berkeley, CA: University of California Press, 1984, 91–109; H. Lefebvre, *The Production of Space*, Oxford, UK: Blackwell, 1991.

3 F. de Vivo, 'Walking in Renaissance Venice', *I Tatti Studies in the Italian Renaissance* 30, 2016; N. Eckstein, 'Florence on Foot: An Eye-level Mapping of the Early Modern City in Time of Plague', *Renaissance Studies*, 30, 2016. Our thanks to these three authors for sharing their articles prepublication. Several collections attest to the recent focus on 'spatial' themes in early modern Italy: F. Nevola and G. Clarke (eds), 'Experiences of the Street in Early Modern Italy', Special Issue, *I Tatti Studies in the Italian Renaissance* 16, 2013, 47–229; R. Laitinen and T.V. Cohen (eds), *Cultural History of Early Modern European Streets*, Special Issue, *Journal of Early Modern History* 12, 2008; J. Paoletti and R. Crum (eds), *Renaissance Florence: A Social History*, New York, NY: Cambridge University Press, 2006. See also F. Nevola, 'Review Essay: Street Life in Early Modern Europe', *Renaissance Quarterly* 66, 2013, 1332–45.

4 De Vivo, 'Walking in Renaissance Venice'.

5 N. Atkinson, 'They Rang the Bells at the Wrong Time', interview by D. Rosenthal and F. Nevola, 2011. Online. Available <http://earlymoderncommunities.org/home/interviews-2/niall-atkinson> (accessed 20 June 2015).

6 There are numerous precedents for the use of nineteenth-century maps. For a wider discussion of digital humanities adoption and the use of early modern maps, see F. Nevola, 'Microstoria 2.0: Geo-locating Renaissance Spatial and Architectural History', in D. Jakacki, L. Estill, and M. Ullyot (eds), *Early Modern Studies and the Digital Turn: New Tools for New Research Questions*, Toronto, Canada: Arizona CMRS and Iter, 2015 [forthcoming].

7 F. Else, 'Controlling the Waters of Granducal Florence: A New Look at Stefano Bonsignori's View of the City (1584)', *Imago Mundi* 61, 2009, 168–85, esp. 168–70.
8 As Else, 'Controlling the Waters', makes clear, the addition of the Cosimo I equestrian monument appears in the second printing of the map in 1594 by Girolamo Franceschi (this is the edition used throughout this collection). M. Cole, *Ambitious Form: Giambologna, Ammanati, and Danti in Florence*, Princeton, NJ: Princeton University Press, 2011, 244–82.
9 A recurring theme in F. Fiorani, *The Marvel of Maps: Art, Cartography and Politics in Renaissance Italy*, New Haven, CT, and London, UK: Yale University Press, 2005, and the more military-political M. Pollak, *Cities at War in Early Modern Europe*, Cambridge, UK: Cambridge University Press, 2010.
10 T. Frangenberg, 'Chorographies of Florence: The Use of City Views and City Plans in the Sixteenth Century', *Imago Mundi* 46, 1994, 41–64; F. Else, 'Controlling the Waters'.
11 D.J. Bodenhamer, 'The Potential of Spatial Humanities', in *The Spatial Humanities: GIS and the Future of Humanities Scholarship*, Bloomington and Indianapolis, IN: Indiana University Press, 2010, 14–30; I.N. Gregory and A. Geddes, Towards Spatial Humanities: Historical GIS and Spatial History. Bloomington, IN: Indiana University Press, 2014.
12 L. Faibisoff, 'The Route of Governmentality: Surveying and Collecting Urban Space in Ducal Florence', in this volume. Since GIS referents have to be unique, complicating factors such as multilevel occupancy – the fine grain of urban living – are somewhat homogenized in the DECIMA-Buonsignori streets.
13 Thanks to Richard Hull (Calvium) for providing a brief account of the technical transfer process on which this paragraph is based: www.hiddenflorence.org/about/about-bonsignori-map/ (accessed 10 June 2015).
14 For a broader discussion of locative media as a digital humanities practice see J. Farman (ed.), *The Mobile Story: Narrative Practices with Locative Technologies*, London, UK: Routledge 2013. Also G. Goggin and L. Hjorth (eds), *The Routledge Companion to Mobile Media*, London, UK: Routledge, 2013, and the special issue R. Wilken (ed.), 'Locative Media', *Convergence: The International Journal of Research into New Media Technologies* 18, 2012.
15 J. Farman, 'Storytelling with Mobile Media', in Goggin and Hjorth (eds), *The Routledge Companion*, 528–37, esp. 529–32, follows M. McCullough, 'Epigraphy and the Public Library', in F. de Cindio and A. Aurigi (eds), *Augmented Urban Spaces: Articulating the Physical and Electronic City*, Burlington and Farnham, UK: Ashgate, 2012, 61–72.
16 T. Presner, D. Shepard, and Y. Kawano, *HyperCities: Thick Mapping in the Digital Humanities*, Cambridge, MA: Harvard University Press, 2014.
17 Locative media's creative practice is the subject of growing scholarly attention, for which see collections in the preceding notes for numerous examples; also useful are the more critical stances of N. Thrift, 'Lifeworld Inc – and What to Do about It', *Environment and Planning D: Society and Space* 29, 2011, 5–26, and M. Tuters, 'From Mannerist Situationism to Situated Media', *Convergence: International Journal of Research into New Media Technologies* 18, 2012, 267–82.
18 E. Muir, 'The Virgin on the Street Corner: The Place of the Sacred in Italian Cities', in S. Ozment (ed.), *Religion and Culture in the Renaissance and Reformation (Sixteenth Century Essays and Studies*, XI), Kirksville, MO, 1987, 24–40; also F. Nevola 'Surveillance and the Street in Renaissance Italy', *I Tatti Studies in the Italian Renaissance* 16, 2013, 85–106. M. Holmes, *The Miraculous Image in Renaissance Florence*, New Haven, CT, and London, UK: Yale University Press, 2013, ch. 3 on the topography of the sacred.
19 See for example A. Paolucci et al. (eds), *Arte, storia e devozione: Tabernacoli da salvare*, Florence, Italy: Centro Di, 1991; scholarship tends to focus only on the images, often indeed cropping out all context from published photographs.

20 B. Paolozzi Strozzi, 'Tabernacolo di Monteloro', Paolucci et al. (eds), *Arte, storia e devozione*, 89–94.
21 For a first tavern called Candeli, which probably closed in the 1470s, see *L'illustratore fiorentino: Calendario per l'anno bisestile 1836*, Firenze, Italy: Tipografia Galileiana, 1835, 105; on the *potenze*, D. Rosenthal, *Kings of the Street: Power, Community and Ritual in Renaissance Florence*, Turnhout, Belgium: Brepols, 2015, for the Monteloro's marker, 19, 168.
22 D. Freedberg, 'Movement, Embodiment, Emotion', in Histoire de l'art et anthropologie, Paris, France: coédition INHA / Musée du Quai Branly («Les actes»), 2009, Online. Available <http://actesbranly.revues.org/330> (accessed 1 July 2015).
23 J. Walton, J. Brooks, and C.R.N. DeCorse, 'Introduction', in J. Walton, J. Brooks, and C.R.N. Decorse (eds), *Small Worlds: Method, Meaning and Narrative in Microhistory*, Santa Fe, NM: School for Advanced Research Press, 2008, 4; C. Ginzburg, 'Microhistory: Two or Three Things That I Know about It', *Critical Inquiry* 20, 1993, 10–35. For recent assessments of microhistory by its practitioners, see S.G. Magnússon and I.M. Szijártó, *What Is Microhistory? Theory and Practice*, New York, NY: Routledge, 2013, ch. 1; S. Bednarski, *A Poisoned Past: The Life and Times of Margarida de Portu, a Fourteenth-Century Accused Poisoner*, Toronto, Canada: University of Toronto Press, 2014, ch. 1.
24 De Certeau, 'Walking in the City'.
25 T. Cohen, 'The Larger Uses of Microhistory', Microhistory Network. Online. Available <www.microhistory.eu/the_larger_uses_of_microhistory.html> (accessed June 19, 2015).
26 S. Schama, *Dead Certainties (Unwarranted Speculations)*, London, UK: Penguin Books, 1991; R. Bisha, 'Reconstucting the Voice of a Noblewoman of the Time of Peter the Great: Daria Mikhailovna Menshikova: An Exercise in Pseudo-Biographical Writing', *Rethinking History* 2, 1998, 51–63; Magnússon and Szijártó, *What Is Microhistory?Theory and Practice*, 2013, 70–72.
27 L. Landucci, *Diario Fiorentino: Dal 1450 al 1516: Continuato da un anonimo fino al 1542*, Florence, Italy: Sansoni, 1883, 57–58 (for beginning of construction).
28 Rosenthal, *Kings of the Street*; on this site and the Red City marker, esp. 17–20.
29 J. Najemy, *A History of Florence, 1200–1575*, London, UK: Wiley-Blackwell, 2008, ch. 6, with earlier bibliography.
30 F. Nevola, 'Home Shopping: Urbanism, Commerce and Palace Design in Renaissance Italy', *Journal of the Society of Architectural Historians* 70, 2011, 153–73.
31 F.W. Kent, '"Be Rather Loved Than Feared": Class Relations in Quattrocento Florence', in W.J. Connell (ed.), *Society and Individual in Renaissance Florence*, Berkeley, CA: University of California Press, 2002, 13–50; M. Jurdevic, 'Civic Humanism and the Rise of the Medici', *Renaissance Quarterly* 52, 1999, 994–1020.
32 For Lorenzo de' Medici's ties to the *potenze*, see R. Trexler, *Public Life in Renaissance Florence*, New York, NY: Academic Press, 1980, 399–418; F.W. Kent and D. Kent, 'Two Vignettes of Florentine Society in the 15th Century', *Rinascimento* 23, 1983, 237–60.
33 S.J. Milner, 'The Florentine Piazza della Signoria as Practiced Place', in Paoletti and Crum (eds), *Renaissance Florence*, 83–104, the relevant passage is at 84.
34 The other is in Piazza della Repubblica, the former Mercato Vecchio (City Centre, Site 6).
35 M.L. Bianchi and M.L. Grossi, 'Botteghe, economica e spazio urbano', in F. Francsechi and G. Fossi (eds), *Arti fiorentine: La grande storia dell'artigianato. Volume secondo: Il Quattrocento*, Florence, 1999, 27–63; E. Welch, *Shopping in the Renaissance: Consumer Cultures in Italy 1400–1600*, New Haven, CT, and London, UK: Yale University Press, 2005; Nevola, 'Home Shopping'.
36 On the Fico and city-centre taverns more widely, see D. Rosenthal, 'The Barfly's Dream: Taverns, Community and Reform in Early Modern Italy', in D. Toner and M.

Hailwood (eds), *Biographies of Drink: A Case Study Approach to Our Historical Relationship with Alcohol*, Newcastle, UK: Cambridge Scholars Publishing, 2015, 14–29.
37 For the 'emperor' of the Prato, D. Rosenthal, 'Big Piero, the Empire of the Meadow and the Parish of Santa Lucia: Claiming Neighbourhood in the Early Modern City', *Journal of Urban History* 32, 2006, 677–92.
38 N. Terpstra, *Lost Girls: Sex and Death in Renaissance Florence*, Baltimore, MD: Johns Hopkins University Press, 2010, ch. 2; M.S. Mazzi, *Prostitute e lenoni nella Firenze del Quattrocento*, Milan, Italy: Saggiatore, 1991; M. Rocke, *Forbidden Friendships: Homosexuality and Male Culture in Renaissance Florence*, New York, NY: Oxford University Press, 1996, 159–61.
39 Rocke, *Forbidden Friendships*, 4–5 and passim.
40 Ibid., 107–10.
41 Rosenthal, *Kings of the Street*, 121–23, 237; more widely, R. Davis, 'Say It with Stones: The Language of Rock Throwing in Early Modern Italy', *Ludica* 10, 2004, 113–28.
42 K. Lynch, *The Image of the City*, Cambridge, MA: MIT Press, 1960.
43 D. Favro, 'Meaning and Experience. Urban History from Antiquity to the Early Modern Period', *Journal of the Society of Architectural Historians*, 58, 1999, 364–73; also G. Clarke and F. Nevola, 'Introduction: Experiences of the Street in Early Modern Italy', *I Tatti Studies in the Italian Renaissance* 16, 2013, 47–55.
44 For an overview: M. Coverley, *Psychogeography*, Harpenden: Pocket Essentials, 2010.

Bibliography

Atkinson, N., 'They Rang the Bells at the Wrong Time', interview by D. Rosenthal and F. Nevola, 2011. Online. Available <http://earlymoderncommunities.org/home/interviews-2/niall-atkinson> (accessed 20 June 2015), 27–63.

Bednarski, S., *A Poisoned Past: The Life and Times of Margarida de Portu, a Fourteenth-Century Accused Poisoner*, Toronto, Canada: University of Toronto Press, 2014.

Bianchi, M.L., and Grossi, M.L., 'Botteghe, economica e spazio urbano', in F. Francsechi and G. Fossi (eds), *Arti fiorentine: La grande storia dell'artigianato. Volume secondo: Il Quattrocento*, Florence, Italy, 1999.

Bisha, R., 'Reconstructing the Voice of a Noblewoman of the Time of Peter the Great: Daria Mikhailovna Menshikova: An Exercise in Pseudo-Biographical Writing', *Rethinking History* 2, 1998, 51–63.

Bodenhamer, D.J. (ed.), 'The Potential of Spatial Humanities', in *The Spatial Humanities: GIS and the Future of Humanities Scholarship*, Bloomington and Indianapolis, IN: Indiana University Press, 2010, 14–29.

Clarke, G., and Nevola, F., 'Introduction: Experiences of the Street in Early Modern Italy', *I Tatti Studies in the Italian Renaissance* 16, 2013, 47.

Cohen, T.V., 'The Larger Uses of Microhistory', Microhistory Network, 2014. Online. Available <www.microhistory.eu/the_larger_uses_of_microhistory.html> (accessed 19 June 2015).

Cole, M., *Ambitious Form: Giambologna, Ammanati, and Danti in Florence*, Princeton, NJ: Princeton University Press, 2011.

Cosgrove, D., 'Landscape and Landschaft', *German Historical Institute Bulletin* 35, 2004.

Coverley, M., *Psychogeography*, Harpenden, UK: Pocket Essentials, 2010.

Davis, R. 'Say It with Stones: The Language of Rock Throwing in Early Modern Italy', *Ludica* 10, 2004, 113–28.

de Certeau, M., *The Practice of Everyday Life*, Berkeley, CA: University of California Press, 1984.

de Vivo, F., 'Walking in Renaissance Venice', *I Tatti Studies in the Italian Renaissance* 30, 2016.
Eckstein, E., 'Florence on Foot: An Eye-level Mapping of the Early Modern City in Time of Plague', *Renaissance Studies* 30, 2016.
Else, F., 'Controlling the Waters of Granducal Florence: A New Look at Stefano Bonsignori's View of the City (1584)', *Imago Mundi* 61, 2009.
Farman, J. (ed.), *The Mobile Story: Narrative Practices with Locative Technologies*, London, UK: Routledge, 2013.
Favro, D., 'Meaning and Experience: Urban History from Antiquity to the Early Modern Period', *Journal of the Society of Architectural Historians* 58, 1999.
Fiorani, F., *The Marvel of Maps: Art, Cartography and Politics in Renaissance Italy*, New Haven, CT, and London, UK: Yale University Press, 2005.
Frangenberg, T., 'Chorographies of Florence: The Use of City Views and City Plans in the Sixteenth Century', *Imago Mundi* 46, 1994.
Freedberg, D., 'Movement, Embodiment, Emotion', in *Histoire de l'art et anthropologie*, Paris, coédition INHA/Musée du Quai Branly («Les actes»), 2009. Online. Available <http://actesbranly.revues.org/330> (accessed 1 July 2015).
Ginzburg, C., 'Microhistory: Two or Three Things That I Know about It', *Critical Inquiry* 20, 1993.
Goggin, G., and Hjorth, L. (eds), *The Routledge Companion to Mobile Media*, London, UK: Routledge 2013.
Gregory, I.N., and Geddes, A., *Towards Spatial Humanities: Historical GIS and Spatial History.* Bloomington, IN: Indiana University Press, 2014.
Holmes, M., *The Miraculous Image in Renaissance Florence*, New Haven, CT, and London, UK: Yale University Press, 2013.
Jurdevic, M., 'Civic Humanism and the Rise of the Medici', *Renaissance Quarterly* 52, 1999.
Kent, F.W., '"Be Rather Loved Than Feared": Class Relations in Quattrocento Florence', in W.J. Connell (ed.), *Society and Individual in Renaissance Florence*, Berkeley, CA: University of California Press, 2002, 13–50.
—— and Kent, D.V., 'Two Vignettes of Florentine Society in the 15th Century, *Rinascimento* 23, 1983.
Laitinen, R., and Cohen, T.V. (eds), 'Cultural History of Early Modern European Streets', Special Issue, *Journal of Early Modern History* 12, 2008.
Landucci, L., *Diario Fiorentino: Dal 1450 al 1516: Continuato da un anonimo fino al 1542*, Florence, Italy: Sansoni, 1883.
Lefebvre, H., *The Production of Space*, Oxford, UK: Blackwell, 1991.
L'illustratore fiorentino: Calendario per l'anno bisestile 1836, Florence, Italy: Tipografia Galileiana, 1835.
Lynch, K., *The Image of the City*, Cambridge, MA: MIT Press, 1960.
Magnússon, S.G., and Szijártó, I.M., *What Is Microhistory? Theory and Practice*, New York, NY: Routledge, 2013.
Mazzi, M.S., *Prostitute e lenoni nella Firenze del Quattrocento*, Milan, Italy: Saggiatore, 1991.
McCullough, M., 'Epigraphy and the public library', in F. de Cindio and A. Aurigi (eds), *Augmented Urban Spaces: Articulating the Physical and Electronic City*, Burlington and Farnham, UK: Ashgate, 2012, 61–72.
Milner, S.J., 'The Florentine Piazza della Signoria as Practiced Place', in J. Paoletti and R. Crum (eds), *Renaissance Florence: A Social History*, New York, NY: Cambridge University Press, 2006, 83–103.

Muir, E., 'The Virgin on the Street Corner: The Place of the Sacred in Italian Cities', in S. Ozment (ed.), *Religion and Culture in the Renaissance and Reformation*, Kirksville, MO: Sixteen Century Journal Publishers, 1987, 25–42.

Najemy, J., *A History of Florence, 1200–1575*, London, UK: Wiley-Blackwell, 2008.

Nevola, F., 'Home Shopping: Urbanism, Commerce and Palace Design in Renaissance Italy', *Journal of the Society of Architectural Historians* 70, 2011.

—— 'Review Essay: Street Life in Early Modern Europe', *Renaissance Quarterly* 66, 2013.

—— 'Surveillance and the Street in Renaissance Italy', *I Tatti Studies in the Italian Renaissance* 16, 2013.

—— 'Microstoria 2.0: Geo-locating Renaissance Spatial and Architectural History', in D. Jakacki, L. Estill, and M. Ullyot (eds), *Early Modern Studies and the Digital Turn: New Tools for New Research Questions*, Toronto, Canada: Arizona CMRS and Iter, [forthcoming].

—— and Clarke, G. (eds), 'Experiences of the Street in Early Modern Italy', Special Issue, *I Tatti Studies in the Italian Renaissance* 16, 2013.

Paoletti, J., and Crum, R. (eds), *Renaissance Florence: A Social History*, New York, NY: Cambridge University Press, 2006.

Pollak, M., *Cities at War in Early Modern Europe*, Cambridge, UK: Cambridge University Press, 2010.

Presner, T., Shepard, D., and Kawano, Y., *HyperCities: Thick Mapping in the Digital Humanities*, Cambridge, MA: Harvard University Press, 2014.

Rocke, M., *Forbidden Friendships: Homosexuality and Male Culture in Renaissance Florence*, New York, NY: Oxford University Press, 1996.

Rosenthal, D., 'Big Piero, the Empire of the Meadow and the Parish of Santa Lucia: Claiming Neighbourhood in the Early Modern City', *Journal of Urban History* 32, 2006, 677–92.

—— 'The Barfly's Dream: Taverns, Community and Reform in Early Modern Italy', in D. Toner and M. Hailwood (eds), *Biographies of Drink: A Case Study Approach to Our Historical Relationship with Alcohol*, Newcastle, UK: Cambridge Scholars Publishing, 2015, 14–29.

—— *Kings of the Street: Power, Community and Ritual in Renaissance Florence*, Turnhout, Belgium: Brepols, 2015.

Schama, S., *Dead Certainties (Unwarranted Speculations)*, London, UK: Penguin Books, 1991.

Shortell, T., and Brown, E., 'Introduction: Walking in the European City', in T. Shortell and E. Brown (eds), *Walking in the European City: Quotidian Mobility and Urban Ethnography*, Farnham, UK: Ashgate, 2014, 1–20.

Soprintendenza ai beni artistici, *Arte, storia e devozione: Tabernacoli da salvare*, Florence, Italy: Centro Di, 1991.

Terpstra, N., *Lost Girls: Sex and Death in Renaissance Florence*, Baltimore, MD: Johns Hopkins University Press, 2010.

Thrift, N., 'Lifeworld Inc – and What to Do about It', *Environment and Planning D: Society and Space* 29, 2011.

Trexler, R., *Public Life in Renaissance Florence*, New York, NY: Academic Press, 1980.

Tuters, M., 'From Mannerist Situationism to Situated Media', *Convergence: International Journal of Research into New Media Technologies* 18, 2012, 267–82.

Walton, J., Brooks, J., and DeCorse, C.R.N., 'Introduction', in J. Walton, J. Brooks, and C.R.N. DeCorse (eds), *Small Worlds: Method, Meaning and Narrative in Microhistory*, Santa Fe, NM: School for Advanced Research Press, 2008, 3–12.

Wilken, R. (ed.), 'Locative Media', *Convergence: The International Journal of Research into New Media Technologies*, 2012.

Conclusion

Towards early modern spatial humanities

Nicholas Terpstra and Colin Rose

This volume has brought together established historians whose work is highly influential in the study of early modern Florence and younger scholars who are pushing the bounds of the discipline in methodological and conceptual ways. By highlighting how new technologies of inquiry, such as HGIS, aural networking, or locative media can expand and extend existing historical scholarship, it offers possibilities for further methodological shifts in how we approach and understand the early modern city. It emphasizes the complexities of early modern data analysis and the particular challenges faced by early modernist 'digital humanists', but it also invites early modernists of all sorts to invest in the skills necessary to employ digital methods appropriate to their research project. It makes the case that HGIS and other digital technologies can improve historical research and spur innovative lines of discovery, and it aims to provide some guidance and caution for aspiring digital historians.

Projects like DECIMA and *Hidden Florence* are never really finished. This book represents a moment in time – a static map – of the state of their development at the time of publication and the academic context in which they emerged. The authors gathered here have described the design, construction, and elaboration of the DECIMA project, including both its underlying database and the georeferenced *Buonsignori* map; shown how the use of DECIMA is opening up new avenues of exploration for ongoing projects in social history; and set DECIMA in the context of a larger group of emerging projects, including *Hidden Florence,* that use sense, space, and movement to analyze the early modern city in various ways. The connecting thread through all of these chapters is that work of this sort lends itself to, indeed depends upon, collaborative research. All of this work begins with individual scholars of history, art, and literature poring over manuscripts and writing alone at their desks, but none of it ends there. Rather, each of these chapters represents ongoing conversations among scholars working to enlarge their research. This is explicit in the coauthored chapters in the collection's central section but is no less true in the others. Each of these projects continues, as the investigators are led in new directions by the results of each successive step of the investigation.

As interest in Digital Humanities expands across all disciplines and periods, premodernists have faced distinct challenges in using its tools, largely because its statistical methods have seemed to work best with large runs of serial data that are not always readily available for the years prior to the eighteenth century.[1] Literary texts offer one exception to this, and many projects have tracked patterns, word use, and imagery as means of tracing linguistic and cultural development.[2] Visualization is also a creative avenue, and archaeologists and architectural historians have used mapping and visualization tools to reconstruct towns and cities in their emergence over centuries.[3] Premodernist historians, both impressed and cowed by massive runs of statistical data with which their modernist colleagues track crime rates, urban mobility, population growth, and financial rise and ruin over decades and across political and geographical boundaries, have had perhaps more work to do. There just aren't that many reliable serial data sets available to early modernists. One exception, of course, is the fifteenth-century Florentine tax records that David Herlihy and Christiane Klapisch-Zuber used so creatively and fruitfully in one of the earliest and most innovative digital humanities projects. Their work on the 1427 *Catasto*, cited by many authors in this collection, transformed Florentine, and indeed much of early modern social historiography; as an online resource, it continues to generate new results many decades after it was first published.[4] Yet, built on years of archival mining and time-consuming and costly data entry, it also serves as a cautionary tale: when on the hunt for big data, be careful what you wish for. It was hard to find historians willing to invest the time in this kind of research, and it is even harder now to find granting agencies willing to invest the funds it requires. Some projects along these lines do continue, most notably the work of University of Chicago political scientist John Padgett to construct a relational database of Florentine family networks of politics and finance through the fourteenth and fifteenth centuries.

Yet, beyond the challenge of finding time, resources, and technical support, early modern historians face the epistemological challenge of their own scepticism. Many resist the notion that answers can be found in the aggregation and manipulation of large sets of numbers and other data. This is not out of Luddite resistance to technology but because their archival research has often shown them that early modern data collection is fraught with compromises and complexities that require that it be undertaken with care. Early modern merchants, families, and bureaucrats often counted in different ways and for different purposes, and the numbers they generated have to be filtered, interpreted, and contextualized carefully. Not an impossible task, but one that often requires more time, training, and expertise than most granting agencies are willing to fund.

The challenges are undeniable, and of course scepticism about early modern data extends further to the difficulty of adequately training those doing data entry in the skills necessary to filter and contextualize it. These challenges underscore the importance of collaborative research extended broadly across disciplines, subjects, and professional stages. DECIMA has followed a collaborative model of resource sharing that aims to counter the pressure and uncertainty that come with resting everything on single large grants from agencies that set ambitious targets and short time lines. It was designed from the beginning to grow by a kind of curated crowdsourcing, and, while technical challenges remain to be overcome before that goal can be fully realized, we continue to consider it less as a fixed project than as an expanding archive and tool. As some of the chapters in this volume demonstrate, the DECIMA team has run queries for many scholars who are interested in setting their own data into a larger framework, and Colin Rose in particular has prepared countless maps that allow these scholars to visualize those data, which in turn become part of the DECIMA database. In this way, data generated by scholars in Florence, London, Toronto, Atlanta, and Chicago have all found their way into the DECIMA database completely outside the framework of a large international grant. DECIMA's research assistants have gained the opportunity to collaborate with leading scholars who are both mentors and learners and who share their own expertise, perspective, and scepticism. The *Hidden Florence* project likewise envisions an ongoing process by which collaborators volunteer to generate new routes that can be added to the app. *Visualizing Venice*, organized by scholars from a number of universities under the direction of Caroline Bruzelius (Duke University) and Donatella Calabi (IUAVenice), has found means of integrating undergraduate and graduate student research in its goal of re-creating both the external elevations and volumes and the internal plans of that city's built environment.[5] Small grants fuel all these ambitious projects, and renewal is never guaranteed. Such projects advance less by rigorous plan than by informal in-kind collaborations, joint workshops, individual initiatives, and an extraordinary amount of *pro bono* labour. Putting these projects online allows them to continue facilitating research and generating results in spite of shifts in funding and personnel. This kind of approach has allowed a tool like the *Online Catasto* to continue as a creative aid to new research, with results integrated in new projects. The projects currently under construction and now emerging aim to take this a step further. While the *Online Catasto* is essentially complete and finished, DECIMA, *Hidden Florence, Visualizing Venice*, and many other new digital projects are deliberately planning for ongoing growth. This kind of open-ended approach allows spatial humanities to continue the practice of qualitative, humanist inquiry and analysis, simultaneously grounding narratives in brick-and-mortar spaces and places and assembling interdisciplinary layers and coordinating convergences that will steadily expand our understanding of how early modern cities *lived*.

This brings us to another of the reservations about digital tools. Some scholars are concerned about methods of data collection and sceptical about whether projects assume the existence of greater transparency in early modern data than actually exists. Others take this a step further. Do projects that rely on big data feed a static view of the early modern city? A number of the essays gathered here evoke Michel de Certeau's contrast between a panoptic vision of the city seen as a whole from above and the city as experienced at street and neighbourhood level, where it is realized at a pedestrian pace and in numerous face-to-face contacts. As we noted in the Introduction, Duke Cosimo I had panoptic ambitions at the beginning of his regime that generated the kinds of censuses that are readily digitized and projected onto a grid. His absolutist drive may not have been directed towards governmentality in its most Foucaultian expression, since he did lose interest after all. Yet when we feed his statistics into our databases, what kind of city does this render? Some digital humanists may certainly cheer the arrival of tools that allow us to survey, plot, and control the early modern city, but would our creation be recognizable to sixteenth-century Florentines? If not, should that be our ambition? The problem goes beyond ambivalence about governmentality and the surveillance state. In realizing Cosimo I's dream, do we risk creating a tidy Disneyfied simulacrum of Florence that flattens it and renders it static?

The final three essays in this collection sketch approaches that aim to preserve the early modern city's three-dimensionality, sensory richness, and sheer chaos. Nicholas Eckstein's contribution helps to frame the future nicely. Eckstein brings in three developing historical currents – the history of emotion, the history of plague, and the digitization of historical narratives like the *Visita* records he employs. Eckstein is able to hypothesize a map of fear – and not just to hypothesize but in fact to create a picture of the mental space of plague-fearing Florence, in which ominous black clouds of filthy vapours hang over large swaths of the city. In doing so, he grounds the fear of plague as represented in his *Visita* records in the circuits of Florentine streets, familiar to their inhabitants and offering both shelter and the conditions of disease. In concert with John Henderson and Colin Rose's chapter, he enables us to see how Florentine fears were well placed: the filthy conditions of San Lorenzo parish did indeed lead to high numbers of plague morbidity among those who lived in that parish's poorer streets. Looking ahead, then, these projects aim to place historical experience into a tangible space, represented in a computer program, that will bring historians closer to the lived and felt landscapes, emotional, social, or physical, in which early moderns moved.

Fabrizio Nevola and David Rosenthal's contribution shows how locative media and the growing ubiquity of GPS-enabled pocket devices allow us to open up historical research to a far larger public. The age of the rigorously researched and engaging historical tour app is upon us, and, as Nevola and Rosenthal note, it should be welcomed not only as a 'high-impact deliverable' that demonstrates history's relevance to sceptical granting agencies and university administrators but also as a tool to give modern tourists the closest approximation to de Certeau's 'practice' of the early modern city that they are ever likely to get. *Hidden Florence* re-creates a Florence that is otherwise familiar mainly to university students and their professors: the Florence of taverns, street-corner games, and local rivalries. Thoroughly documented and woven into a platform that transports users from the modern-day Ponte Vecchio into the Buonsignori map, it offers a way of seeing beyond the packaged Renaissance-land of the modern tourist centre. Projects like these demonstrate how we can disseminate sophisticated historical research through new media technologies in order to reach new audiences. And these audiences are not simply modern tourists. When projects like *Hidden Florence* focus on *movement* and immerse their audience in the daily journeys and lives of historical subjects, they can engage archival historians in the experiences and contexts that lie behind and shape their documents.

This brings us further into the history of senses, and Niall Atkinson's essay shows us how digital tools can advance exploration of Florence's soundscape. The histories of sense and emotion face the challenge of meaningfully historicizing these highly subjective phenomena. Historical GIS and other platforms visualize documented experiences of the senses and allow historians to query and manipulate those visualizations. Atkinson shows how the social space of Florentine parishes was imagined and practiced by reference to a sonic messaging system that is lost to us now but that went beyond simple time-keeping to being a language expressing political, religious, and social order. Atkinson helps us to hear the bustle of commerce, politics, and rebellion that animated early modern Florence. Placing historical experiences of sense and emotion onto the historical landscape through HGIS and other platforms benefits these expanding inquiries, while giving us a deeper reading of experiential documents grounded in times and places.

Historical GIS foregrounds physical spaces in social historical studies and so lends further dimensions to the great body of sometimes telegraphically sparse documents detailing the lives and *travailles* of early modern people from the sick to the high and mighty. This is perhaps an obvious point but one that is worth underscoring. Far from rendering a more static and one-dimensional city, digital platforms that bring together visual, sonic, and documentary materials can reveal unexpected connections and trigger new questions about how early moderns moved through their cities and experienced them in parts and wholes, constructions and demolitions, smells, fears, and sounds. This volume has aimed to show how existing historical projects can be extended by moving analysis on to a spatial platform. HGIS can reconceptualize the way families organized property holdings by tracking the convents where they placed their daughters and can show just how closely prostitutes skirted the regulations on where they could live and practice around those convents. It helps us hear how noisy sounds constructed space and see the areas that generated fear as silent plagues scythed their way through streets and neighbourhoods. The essays here have explored digital mapping in the early modern city, and the availability of maps and other documents can tend to privilege urban and national histories over rural or local studies. The challenge then is to reconstruct, from archaeological and documentary evidence, spatial profiles of rural districts in as many areas as possible, creating further opportunities for interdisciplinary historical research. In rural as in urban history, digital tools can help us engage with *space* in its physical extension, its sensory dimensions, and its emotional sense.

In 1561, the anonymous scribes of the *Decima* walked through the streets of Florence, knocking on doors and collecting information about who lived inside. A singular project by Cosimo I, the *Decima* demonstrated Medicean governmentality and an impressive administrative prowess. The scribes created a static record of a living city, reducing individuals to 'mouths' needing food, but they also created a living document that moves through that city in an almost narrative form. Twenty-three years later, in 1584, Stefano Buonsignori, on the orders of Cosimo's heir Ferdinand I, climbed the hills around Florence and, using the best tools available to him at the time, created a detailed and admirably accurate picture of the city and its homes. His map proclaims the glory of the city and its civic spaces, but it also forces the viewer to dwell on the dwellings, on the clusters of lean-tos and sheds that populated the city's garden spaces, and to contemplate the grim realities of living in the densely packed and poorly drained early modern city.

Conclusion 215

The digital tools available today allow us to combine these two visions of the city – the *Decima*'s panoptic governmentality and Buonsignori's mixed urban form – to re-create many others. The ability to place quantitative, qualitative, and visual sources into a single frame of analysis is the core of HGIS and of much of spatial humanities generally. Are they as revolutionary as the rhetoric of grant proposals sometimes forces us to claim? Likely not. In practice, a close look at some digital mapping projects reveals that for all their value they may not be quite as radically new as advertised – numbers alone don't make a revolution. Digital tools can extend and enlarge the humanities by fostering connections and conversations that in turn open up new questions that we can't at this point anticipate. The chapters in this volume look at projects emerging from the community of early modern Florentine historians, but the example of developing tools collaboratively that allow us to recognize connections we hadn't seen before, to ask questions that hadn't occurred to us earlier, and to share findings in ways that narrow the gap between academics and the public is not limited to any particular time or place. The real revolutions still come out of conversation and collaboration, and they usually catch us unawares.

Notes

1 The pioneering University of Victoria Digital Humanities Summer Institute had seven participants in 2001; it now numbers well over five hundred every year and stretches over three weeks. Online. Available <www.dhsi.org/archive.php> (accessed 23 August 2015).
2 P. Withington et al., 'Commonwealth: The Social, Cultural, and Conceptual Contexts of an Early Modern Keyword', *The Historical Journal* 54, 3 (2011), 659–87.
3 C. Clarke, ed., 'Mapping Medieval Chester'. Online. Available <www.medievalchester.ac.uk> (accessed 25 August 2015).
4 D. Herlihy and C. Klapisch-Zuber, 'Florentine Renaissance Resources: Online Catasto of 1427'. Online. Available <http://cds.library.brown.edu/projects/catasto/> (accessed 23 August 2015).
5 *Visualizing Venice,* Online. Available <www.visualizingvenice.org> (accessed 23 August 2015).

Bibliography

Clarke, C. (ed.), 'Mapping Medieval Chester'. Online. Available <www.medievalchester.ac.uk> (accessed 25 August 2015).
Herlihy, D., and Klapisch-Zuber, C., 'Florentine Renaissance Resources: Online Catasto of 1427'. Online. Available <http://cds.library.brown.edu/projects/catasto/> (accessed 23 August 2015).
Visualizing Venice, Online. Available <www.visualizingvenice.org> (accessed 23 August 2015).
Withington, W., et al., 'Commonwealth: The Social, Cultural, and Conceptual Contexts of an Early Modern Keyword', *The Historical Journal* 54, 3 (2011), 659–87.

Index

Abbandonate 46
Acciauoli, Benedetto 160
Alberti, Leon Battista 151–3
Alessandro I de' Medici, Duke 2, 111
Altoviti 98–101; property holdings 100 fig. 5.5, 101
Altoviti, Antonio 3, 90; Bindo 68; Filippa di Gentile 99; Francesco 101
Ammannati, Bartolomeo 2
Animated Atlas of African History 135
ArcGIS 17, 93, 140, 159
ArcMap 135, 137–40
Atlas of Early Printing, The 135

Bargello (Palace of the Podestà) 111, 157
Benzi, Antonio 173
Black Death *see* plague
Bologna 127, 132–3, 170–1
botteghe (artisanal workshops) 6, 19, 81n13, 202
brothel 4, 9, 110, 113, 118, 120–2, 123n19
Buonsignori Map 6, 10, 17, 20, 34, 43, 51n27, 169, 172, 181, 190–4, 210, 213; accuracy of 5–6, 16–17, 33–4, 40, 80, 133; comparison to modern maps 133, 181; figures 5, 20, 44–6, 27, 130, 158, 175–6, 188, 191, 194, 201; history of 4, 16–17, 80, 193, 214; idealizing geometric space 162–163; layering data on (*see* DECIMA, creation of); representation of space 19, 21–3, 34, 39–40, 43, 48–50, 187, 191; resolution of 29; use of by DECIMA 6, 19–22, 23, 33, 44, 60, 149, 183, 190–4, 210, 213
Buonsignori, Stefano 16–17, 33, 49–50, 80, 187, 190–1, 214–15

cadastral map 6, 133
campioni (registers) 49, 64, 66
Canigiani, family 98–101

Canigiani, Lena di Francesco 99
Carducci, family 98–9
Carducci, Lorenzo 177; Paola di Lorenzo 98
Carocci, Guido 151–4, 155 fig. 8.4
Catasto 2, 4, 7, 10, 34–8, 48, 154, 173–7, 211–12
census 3, 7–9, 17–22, 26, 28–9, 35, 42–44, 53–4, 60–2, 64, 75, 80, 87–92, 108, 116, 132–4, 149–51, 154, 173, 192, 212; *see also* census data on; convent; *decima*
Certeau, Michel de 35–6, 174, 189, 197, 200, 203–4, 212–13
Ciompi (wool guild) 198, 200; *see also* Ciompi Revolt
Ciompi Revolt 160–2, 164–5, 197–8, 200
confini 173, 175, 177, 179
confraternity 3, 8, 25, 65, 173, 187, 196; as landlords 28, 72–3
confraternity of the Misericordia 128, 131
contado 171, 175, 183
convent 3–4, 8, 20, 24, 92–3, 107–9, 114, 214; census data on 4, 68–9, 73–4, 87–95, 96, 102, 103n2; landlords as 63–4, 68, 72–3, 75; mapping of 91–3, 95–8, 107; reform 3; socio-spatial networks as 87, 89, 94–6, 98–101, 110
Convertite 116, 123n20
Cosimo I de' Medici, Duke 1–5, 7, 9, 19, 28, 34, 36, 190, 212–14; convent census and 87, 90–1, 102, 118; *Decima* and 37–43, 53–4, 121, 214; landowner as 69, 71; prostitution and 107–9, 111–14, 116, 121
Cummins, Neil 136

data 1–11, 15–30, 31n19, 53–62, 95, 134–41, 150–1, 154–5, 157, 161, 175–6, 179, 193, 210–12; accuracy of 35, 38, 158, 170, 172; *see also* DECIMA; *Decima; Catasto; Estimo*

218 Index

Dati, Goro 154, 156, 160, 162
Del Giocondo, Caterina di Amadeo 99
Del Giocondo, family 98
DECIMA 1, 4–7, 15–18, 29–30, 34, 50, 53–62, 67, 109, 115, 141, 151, 154, 164–5, 192, 204, 210–15; creation of 5–8, 16–20, 22, 24, 27, 50, 57–62, 81n13, 93, 95–6, 115–22, 134–40, 151, 154–5, 156–7; figures 158–9, 161; micro-analysis 16, 22–9, 98–101, 136–9; related apps 190–3 (*see also* *Hidden Florence*); sources 1–6 (*see also* Decima); tables 139; use of 7–11, 24–8, 33, 49, 60–4, 75, 80, 96, 102, 108–9, 118, 121–2, 125, 134–7, 141, 169
Decima 5–8, 10–11, 20–1, 24, 36–43, 51n27, 54, 57, 60–2, 77, 80, 81n3 n5 n15, 83n32, 102, 116, 118, 151, 165, 210–25; data from 16–19, 21, 26, 31n19, 34, 39–43, 48–9, 53–8, 63–5, 67–8, 71–2, 89, 91–5, 108, 154, 175, 193; figures 55, 59; governmentality and 18–22, 33, 38–9, 43–9, 89, 121–2; history of 1–5, 37–8, 64; Magistrato della Decima 34, 37–8; mapping of (*see* DECIMA creation of); tables of 53, 67, 72–3, 75; textualized mapping 38–9, 41, 43, 48–9, 61, 108
Decima ricerca see Decima
digital humanities 1, 211; *see also* spatial humanities
digital mapping 1, 5, 7–11, 49–50, 53, 87, 89, 91–6, 101–2, 108, 109, 115, 117, 122, 134–6, 151, 164–5, 166n12, 169, 210, 214–15
Drago Verde (Green Dragon) 36, 78, 80

Eleanor of Toledo 68
Estimo 37, 38

fear 10, 17, 117, 169–84, 178, 182–4, 213–14; governmentality in relation to 117, 183–4; 'grandissimo timore' 170; mapping of 169, 171–2, 175, 181; *see also* plague
Ferdinand I de' Medici, Grand Duke 214
Ferdinand II de' Medici, Grand Duke 123, 125, 128, 141
Firenze Città Nobilissima 6
Florence 1–11, 22, 29, 33–4, 43, 102, 108, 110, 113–14, 121, 162, 203, 210–15; neighbourhoods of (*see* individual neighbourhoods)

Foucault, Michel 35, 50n6, 212
Francesco de' Medici, Grand Duke 4, 190

Genoa 170
geodatabase 140
geography 10, 15, 39, 49, 80, 135, 165, 203; *catasto* and 7; Florence of 20, 34, 39; governmentality and 9, 21, 34–5; social 18–19, 22, 36, 62, 149, 200; textual 35, 38–9, 41, 48–9; urban 3, 35, 43, 48, 96
ghetto 4, 153, 182
Giannetti, Antonio di Filippo 3, 42–3
GIS mapping 1, 6–8, 18, 27, 53, 62, 89, 102, 137–40, 154, 192, 205n12; *see also* ArcGIS; HGIS
gonfalone 15, 20–1, 35, 37–8, 151, 178
Google Earth 159, 160, 172, 176, 181
governmentality 3–4, 7, 18–22, 33–6, 43–50, 50n6, 121, 212–15
Grascia 110
Guidi, Giovanfrancesco 170
guilds 25, 110, 162, 200; individual guilds (*see* Ciompi, Grascia); landlords as 8, 72–3

Health Board 128, 133, 169; *see also* Sanità
Herlihy, David 2, 174–5, 211
HGIS (historical GIS) 1, 7, 9, 15–16, 18, 21, 26, 28–30, 40, 134–41, 204, 210, 214–15
Hidden Florence 2, 4, 6, 10, 187, 188 fig. 10.1, 190, 197, 200; Bounsignori's map and 190–4; navigating space and sense 177–8, 189, 192, 193–4, 203–4
homosexuality 123n19, 202–3
hospitals 68, 70, 72–3, 91, 125–6, 131

Jews 4, 110, 153

Klapisch-Zuber, Christiane 2, 174–5, 211

Lanci, Baldassare 2
landlords 8, 28, 80, 82n23, 95, 97, 129; institutions as 63–71, 74, 75, 96 (*see also* confraternity; convent; guilds; monastery; Ospedale degli Innocenti); private 71, 73, 78
Landucci, Luca 197
lazaretto 125, 131–2
Litchfield, Robert Burr 5–6, 22–4, 26, 126, 132
London 125–7, 129–33, 136

Index 219

Magistrato sopra i monasteri 90
Mapping the Republic of Letters 135
Medici, Alessandro I *see* Alessandro I de' Medici, Duke
Medici, Cosimo I *see* Cosimo I de' Medici, Duke
Medici, Cosimo de' 2
Medici, Ferdinand I de' *see* Ferdinand I de' Medici, Grand Duke
Medici, Ferdinand II de' *see* Ferdinand II de' Medici, Grand Duke
Medici, Lorenzo de' 37, 198, 200
Medici, Piera de' 93
Milan 127, 160
mobility turn 189, 203
monastery 8, 18, 28, 56, 109–10, 113–14; landlords as 63, 69, 72–4, 78; *see also* individual monasteries

Nove conservatori (Nine Conservators) 3, 37
nuns 16, 42, 87–103, 109, 131, 193; responsibility if 99–101; *see also* convent

Onestà (Office of Decency) 107–8, 111, 113, 116–18, 121–2
Online Catasto 211–12
Orbatello 107, 109
Orbis Urbis 6
Ospedale degli Innocenti 60, 74, 76–7
Otto di Guardia (Eight of public Safety) 110

Palazzo dei Priori 4, 154, 157
Palazzo Pitti 2, 19
Palazzo Vecchio 19, 190; *see also* Palazzo dei Priori
paleography 8, 54–7, 61
parish 9, 15, 19, 21, 29–30, 38, 89, 161, 164–5, 178, 187, 210–15; churches 20–2, 63–4, 82n30, 156–8, 162, 199; convent 91, 63–4, 91–5, 100–1; mapping of 19–22, 42, 95–8, 119, 136–7, 150, 154, 160–1, 187, 199; plague and 129–33, 136; social makeup of 100–1, 130, 132–3, 150–1, 165, 178
Paul III, Pope 90
Piazza della Signoria 158, 190–1, 193, 200
Pisa 37
plague 9–10, 125–43, 170–85, 213–14; data on 127, 129, 131, 134–40; fear and 169–73, 178, 181–3; figures 136, 180; mapping of 125, 130–3, 135–40, 172; parish response 127–34, 136, 178, 182–83, 184n8 (*see also* Sanità)
Podestà 110, 157
portate 173, 175–6
property 25, 28, 68, 73, 75, 80, 81n10, 82n17, 82n23, 82n30, 102–3, 108; DECIMA and 16, 214; *Decima* and 37–42, 48–9, 54, 65, 71–2; figures 79, 95, 119; mapping of 18, 138–40, 95–8; market 63–4, 66–7, 69–71, 118; ownership 7–8, 76–80, 89–91, 93–4, 101, 120–1 (*see also* landlords); tables of 67, 70, 72, 73; taxation of 34–5, 65–6
prostitution 9, 98, 107–9, 202; landowners 117, 119–21; license fee 113; mapping of 115–20; noise and 114–18; regulation of 107, 110–15, 119–21, 123n19, 153 (*see also* Onestà); sumptuary legislation and 114; tassa maggiore and minore 116

quarters *see* by name of quarter

rent contract 64–6, 71, 75, 80; livello and pigione 23, 65–6, 69–71, 75, 80, 81n12, 82n29
reveller-warriors 80
ricerca see Decima
Rogation procession 156, 159, 161, 163
Rondinelli, Francesco 126, 129
Rome 6, 117, 126, 151–3, 162–3

San Giovanni, city quarter 20, 53–9, 65–7, 76, 92, 99, 129, 132, 151, 180
Sanità (Officers of Health) 131, 169–73, 179, 182–4
San Jacopo di Ripoli, convent of 93, 99
San Jacopo, order of 76, 78–80
San Lorenzo, parish 9, 125, 130, 132, 136, 139, 213
San Pier Maggiore, convent of 92
San Pietro, monastery of 28
Santa Croce, city quarter 17, 19, 43–8, 53–4, 56–7, 66–7, 93, 151
Santa Felicita, convent of 92, 99–100
Santa Maria degli Angeli, monastery of 76
Santa Maria del Fiore (il Duomo) 19, 64, 161; cathedral chapter 71, 76; landlord as 76–7
Santa Maria Novella, city quarter 7, 15, 19, 22–9, 39, 43, 53–4, 57, 61, 66–7, 77, 93, 99, 151, 171
Santa Maria Novella, convent of 69, 75

Santa Verdiana, convent of 93, 100–1
Santo Spirito, city quarter 20, 53–7, 65–7, 78–9, 92, 99–100, 151
Savonarola 3, 111
scrivani (scribes) 54, 56
sex trade *see* prostitution
socio-spatial relations 87, 91, 94, 96, 98
Sommai, Girolamo 68
sound 6, 9, 33, 114, 118, 149–51, 157, 164, 192; mapping of 154–9, 161, 163; *see also* soundscape
soundscape 9, 149, 157, 159–60, 162, 165, 213
spatial humanities 7, 108, 115, 122, 210, 212, 215
spatial turn *see* HGIS; socio-spatial relations; spatial humanities
stima see taxation
Strozzi, Alessandro 77
Strozzina, Bettina 107, 109, 121

taverns 6, 16, 29, 107, 110, 196, 202, 213
Taverns Project 6
taxation 16, 23, 34, 37–8, 38, 61, 64–9, 80, 81n10, 89, 93, 99, 116, 173, 187, 211
textile weavers 22–5, 29
Thirty Years' War 127
Tuscanisms 55, 60–1
typhus 128

Ufficiali di Notte (Officials of the Night) 110, 202–3
Uffizi 2, 4

Vallombrosan order 93, 101
Vasari, Giorgio 2
Venice 126–7, 170
Villani, Giovanni 155, 162–3
Visita (Visitation) 87, 90, 101, 173, 174, 177–84
Visualizing Venice 6, 212